MARNI JACKSON

The
MOTHER
Zone

VINTAGE CANADA

For my mother and father

VINTAGE CANADA EDITION, 2002

Copyright © 1992 by Marni Jackson

Published by arrangement with Macfarlane Walter & Ross, Toronto, Canada

National Library of Canada Cataloguing in Publication Data

Jackson, Marni
The mother zone

ISBN 0-679-31214-5

1. Motherhood. 2. Mother and infant. 3. Mother and child.
4. Jackson, Marni. I. Title.

HQ759.J23 2002   306.874'3   C2001-904294-9

Lyric excerpt from "Alexandra Leaving" appears by
kind permission of Leonard Cohen.

www.randomhouse.ca

Cover illustration by Phil Borges/Stone
Cover design by CS Richardson

Interior designed by Louis Fishauf
Typeset by Tony Gordan Limited

Printed and bound in Canada

2 4 6 8 10 9 7 5 3 1

Contents

Acknowledgments

PORTIONS of this book began as magazine articles, and I would like to express my thanks to the following editors: Marq de Villiers and Lynn Cunningham at *Toronto Life*, Anne Collins, John Fraser and the staff at *Saturday Night*, Carole Sherman at *Destinations*, and Dawn MacDonald at the erstwhile *City Woman*. They flinched not at "soft news."

I'm grateful to Alan Mirabella of the Vanier Institute of the Family for research in the early stages of the book. Most of all, I thank a number of generous and opinionated friends and writers, whose honesty and humor kept me on course: Judith Timson, Cathleen Hoskins, Carole Corbeil, Maggie Huculak, Annie Kidder, Dorothy Bennie. Special thanks to those who read parts of the manuscript and offered editorial advice: Olive and Clyde Jackson, Anne Mackenzie, Jill Frayne, John Greyson, Alice van Wart, Jackie Burroughs, Maggie Gilmour, and Ian Brown.

I owe the existence of this book in more ways than one to my editor, Anne Collins. Another writer once described her editing style as "more like getting a massage than going in for surgery" and I agree. During the writing of this book we have gone through a birth, a death, and a pharmacy's worth of antibiotics, and I'm very grateful to her.

I would also like to thank my agent, Lee Davis Creal, for her enthusiasm, and my publisher, Jan Walter, for her patience and support at every stage. Bill Strachan of Henry Holt and Company in New York gave me excellent editorial guidance as well. Wendy Thomas did a thorough and spirited job of copyediting.

At this point, an author usually thanks someone in her family, "without whom the book would never have been completed." It is fair to say that this has never been truer than in my case. It may not be normal to thank one's "material," but I have a thousand reasons to be grateful to my son, Casey Johnson, and to my husband, Brian Johnson. Both have been unbelievably tolerant and forgiving of this long, strange process. Brian Johnson, in addition to his numerous other roles, has been a wonderful editor. Sometimes it takes a writer to live with one.

Amnesia: an Introduction

SUNDAY, 7 a.m. This morning we had the dead mouse problem. Casey raced into the bedroom, great round tears coursing down his face.

"He's dead, we killed him," he said weeping red-faced into my nightgown.

"Who, the hamster?" I asked. The hamster was elderly and had been breathing funny.

"No, the mouse, my mouse. I wanted to catch him and let him go but the glue on the trap didn't dissolve like it was supposed to and his nose got stuck and he died. I killed him!"

Primal tears. Brian, wearing a sweat shirt and a towel, came into the room with a rueful look. Yesterday the two of them had gone off to the hardware store to get a Humane Trap.

"But the thing looked like no self-respecting mouse would ever set foot in it, and it was seventeen dollars," Brian explained. "So we bought these little sticky traps instead. The mouse gets his feet stuck, then you take him outside, pour some water on the trap, and the glue is supposed to melt."

"But he got his whole self stuck instead," Casey moaned. "I feel like I killed him."

"Well, technically, it's my fault, Casey," Brian said. "I didn't want to spend that much on a mousetrap so I bought the cheap one. It's not your fault."

Casey pressed his face into Brian this time.

"What do you think a mouse's life is worth, dad? Four dollars? Twelve? Isn't it worth seventeen at least?"

Frankly, no, I thought. Brian and I exchanged a look, the Glance of Shame.

"He was so friendly and tame," mourned Casey.

It was true, we had grown used to the mouse doing his circuit, from his stove niche to the fridge niche and up the heating vents. If we sat quietly at the kitchen table, he would race around, well aware that we were watching him. We had had a relationship of sorts with the mouse and now he was snout-down in a saucer of glue.

"I didn't want to kill him, I just wanted to get close to him," Casey said, unleashing a fresh torrent of sobs. These were the death sobs, I had seen them before.

"I think he knew you were nice to him," I said. "He saw you letting him run around."

"He really did seem to know me," he agreed, pausing to cough. "What did you do with him, dad?"

"He's in the garbage."

"Can I bury him?"

"I suppose so, if you want to."

"Didn't you want to bury your father?"

"Well, that's different. Anyway, we didn't bury him."

"What happened?"

"Uh, we burnt him. He was cremated."

"Don't you bury the ashes?"

"What did happen to your father's ashes?" I asked.

"I don't know. I don't have them."

"Are you sure they're not around here somewhere?"

A withering look. "*Yes*, I'm sure."

"Bury him deep in the garden and he'll make the flowers grow bigger," I told Casey. Mother talk.

"Maybe it'll bring me good luck." Already, he was counting the possible dividends of this little tragedy. I could see the engines of his optimism at work.

"It was my fault," Brian said. "I was just being cheap."

"Anyway, there are probably lots more mice in the house," I added, in that desperate we-can-always-get-another modern way.

"If there are," Casey said, hope back in his face, "can we buy the seventeen-dollar trap?"

His father and I looked at each other. The logic, the merciless logic of the heart.

"Yes."

*   *   *

When I was thirty-seven, I had my first child, a boy who is eight years old at the moment. All of a sudden, this former baby is as tall as a bulrush, tall as my chest. Everything changed when I had him — as I expected it would — only in ways I didn't expect. And as he gets older, everything is changing again. I notice that I am busy forgetting all the minutes and hours and days of the time when I was more a mother than anything else.

I'm not alone in this maternal amnesia. Ten years ago, when Adrienne Rich published *Of Woman Born*, she remarked on how there were endless amounts of secondary material on the concept and institution of motherhood, but very few primary sources: books on motherhood written by mothers. Even now, when we are drowning in first-person confessionals about dysfunctional families, this conspiracy of silence around ordinary motherhood remains. Parenting books by experts proliferate, but the reality still comes as a surprise to every woman who goes through it. Motherhood may have become an issue, but it's not yet a narrative.

During my prenatal reading binge, I looked in vain for this missing voice. Leach, Spock, Brazelton, Kitzinger — all invaluable, all not enough. And only a narrow band of literature could shine a light on the things I was feeling and thinking. (Did the Brontë sisters have children? Bramwell doesn't count.)

There seemed to be a hole in the culture where mothers went.

Then, when their kids went off to school or stopped having ear infections every three weeks, they emerged from the mother zone, and like everyone else, they forgot where they'd been. Amnesia surrounding motherhood is the rule, not the exception.

It appears to be as easy and natural to forget those early days with a baby as it is to erase the pain of childbirth. We become adept at forgetting the real texture of childhood, until mothers are buried in that forgetting, too. Best to forget the nights alone in the emergency department, or the intense, too-tiny world of other mothers going through the same things, talking loudly and riotously at a party.

We forget those moments in late November, in the park, wrestling the stroller through the first sticky snowfall as the sun sets and four more hours of building block towers remain before the baby's bedtime. Or the sense of having been through so much in one day, and yet of having nothing at all to say to your husband when he comes home. Like a passionate affair that ends and gets redefined as a fluke, a mother also learns to forget the erotic bond she once had with her baby — a perfect intimacy that may never be recaptured. All the raw extremes of emotion are smoothed over and left behind, on the island of motherhood.

With cunning reverse psychology, our culture encourages this amnesia, simply by excluding mothers from its most conspicuous rewards — money, power, social status. Everything from the shameful wages of day-care workers to the isolation of the at-home mother is evidence of how, despite lip service and pedagogical theories, our culture remains inimical to children and to the people raising them.

So it becomes more rewarding to forget, and the true drama between mother and child is slowly replaced by the idealization of motherhood. The sentimentalizing of her relationship to her children begins — along with the guilt when she won't, can never, conform to the ideal. Motherhood ideals change from generation to generation but whatever they are — the old having-it-all myth, the new retro-mom fantasies — they will elude her. The real shock is that mothers themselves participate in this self-betrayal. Throughout the writing of this book, I kept confronting this.

I worked at home, or tried to. My son spent a lot of time at home with me — at first by design and later as a result of illness. I found myself inhabiting a paradox: I was a full-time mother with a full-time job. Surrendering to one always felt like a betrayal of the other, and yet, I was both. The contradictions abounded — I was happy, but this new core of happiness was accompanied by an unexpected sense of isolation and loss of self. I was lost, and found. Being a mother chipped away at the iron-clad ego you need to write. Why even bother? Things seemed to go much more smoothly when I gave in to the baby instead. As Emily Dickinson, a productive non-mother, once wrote, "Drowning is not so pitiable as the attempt to rise."

Measured against the awesome selfishness that writing demands, I could gauge my disappearing clearly.

Since I had only one child (so far) and a willing husband — a writer, too — this melodrama of the waxing and waning self seemed rather indulgent. Millions of women before me had gone about having their children without a fuss, and not one of them felt compelled to call their agent. What was the big deal?

The answer, I'm convinced, is that no one is prepared for the experience of motherhood. My mother was surprised, too. The more myth we generate, the greater the shock when it happens to us. But the new-mother script is still the same, whether it refers to the pain of labor, the swoon of emotions or the subtle hydraulics of breast-feeding: *why didn't anyone tell me it would be like this?* There's no preparation for the alchemy of the self that takes place during motherhood.

Some women head into the experience of having a baby planning to run it like an executive, scheduling "time for themselves" and plotting their "return to normal." What the time-managers among mothers forget is that raising children is also a muddle, a feat of the imagination, a Russian novel-in-progress.

Much thought, sometimes just in the form of fantastic scenarios of doom, goes into the daily work of raising children. Child-care books emphasize the management of motherhood and the administration of childhood. This Bus-Admin approach has generated new myths almost as potent and misleading as the old white-picket-fence ones.

In fact, I've tried to avoid using the word "parenting" in the body of this book because it suggests that mothers and fathers play interchangeable roles. But "parenting" is a euphemism, I'm afraid. Even in so-called equal-opportunity households, it continues to be women who do most of the child-raising work — the planning, the thinking, the birthdays, the *authorship* of family. Men can and do make good mothers, but not many choose to go that route. Why should they, when motherhood has become defined as a "maternal leave of absence" from the real world? Until the status of motherhood changes, the absolutely crucial participation of men in the daily work of raising children is going to continue to be slow in coming.

Even to write about motherhood, I learned, is perilous. You run the risk of re-sanctifying it, or luring women out of their fragile new powers and back into the home, in search of some vanished notion of family. You risk raising the ghost of the biological imperative. You risk idealizing the nuclear family and excluding other models — blended, extended, communal or gay. You make child-raising sound like the only reasonable destination for a grown-up, which it isn't. On the other hand, to overlook the biological side — the way pregnancy, birth, and breast-feeding affect mothers — is to disembody women yet again. For the past twenty years, access to jobs and reproductive choice have taken priority — a "mock male" period that was not an aberration or a cul-de-sac, but a necessary phase in the evolution of feminist thought. But this put too much distance between women and the family, between women and their bodies. Now there is a willingness to explore differences between the sexes as a source of strength. We can imagine equality that is not predicated on sameness. And one way feminism can continue to evolve without falling prey to a static ideology is to stay true to the female body, a crash course in constant change.

The first lesson the body teaches us is to abandon generalizations. By telling the story of one particular family, I want to remind women once again to trust their own feelings and thoughts, regardless of social pressures. But by sticking to my own story, I lay myself open to all sorts of charges, of course. Collectors of this sort of thing will find evidence here of weak ego boundaries, the enmeshed mother, the wheel-shaped family system, psychic hovering, old-fashioned neurosis, co-dependency on everything from margaritas to bad TV, lack of individuation, opening the refrigerator too often for no good reason, and occasional forays into borderline psychosis. Not only will I refuse to behave as a maternal role model, I intend to flaunt eccentricities that fall well short of the universal. But somewhere in the middle is a good-enough mother, with the usual emotions, doubts, and desires.

Doubt, along with years of the Endless Ear Infection, caused me to drop the thread of this story over and over, until the book began to look like some domestic artifact itself — a quilt, a photo album, a dog-eared object worked on at odd hours and in vastly different moods. As Tillie Olsen wrote, "Motherhood means being instantly interruptible, responsive, responsible." My divided self was replicated in the separate piles of manuscript that slowly began to grow in the corners of my room.

The decision to use my own family instead of a fictional one wasn't easy, but to write fiction, you have to inhabit a book in the same way that a baby inhabits you. It requires continuity, time, and idleness, three things a mother sheds. The deciding factor, though, was my desire to restore the first person to a subject that has so much otherness, so much third-person expertise brought to bear on it. How can something become fiction before it has been named? Modern motherhood is still *terra incognita*, awaiting its raconteurs, explorers, and household anthropologists.

Of course, the pressures on a citified two-job, one-child household are not to be confused with the physical work, economic obstacles and emotional pressures borne by bigger families, single mothers, poor mothers and everyone else living outside the white middle class. *Mea culpa, mea maxima culpa*; I am a person of pallor, a demographic dominatrix, whether I like it or not. But writing for a living — especially about mothers — is a taste of marginality. It's also a useful metaphor for what every mother has to do, regardless of her situation. She has to find her own voice. Sometimes the surrender and sacrifice of motherhood turn out to be the easy part.

The changes in family have come so fast and furious it's easy to forget that childhood is an invention of this century. Everything from psychoanalysis to the newly acknowledged scars of incest and childhood abuse has made the point that what happens in childhood matters. It matters terribly. No wonder parents take their job so seriously these days. The gravity of the task of raising kids along with the scariness of the world they are born into have sent parents into an acquisitive tizzy, gobbling up skills, strategies, pedagogical theories, and expert advice.

The result is that we try to master and manage family, and to fit children into our lives. But the obvious continues to elude us — families are not puzzles to be solved, they are the place where we struggle to love. Motherhood is not a separate, pastel wing of emotion; it is a relationship as tricky and passionate as any other kind of love. We keep aiming for happiness as a state of equilibrium, but the first useful thing children teach us is that everything that works today won't work tomorrow. Family requires improvisation. We chase the shifting point of balance between individual freedom and the absolute dependence of an infant, between the hunger for intimacy and the need for solitude.

I still find myself trying to live up to some calm maternal archetype who wakes up one morning tattooed with Patience. But nothing about motherhood is bestowed, except conception, which continues to be a miracle. Nothing is instinctual, except, perhaps, that first irrational urge to have a baby. Fathers can mother. Adoptive parents ride the same roller coaster. Anatomy still isn't destiny — but biology has to count for something. How can we recast motherhood in a way that no longer idealizes nor demeans the experience — in a way that takes feminism into the future, not the past?

Motherhood is an unexplored frontier of thought and emotion that we've tried to tame with rules, myths, and knowledge. But the geography remains unmapped.

I know why. Mothers in the thick of it have no time or brain cells left to write it down, to give it life. Now that I have the time, time has me: amnesia moves in. So on the cusp of being too much inside the story and too far beyond its greedy embrace, I will tell as much truth as I can. The rest is fiction.

mating

1.   Body

I HAVE a normal, that is to say abnormal, female obsession with my body — how it feels to be inside it, how it looks to other people. I think I was about twelve when I began to find ways to disown it. But there was nothing wrong with how I looked. No complaints, no family tragedy. What, then? Why did I feel as if someone else had drawn the shape I lived inside?

My version of anorexia was to wear a girdle at all times, which was not unusual among high-school girls in the early sixties. It was how we held our stockings up, for one thing. I wasn't fat, but I was already alert to the messages, overt and subtle, all around me, that it was best to keep the territory between navel and knees tightly under wraps. So I decided that I owed it to the world to wear as many pairs of pants as possible.

At the 1991 Cannes Film Festival, Madonna dropped her wrap and displayed to the gathered press the ultimate shield, an old-fashioned, long-legged girdle. It was a reverse strip and a joke I understood. I wore mine under everything, even in summer. At camp, at the age of thirteen, with braces on my teeth and shirred elastic under my shorts, my nickname was G.K., the Girdle Kid. The braces were supposed to push my eager teeth back into line, and the girdle would take care of the rest.

I looked exactly like what I was, in fact: a round-armed, milk-fed, well-cared-for middle-class white girl with a bevelled blonde flip, who lived with my intact family — two parents, an older brother, a younger sister — in a small town on the shore of

Lake Ontario. My father was an engineer who worked hard to make home a refuge from the treacherous world beyond the hedge. My mother stayed home where she poured endless creativity and thought — it used to be called *household science* — into the raising of her children. In fact, the only thing I can possibly claim to be in recovery from is the unrelieved WASPness of my childhood. It felt like a weird kind of racelessness, to be raised with "everything" and yet be deprived of other voices and cultures.

But I didn't know that then. I enjoyed school. Late at night I ironed my Susan van Heusen blouses down in the basement, with my hair rolled around orange-juice cans. Boys went out with me. I was big on kissing, could kiss for hours even through my braces, but the fact that my left breast was a tiny fraction smaller than the right one quickly settled the whole sex question. I viewed this flaw, invisible to everyone but me, as a genuine disfigurement. Sorrowfully, I explained to attentive boyfriends that there was something very wrong with my breasts, something I couldn't reveal to them. Between the snap of the girdle and the mystery deformity, there was not much left for us to explore.

Instead, I wore padded bras that always curdled in the dryer; I sewed tiny plastic pillows into the cups of my bathing suit. One summer, I went water-skiing. When I tried to cross the wake, I fell and came back up to the surface to see the two pillows, like buoyant croissants, floating away in opposite directions along with the skis. My pretend body, adrift. The boys were too busy hydroplaning to notice, so I let the skis go and went after the breasts.

Real sex I associated with catastrophe — the spooky disappearance from school of the unwed mother, or the teen dementia of Natalie Wood in *Splendor in the Grass* trying to drown herself in the tub. My yearning for some kind of sexual connection, for some passionate fit with the available world, led me instead to moody cravings for Art.

I fell in love with poetry. My parents took me to art galleries where I stood for longer than was strictly necessary before each painting. I read Leonard Cohen's first novel and wrote him a short, lambent note of congratulations, to let him know that at least one hugely intelligent reader understood him. On Friday nights my girlfriend and I would descend to the rec room, where we would drape a red scarf over the pole lamp and lie in a sublimated swoon listening to Johnny Mathis sing "Chances Are."

Still, I could feel the friction between my stateless desires and the constructed shape I moved around inside. My body housed a loneliness that I tried to solve by reading, by kissing, or by listening to Thelonius Monk. I learned to dance to Chuck Berry, but Erik Satie made me feel old and melancholy and precise. I read Camus and Sartre, whom I instinctively understood, in my state of muddled self-invention. They also conferred a special status on me that I would take refuge in for years — the intellectually precocious girl. An apprentice guy, in a panty girdle.

The more I fulfilled the requirements of my time and place in the world, the more I split and lost focus until I felt like one of those 3-D post cards, where the image is blurred until you hold it at exactly the right angle. Nothing was holding me at the right angle. My parents had raised me with unusual love, intelligence, and tact, but they were stuck in history too. So there was absolutely no one or nothing to blame for my sense of dispossession. The frame of the picture — the culture itself — was still invisible to me.

Sometimes, a boy would deliver me home, we would kiss in the driveway for a while, and then he would go off to visit one of the girls who went all the way, girls inevitably called Suzie or Sherrie. Toward the fast girls I don't remember feeling what I was supposed to feel — disapproval, superiority. I felt curiosity and even awe. They had guts, they knew something I didn't.

The three Baxter boys were notorious for this split shift of the show-date and the late-night girl. The B's, as we called them, lived on the lake in a veritable mansion with a circular driveway, behind stone gates. Their mother seemed permanently bewildered by the fact that she had ended up at the mercy of these three smart, wild boys who lived in her house.

When I was fourteen, I briefly dated Bobby, the middle Baxter boy. He dated everyone, sooner or later. One day he came over to our house.

"Hi, Miz Jackson," he said, passing through the kitchen. "That sure looks good." My mother was baking something. All the Baxter boys flirted easily with the mothers. My mother pointedly asked after his family and then suggested we go down to the rec room, "where it was cooler." My parents went out of their way to give me privacy. They felt it was better to have me fooling around in the basement than dying of carbon monoxide poisoning in lover's lane, where madmen with hooks for hands would try to kill me.

We descended to the rec room.

"Let's play Dark," Bobby suggested.

"What are the rules?" I asked, and he flicked off the lights.

"You stand at that end of the room, I stand at this end, and then we run together in the dark," he said.

I laughed. We ran into each other, and he wrapped his arms around me. He was tall. Then he began growling into my neck and sucking on the tops of my shoulders.

"That's it, that's Dark." He put a leg up behind my calf, like a kid wrestling, and in a flash he had me down on the shag rug. He carefully laid his big bulk on top of me, as if I were an air mattress.

"I won," he said, burrowing with his tongue in my mouth. I was amused. Upstairs I could hear the hysterical hssss of the pressure cooker full of carrots on the stove.

Such straightforward aggression relaxed me for some reason, and I merely slapped away his hands as they dove without further ado into my shorts.

"Sorry," I said, "out of bounds."

"You mean to say nobody's ever got into your pants?" he

asked incredulously. Propped up on one elbow, he then went on, with admirable candor, to explain how it was possible for a girl to "climax" without "going all the way." I greeted this with the same derision I had felt for the astonishing news, many years earlier, that penises somehow found their way into vaginas. Camus would not approve. I accused Bobby of false advertising, and we went on amiably necking. He didn't mind; there was always Suzie for later on. I was the day-girl, the conversational primer. Suzie was the real thing.

As soon as he left, however, I went up to my room and consulted *The Wonderful Story of You*, which my mother had conspicuously made available to me. I lingered, as usual, over the quaint bulbs and tubings of the male genitals and found a reference to this putative "climax," along with a description of what you had to do to have one. Once again, it was words that did the trick first.

When I got older, I thought petting was paradise, a duty-free ride to the end of the line. I liked nothing better than to see the fog creep over the back window of a car. But real sex was still out of bounds until I went to college. My threadbare virginity had little to do with emotional maturity, I think, or degrees of love. It was based on a conventional fear of pregnancy — this was pre-pill — and a shame-tinged self-consciousness that kept me safe inside the tower of my body.

*   *   *

Not surprisingly, I developed a flair for acting. I rinsed my hair black and played a rather moving Anne Frank in our excellent, if profoundly non-Jewish high-school production of the play. In university, I auditioned for *Ondine,* by Giraudoux. I was hoping for a speaking part. After I read, the director said that he would like to cast me, but in an offbeat role — as a statue of Venus. Big entrance, but no lines. It was the Mute Venus, or nothing. I said yes.

Miscast again! I concocted a more Venusian pair of breasts to wear under my outfit, which was a white body-stocking in chiaroscuro, with a scrap of chiffon and a towering white wig. My role was to squat under a riser on stage for the duration of a long scene, waiting for a magician to conjure me up as a special effect. During the blackout, I scrambled up onto a big plywood half-shell, where I assumed my pose. Thunder rumbled, the lights strobed, rose petals fell from the sky, and the magician brought me to life. With a Mae West roll of the eyes I slowly descended from my half-shell and exited.

*　　*　　*

The statue act lasted for a good part of my twenties, as I went around half-frozen, a busy head floating on a body that had a few roped-off erogenous zones surrounded by unhappy flesh. It wasn't until I was almost forty, I think, that I felt at home in my skin. This began earlier with one or two men who loved me unreservedly, but what finally broke up the ice in my body was birth and the revolution of self that accompanied it. For someone like me, living with Camus and the boys in my head, it took the ordinary, animal feat of having a baby to get me back inside my body.

Not that birth or new motherhood felt like healing at the time. At the time, I thought I was going backward. I felt eclipsed by this intense new form of love.

But now, when people touch me, I feel them touching me all the way through. I feel them. I'm no longer the little larva inside the jumping bean, waiting for some warm hand to make me come to life. The third person who lived inside me, back when a woman's body belonged to everyone but her, is only a ghost of a voice now — a ghost that can still rattle me and leave me lost, but it no longer dominates.

The sexual etiquette of the sixties didn't help matters at all. In 1969, when I went on a post-grad trip through Europe with my cruel writer boyfriend, sexual betrayal wasn't considered grounds for self-destruction. When he slept with someone else — the hated Betty — more or less under my nose, my job at the time was not to feel much of anything. Jealousy and tears were proprietorial, unseemly reactions. So I conspired with him against my grief and my unfashionably broken heart. Even several months later, when we amiably split up and I went back to Canada, I was pretty sure I felt next to nothing. Then, as I clicked through the turnstiles on the subway headed home, a whole host of tics and palpitations and psychosomatic disorders began — the revenge of a twice-betrayed body.

My heart began to race and pound, and close quarters put me in a sweat. At the age of twenty-two, I was convinced I was headed for a heart attack. Sceptical doctors would give me EKGs and Valium. I walked around with a vague sense of being in mortal danger, and for the next few years, my body became an unpredictable traitor who could turn on me any time — after a work deadline or in a supermarket line-up. Girlfriends would insert me into warm baths, dates would order Scotch. Several decades of standing in bookstores flipping through self-help books have since informed me that these were nothing more than panic attacks. This is normal. This is what happens to unresolved, unexpressed grief and damage; it goes visceral and attacks the body. In a way, it was a sign of health, that my body refused to be lied to. Slowly, painfully, I was waking up.

I figured all this out — indeed, I was my own best example of the mind-body split, a concept that consumed me for years. But I didn't know how to mend it. Meanwhile, I went on falling in and out of love and working. I worked for a small publisher, wrote book reviews for the newspaper, and free-lanced for magazines. I was proud of the fact that I could support myself by writing.

At the height of heart-attack time, I went back to my parents' home for a visit, where I descended to the basement — the suburban sublimation room — to work on a large collage. Pieced together from magazine images, it was a textbook study of repression, longing, and dissociation. In the center was a woman behind a pane of glass, looking out. Fences, prison bars, clear containers proliferated, along with pictures of wild animals in flight.

My mother observed this little artistic outburst and prudently said little. She painted too. I was less tactful when I saw her gorgeous painting of bulrushes — wonderful, pink columns rising out of a green background. I ventured to remark in a joking way that the bulrushes looked phallic.

Her unconscious was so completely in control of the situation that this came as news to her. The next morning, I went down and saw that she had scraped the bulrushes off the canvas and started over, because, she explained, now she couldn't see the painting any other way.

She saw bulrushes; I saw penises. Was I seeing through her, or was she seeing through me? The mystery continues.

2.   Skin

IT WAS one of the first warm days in spring, shortly after I had moved in with him. I glanced out the window and saw him beautifully shirtless, like the sight of new leaves on trees. Drumming had given him nice muscles.

He was sitting in a lawn chair with a knife, scraping away at a goatskin, a messy and atavistic chore he liked to perform outside in the sun. There were skins drying on the lawn and more dry, stiff ones in the basement. The goatskins were for his drum, a bulbous African instrument called a djembe. (This was, I hasten to add, fifteen years before the phenomenon of organized Male Drumming.)

When I met the future father of my child, his first and most complicated relationship was to this drum, which he admitted was a fetish, and a transparently phallic one at that. You put the thing between your legs and play it with your hands. When I watched him perform with his band on stage, using one hand to push up his glasses without losing the beat, I was appalled and transfixed: carnal exhibitionism in an English-born, Canadian-raised, private-school boy. What next?

Looking out the window, I admired his diligence, and his chest. But it drove me crazy that he devoted his spare time to sitting in the sun, oiling his own skin or the drum, while I languished inside, trying to work. He had such an obsessive passion for music and such a mild, convenient thing for me — or so I thought, as I watched him when the crocuses were not even open and he was already out there on the lawn, half-naked. I was jealous of everything else he touched.

*   *   *

When we met, I was a thirty-two-year-old writer heading into baby lust, and he was a twenty-nine-year-old journalist turned musician. His band was touring and had ambitious plans for rock stardom. Babies were the last thing on his mind. Just as I was beginning to revise my future, he was busy subverting his past.

After ten years of private school in Toronto, he had gone off to college where he intersected deliriously with the sixties. Along came Marx and the boys; he discovered that he had been stuck in class in more ways than one. He dove into student politics, had great all-night sex with argumentative women, and edited the campus paper. He began to favor open-necked velour shirts. It was a great feeling, to have the world on the end of your tongue.

After graduation, he made his way to Montreal, where he worked as a labor reporter on the local English newspaper. This was the mid-seventies, when leftist dreams of revolution were being validated by a wildly insurgent labor movement. Soon he was playing both sides, mild-mannered reporter by day, flaming revolutionary by night. But the strain of commuting between these two worlds, along with the *dérèglement* of the usual drugs, took its toll. He called a televised press conference to denounce the "bourgeois press," quit his job, and walked off into a blizzard. A Paul Bowlesian trip to Sicily with his girlfriend followed by her departure was the *coup de grâce*, and he went benignly crazy for a while.

Nobody was too worried — in those days, dementia was part of having fun. Instead of checking into the nearest hospital, he took the train to Toronto and moved in with a few friends.

Before he left Montreal, a Haitian drummer had given him lessons. He had practiced, diligent as a cobbler, obsessive as a madman, until he was good at it. When his political friends formed a band, he joined, and eventually they came to Toronto, too.

Any writing he produced now was not going to be tied to the wheel of journalism. He churned out poetry and a meticulously paranoid novel and walked the streets, where he received personal messages from the radios of strangers. Only a thin membrane existed between him and certain universal secrets. All in all, he still maintains, it was a great time. He was free, free of consequence, the angel that hovers over family. The air itself was ripe with meaning.

By the time I met him, he was a man in the happy grip of obsession — a cross between Trini Lopez, Peter Jennings, and Keith Richards. He wanted to drum, not talk. He wanted to dance, not push words around on the page. I sympathized and saw him as a writer in flight from the awful daily consciousness of writing, not to mention the phony objectivity of journalism. At the same time, it all seemed so . . . contrived, somehow, a toying with madness. Maybe he'd read too much André Breton. I'd *done* surrealism, and found it a cold and supremely rational re-ordering of reality. Or so I told him, with breezy arrogance. Surrealism was for guys.

Even though we had both managed to stay out of conventional jobs or marriages, we were not of the same political hue, when you came down to it. His ideas were rooted in class analysis; tiffs over housework were not to be confused with Issues. As for me, I was a feminist, although a heretical one. I never subscribed to the seventies' androgynous ideal and I had a weakness for cowboys. I was hoping we could come round to a more enlightened gender gap, one that honored differences.

At first his reverential faith in art, magic, and poetry drew my scorn; I didn't want to see art as a cabal. To me, this was more corny left-wing male-*artiste* ideology, a Rimbaud impersonation. I thought art was inseparable from the ordinary stuff of life, including laundry. Especially laundry. In short, our pretensions took different forms.

But I recognized myself in him, trepidatiously. I recognized his WASP longing to be someone else — to change skins. I approved of his urge to shed self-consciousness and his appetite for experience. I just didn't want to be gobbled up in the process.

To make some money while the band got going, he wrote a column on the urban scene for the Toronto *Globe and Mail*, where his reckless, over-amping imagery first caught my eye. It was like coming across a belly dancer in a tony restaurant. He had also published a book of poems, written with a lyrical malice he didn't betray in person. There was a combination of soft and hard in his writing, and in his face. First I fell for the words, then I had to deal with the rest of him.

It was 1978. We met through friends, at a bar where his band was playing. Then we ran into each other at a gallery called A Space and went out for coffee in a fluorescent-lit falafel place on Yonge Street.

We talked, or rather he talked, about his adventures on a Caribbean island with voodoo, local shamans, and live volcanoes. He seemed quite enchanted with the connect-the-dots of his own life, and his monologues had a writer's crafty innocence. He was hogging the naiveté.

As I listened to him talk and watched his open face, I felt a welter of confusing emotions, not the least of which was fear — the sort of alarm one feels in the tropics. To me, madness was something to be kept at arm's length — not *fun*, not this vocation. He seemed rich, humid, and impenetrable, like a jungle. He chewed his food with too much relish. He approved of pleasure. Perhaps I thought I could stay safely hidden around this attractive narcissist.

And who was I in his eyes, at first? A writer as well, a cool, sarcastic blonde in glasses with breasts the right size. (Ah, but little did he know . . .) Obviously, we were on different rides altogether.

Then, after a week of reviewing his numerous flaws, I picked up the phone and called him. I said I thought perhaps we ought to get together. There was a benefit dance at the Rape Crisis Centre, I said, we could meet there. (We were nothing if not era-specific.) He informed me that his band was already playing for the benefit. I hoped he wouldn't turn out to be too competitive in this area.

The warm-up band was called, unfortunately, Wolf At The Door. Then Limbo Springs, his band, came on, and I stood at the back and watched. They played their own music, a mix of reggae and rock that was fun to dance to. But I was appalled by how *on* he was on stage — it was like watching someone take a bubble bath. I stood there making decorous little circles with my hips as they played. Meanwhile, the latent exhibitionist in me writhed, in recognition and secret envy.

One of the band members was married, and his wife brought along their new baby, in a basket. I remember that.

When the set was over, Brian jumped off the stage, came over to me, and took my hand in his. This was quite proprietorial, I thought, considering we had barely met. We danced a bit, then walked around the corner to a restaurant. This time I don't remember what we said. It already seemed to be a given that we would spend the night together. For one thing, this was what you did in 1978, if you met someone attractive. Strange as it may sound, regular sex was once considered part of mental hygiene. But I detected something else at work too, a somnambulistic feeling, a sense of gravity taking over.

We went back to the co-op house I shared with assorted faculty philosophers and grad students. I liked my strange, convivial housemates. One of them was the great-grandson of Whistler and liked to eat raw bacon while sitting on the edge of the tub. Miraculously, that night no one was home. We sat downstairs on the couch and without further ado, he took my foot in his hand. He certainly had a way with my extremities.

I took him up to my room — two rooms, actually, a little converted kitchen and a white sun porch where I slept and worked. The porch was tongue-and-groove, a cockpit of windows that overlooked the Italian gardens of our neighbors. My bed with dark green sheets was the exact width of the room. I was shy but determined not to be, according to the etiquette of the day. It was mid-February. Whenever we rolled against the edge of the bed, we could feel the cold radiating through the uninsulated wooden walls in waves, like heat. Hot and cold, like two strangers abruptly fused in sex. Both of us were haunted by other people, the last ones to leave us. Still, much is said through the skin, things you can't ever take back.

*   *   *

The next morning I felt light and lithe, as if the future were a simple board game that required momentum, nothing more.

There was someplace I had to be that day. As we walked to the bus stop, he was talkative, going on about the importance of the month of March and his affinity for the letter "M." I began to have doubts again. He wore a sheepskin coat with no buttons, and as he held his coat together with his hands, his teeth chattered. Don't let your teeth chatter like that, I thought, it's a plea for me to keep you warm. He was so tall and cheerful, a well-fed man. Already I was feeling cornered and lovesick. Why did love feel like going under to me, while it seemed to buoy him up?

We began to see each other — or rather, I began to show up wherever the band played; if I was lucky, I got to dance on some dime-sized dance floor. Or else I sat getting sodden on beer through two or three sets, waiting for the night to end so we could go home and get into bed, the only place we made sense. I don't remember many real dates, like going out to a restaurant or a movie. I just remember the weird and often humiliating role of being "with the band."

When we did go out, I was amazed by his amiable silence. He was like a closed-circuit TV, tuned in to certain rhythms in his head all the time. I used to amuse myself on the subway or walking along with him, wondering how long it would take before he thought to speak.

Life outside the band was not a problem for him — indeed, it scarcely existed. The band paid its members their rents and set amounts of spending money. There was no need for a wallet, or even social insurance. The band was family, work, and state. I was the girl waiting for him back in his room.

He lived in a co-op too, a pretty white corner house with a kind of turret. It was a very pleasant household until I moved in, and then couple chemistry went to work — furtively quiet sex and loud arguments about money that lingered in the house like cigar smoke.

The first night I spent there, I had to get over being appalled by his room. It was small, with a recessed niche where the window was. A Moroccan woven runner was pinned to the wall and trailed across the floor as a rug. There were pale water colors, druggy collages, and a picture of Debbie Harry. The room also had a secret vestibule, a windowless cubby that he used as his office. The fact that he worked in a closet was the clincher: it mirrored his implacable introversion. My room was all windows, and the wind blew right through it.

On the desk were dusty objects, beads, photos, letters from Italy, scraps of calligraphic poetry. A collector's room. The objects meant much to him and seemed blurred and opaque to me. Somebody else's life.

His bed was a two-inch slab of foam with a flannel sheet and a Guatemalan blanket for a spread. The floor was soft with dust at the edges. What am I doing here? I asked myself, as I took off my coat. But when I lay down, the bed turned out to be deliciously comfortable, and the room revealed its logic. A ribbon of coolness from the hall crept under the door and across us. He told me two provocative stories about his past. His body felt warm, and not at all mute. Through the window, I could see the mauve city-night sky and the bare winter branches of the tree overhead.

3.   Getting Pregnant

OUR COURTSHIP was not the stuff of which photo albums are made. I was shocked to find myself in love with someone willing to risk losing me. So I would leave, come back. Leave, come back, like destiny's yo-yo. I tell myself now that I must have seen the gleam of the good father in him. But I didn't. Right from the start, I lavished lusty hatred on him, because he made it perfectly clear that he preferred a *drum* to a baby. His resistance on the reproductive front made for some poisonous fights, as I tried to intellectually manhandle him into position.

When he went on tour, which was often, I even did my best to fall in love with other, more suitable mates. For a time, this strategy worked all too well. Both of us flirted with losing each other, lobbed revenge back and forth. But he was there in his body, which is what hooked me and kept me hooked. I knew that he had a stubborn mind and a muscular heart, and maybe he would open them up to me someday. Well, I didn't know it then, but I could see the evidence, at least, in his clear passion for writing and music. I always wanted to spell things out, and he was tired of consciousness. Now he wanted it all to happen physically, or musically.

I would sometimes tag along when they went on the road, to some small-town bar up north, where girls wearing the all-pervasive Farrah Fawcett hairdo and too much blue eye shadow would linger in the dressing rooms. After every gig, the Hairdos would drift into the back rooms, perch on the sprung sofas. Then I would show up, the bad-tempered bride with sensible bangs, to claim my boyfriend, the lapsed writer, the mad drummer.

I didn't want him to give up music, although it must have looked that way to him. And I didn't care about getting married, or waffle irons, or anything like that. It was the heart, an ability to stick around, and the friendly, highly motile sperm I was after: the minimalist approach to marriage.

He saw the creative life as incompatible with family. He had a point, although I refused to accept his dichotomous view of things: art vs. journalism, fun vs. family, freedom vs. "settled down." I felt I was being typecast as the practical homebody, whereas until meeting him I was a traveler too, an adventurer. I was like him. But now the urge to have a baby was turning me into some kind of enemy.

I moved in with him, and we fought almost every night. As the band was running out of money, I felt I was running out of time. It was tempestuous, sad, and wearing. When I wasn't plotting my own escape, I wondered why he didn't leave me.

Looking back, the thing that also kept us stalled was my insistence that he match my desire for a baby, cell for cell. I wanted him to want one in exactly the same way, and to the same degree, as I did. Otherwise, I wasn't convinced. It didn't occur to me that men might come at the idea of fatherhood from a different angle. Perhaps for men babies are just an idea, an abstraction until they hold them in their arms. But the initial urge, the detailed, irresistible, and irrational longing, was mine. It was physical, like hunger. I refused to admit that this difference could exist between us and not be a failure of love. I needed him to be as sure and single-minded, if not more so, than I was. So there we were, in limbo.

Four years passed in this fashion. I was thirty-six. We had moved into our own apartment, and he had started to free-lance again. The band had turned down a recording contract to pursue success on their terms, but debts eventually forced them to call it quits. Brian decided that, generally speaking, in principle, the idea of a child might not be so bad. It could happen — no need to set a specific date, yet. The bull was in the chute, at least. (Crass biological analogies are in order here.)

But how I resented my role in all this, which was to arrange for timely coition. I had to be ruthless and administrative about it, while he got to be vaguely spontaneous. Already, I was up there in the mother zone, overseeing, planning.

It was September and coming around to ovulation time again on the old Wheel of Fortune. I decided we would give it a whirl in two days, on a Friday. He didn't say no. Except — except — he was playing that night, at an event down at the Cameron Hotel, an artist's hangout. Once again his performance night clashed with ours.

Friday night arrived. We went down to the Cameron, he did his set, and we were about to go home around midnight. I was almost but not quite dragging him through the front room in the direction of the streetcar, the one named Desire, when he caught sight of Mojah, a drummer friend who had just arrived. "I'll be right there," he said to me and headed for the back room.

I waited. Then I heard drums. They were playing together! He had forgotten about me and our momentous unborn child. I was furious. I could have pried the tiles off the floor with my bare nails. I went outside into the raw, wind-whipped fall night, where I waited in a radioactive rage for the Spadina bus.

An hour or so later, he came stealthily up the stairs to our third-floor bedroom — the innocent, tired, satiated musician coming home to the trusty flesh of his somewhat demanding girlfriend. I said I needed him not just to capitulate, but to choose. I accused him of all sorts of other sins, then turned my back on him, and myself, and us. There was a spare bed next door. I crawled away into it and congealed into a solid block of sleep.

Saturday morning, we had to face the fact that we were going to a friend's wedding, which was a two-hour drive north. Well, it's now or never, I thought, still seething from the previous night.

I went into the bedroom and sullenly asked him to join me

on my pallet next door. He was sleepy and unrepentant, but the idea of making love in the morning, like a cup of hot coffee, perked him up. After all, this was sex, the easy part, not just another fight. We have to step on it, I said, or we'll be late for the wedding. I was shut down and stone-faced as we began to make love.

But then something took over. Soon there was nothing ambivalent about what we were doing, nothing halfhearted at all. Babies spring from heat, not ideas. I felt myself fall into the buoyant net of something bigger than our two battling egos. My anger, his resistance, were just part of a tedious game we had played with each other, like children. Our own childishness dissolved in this attempt at child-making, and we came out of it on level ground.

Then we leaped up and began racing around getting ready to go to the wedding. In our newly purchased, three-hundred-dollar used Volvo, we drove up the parkway, with the engine laboring. On the fringes of the city, the unthinkable happened. The car slowed down and trolled to a halt. Since I was in the throes of imagining myself pregnant, this was a sign, and what it said to me was: you have just bought a used car that will break down in the fast lane of the freeway. We will never leave town and reach a better, sweeter place.

Brian took over, suggesting we rent a car and carry on. We would still make the wedding in time, he reassured me. The Volvo was towed off, a new car arrived, and we sped on, distraught but persistent. By driving at frightening speeds through the strobing autumn colors of northern Ontario, we arrived at the church just before the bride appeared.

As we sneaked into a back pew, I wondered exactly how long it takes for the sperm to collide with the lost moon of the ovum. Somewhere between the smoky bar of the previous night and the small-town wedding, our son was conceived, in helpless love and human anger.

*   *   *

Then came the dreams. Shortly after the wedding weekend, I dreamed I was "put in charge" of a baby. Note the passive voice. He pissed up into the air and wet the blankets: a boy. I cleaned it up. Prophetically, I saw my first maternal gesture as cleaning up pee. Another night I dreamed I found myself responsible (the passive, again) for a rather large, blond baby with a forceful, merry personality, who stood up in a somewhat looming fashion in his crib. My father then came by and suggested we go to the driving range and shoot off a few buckets. This I did, with the guilty thought that I ought not to leave the baby alone for too long. A transparent eternal-daughter dream! Also, I correctly saw a Sunday at the driving range as the opposite of motherhood.

Two weeks later, another dream: I did have a baby, in fact, a tiny thing, but it mutated rather charmingly between a little weasel that lived under the sink, to a kind of . . . anchovy, which I lovingly applied to my breast like a poultice. I was quite fond of this distressing creature. I think I was dealing with the evolving life inside me as best I could.

When I decided I was pregnant, I was at a northern lodge being used in the off-season as a writer's retreat. I was trying to finish my first novel, the one about white girls, black men, Dalkon Shields, racism, bush medicine, and cultural colonialism. The first IUD novel of its time. I had my quire of fresh paper, my old Selectric, and I was steaming along. Then, in mid-sentence, as it were, I stopped. Something was happening to me, all over.

It wasn't just that my breasts were sore and my legs seethed with restlessness at night. A knitted cap seemed to have settled on my brain as well. Never think that pregnancy is just a spare room in a woman's house; it changes everything — the heat, the light, the furniture. And why shouldn't it? The idea that we ought to gracefully override pregnancy as something a modern woman can and ought to "handle" is a clue to our devaluation of the body itself.

So there I was, up in the woods, writing about colonialism and sex while I weighed my breasts in my hands and wondered why my pants were getting tight. Well, of course, I didn't wonder, I worried. After five years of haranguing, it was now my turn to be ambivalent. Perhaps it was true, then; perhaps I was going to have a baby. Now what?

Scrupulously, I wrote each day, for long hours. It was typing. At 5 p.m. when I went down to the sleepy lodge bar, beer no longer tasted right. Coffee was too acrid. There was a swarming in my pelvis — "vascular engorgement," as they say in the books — that kept me physically, impersonally, aroused all the time. I confided in another writer, an older woman with two grown sons. "The waist was the first to go with me," she said. "That and the brain."

I consulted the mirror. My face looked as if it had been sublet to a new tenant. I looked deeply preoccupied, not to mention vaguely alarmed. My eyes were gray and said nothing. Little wisps of nausea were catching up to me.

In the lobby of the lodge was a phone booth, the only one available. Brian was out of town on a writing assignment, but when he got back to town, I called him.

"Well," I began briskly, "I think I'm pregnant. My period's a week late."

There was a rather heartbreaking pause.

"Huh," he said. "Amazing." I might have remarked on the unusual number of raccoons in the area.

"Is that all you have to say?"

"It's, it's just a bit of a shock. I don't know how I feel yet."

I recognized this to be true of myself as well, but I wanted one of us to be good on this. The conversation staggered on a bit longer.

"I've got to go," I said, "someone needs the phone. I'll talk to you tomorrow." I hung up and spent the evening bitterly facing a future that might or might not include a father. Well, never mind, the deed was done. I would manage, somehow. I had bleakly oriented myself to single parenthood by the next morning when Brian called. His voice had wings.

"I tried to call back yesterday, but no one answered. I'm sorry I didn't respond last night," he said. "I was in shock. But I feel good about it now. When I got off the phone, I felt this great wave of both joy and sadness."

The first of ten thousand tears came into my eyes. Well, we weren't able to be there for each other at the same time, but perhaps we could be there separately, for each other, now and then.

When I got back home, it was confirmed. We went to dinner — a date, at last — at an Italian restaurant for a rather subdued celebration of our uncertain future. There was no discussion of money, or houses, or the fact that we didn't own a couch — just a toast to the two of us, now rapidly divided into three, for having survived this long.

*   *   *

Then I phoned my parents. "Oh boy," my dad said with a dark helpless chuckle, "you're in for it now, I guess." Brian phoned his parents, speaking in the chipper fashion he reserves for them. Isn't that marvelous, they responded, isn't that exciting. They were the soul of decorum. Nobody breathed a word of censure about our unmarried state, since both our families were conditioned to Support Us in our bewildering and protracted pursuit of personal happiness. But it must have crossed their mind that this baby business might be another passing fad, like bell-bottom jeans.

Much later, it occurred to me how precarious it must have looked to anyone from the outside. But to me, it was an utterly serious commitment to have a child together. It was deeper than marriage. It would be all of our life, or a huge mistake.

*   *   *

Which would it be? Perhaps a therapist would tell me. I remember being pregnant and walking to the office of my new therapist, who urged me not to "ventilate" so much. He was an anti-ventilationist. I told him that I preferred to express anger rather than be repressed. The word repression clearly irritated him. He was Scottish, dark-suited and fat, and no doubt monumentally repressed himself, but he turned out to be helpful. He suggested that anger begat anger, and it would be in my interest to cultivate a little domestic harmony right now. If I planned to stay with Brian, perhaps it would help matters not to browbeat him every evening. I could see the simple wisdom in this.

But first, I did a lot of weeping. I wept out of chastening fear and confusion and because of my body's implacable new tyranny over my life. I was overjoyed in my cells to be pregnant, but afraid that I was with the wrong man, because he might leave me, or not help me in this new task. The shrink kept suggesting to me that I was happy, happier than I've ever been.

"I studied under D.W. Winnicott, and his research was based on thousands of pregnant women, and they were statistically happy," he reminded me. I suppose I was lucky he studied under Winnicott, a writer on childhood development whose books I later came to cherish. It meant he had a professional interest in pregnant women, which was rare enough. I countered with some anecdotes about how strangers on the bus lean over and tell you horror stories about awful births, but he simply listened, his face faintly reflecting the institutional green of his office walls.

His office was in a hospital. To reach it I had to pass through a sequence of push-through double doors that connected the different wards. Other red-eyed women sat in his waiting room. I was impressed and disturbed by the number of females I encountered on the psychiatric floors. The more unavoidably female one became — pregnancy being one example, birth and menopause being others — the more one became a candidate for mental anguish, it seemed.

As the days passed, I filled up with nothing but time. I stopped picking fights. I stopped attacking Brian. This was a calculated decision on my part, a strategy to avoid being abandoned, even though Brian still fondly attributes this to my pregnancy. "You were never as happy as when you were pregnant," he says. When he says this, I can only think of myself stretched out like a manatee on our double bed, sleeping in the afternoon. I was certainly happier than I had been, and grateful for our lucky conception. But I can't equate that otherworldly, passive time as my personal standard for joy.

Pregnancy ends the illusion of autonomy. You are housing somebody else, a living presence. The growing baby shoves aside your guts, pushes up the lungs, rolls you over during the night. It's a third party to the relationship long before the father suspects. He may sing to the baby and converse with your belly, but it's still just an idea, until the baby is born. For the woman, it's already the root, the core around which she walks and dreams.

I read omnivorously. I read Sheila Kitzinger on breast-feeding and Penelope Leach on baby care and, in the afternoon, "Kathy Goes to Haiti" by Kathy Acker, about having lots of sex in a hot country. During mid-pregnancy our sex life became tropical, too, until hugeness eventually intervened. I ate constantly and absent-mindedly. I would find myself standing at the counter, tearing the meat off a roast chicken with my hands. I lay in the bathtub and contemplated the marble basketball that rose above the water line, and the baby inside, going through motions I could not only feel, but see.

Every day I would work — write a book review, work on the stage show I was collaborating on — and in the late afternoon, I fell into the syrupy thick medium of sleep. In a way, sleep was truer to my central work, the knitting together of cells and bones, the deep molecular imagining of the baby. I had no ideas about this stage at all. When I was awake, I was fixated on learning the basics, like how to deal with the cut cord, or how to shampoo a baby without drowning him. This I had never done. As part of my middle-class deformity, and the happenstance of my own family where there are seven years between each sibling, I had never taken care of babies myself. I was ignorant. But I was good at research and assumed that was all that was necessary. So I read.

I caught the eye of other pregnant women on the street, and complex emotions passed between us. I gained forty pounds. My sinuses swelled and ached, the usual hemorrhoids settled in. In pregnancy, the body parks itself in the middle of your mind and won't budge. Still, I can't remember precisely how I felt apart from a calm and profound distraction. I was nothing more, or less, than pregnant, which I think of like this: ( ).

Up until this point, Brian and I had behaved rather like competitive, passionate siblings. We saw our roles inside the relationship as almost identical, which was how I thought it ought to be. But as a pregnant woman, I became different from him. Now I was someone who ate like a wolf, napped like a cat, and dreamed like a madwoman. I began to switch from someone who thought she could walk out the minute things weren't up to scratch to a temporarily weepy, dependent soul. The closer the birth came, in fact, the more I admitted that I needed him — and this was a logical, visceral need, not the old toxic longing. I counted on him to help me through this experience. At the same time, Brian was writing more, and working harder. It was sinking in; he was going to have to help *take care of someone else*. It occurred to me that things were getting rather retrograde — I was making curtains, he was bringing home the bacon. But far from being appalled by this gender gap, it felt equal and came as a relief. For this brief biological passage, I had my territory and he had his. We were embarked on something mysterious together.

4.   Birth

I T WAS early July. Hot. Pictures of me at my shower reveal the sensible short hairdo, and those estrogen-inflated lips. My jaw was heavy, like my pelvis. One of my friends gave me a huge banner with a Madonna (the original Madonna) painting on it with the slogan The Mother Club. Most of the women there had yet to join it.

The due date came, and went. I can't remember how the days passed until I could lumber up to bed again and dream my inhabited dreams. In the last week or so, the hormonal veil lifted, and I went back to coffee, tasted wine. The pregnancy was wearing off, like a drug.

On July 2, I felt some cramps. I was already "effaced," as they so accurately put it — the cervix had softened in preparation for the passage of the baby's head through that pencil point. The baby was down and in position.

Down the street from us was a demonstration to protest the attacks on the country's first free-standing abortion clinic. I made a sign that said "Pro baby and pro choice," and Brian and I strolled down to take part in the gathering. A local paper took a picture of us. Brian, unshaven and wild-haired, looked like a lapsed Trotskyite, and the gleam in my eyes was quite demented as well. I was huge, holding our unholy sign, the waist of my detested maternity pants showing through my big red T-shirt. As I stood outside the clinic in the heat of the chanting crowd, while police lounged in blue cruisers parked in the lane, the mild pains began to acquire a distinct rhythm. After a while, we walked back up the street as the tightening at the bottom of my belly came and went, came and went.

That night we watched Barbara Frum on "The Journal," and I lay on the rug. I began to time the contractions — nine minutes, twelve, six, then nothing for twenty minutes. Obviously free-lance contractions. The hormone cocktail of labor also triggered the start of a migraine headache — the blood vessels in my head were clamping down as my cervix strove to open up. I thought it was entirely characteristic that my head would try to upstage my belly at this point.

The cramps soon acquired a tiny narrative arc, with a beginning, middle, and end. This is probably it, I told Brian. He immediately did as the books instructed and flew to the kitchen to make a bacon sandwich to keep up his strength. The oily, migraine-stoking odor of the bacon snaking up the stairs is something I can smell to this day. So, I thought, this is the way it will be — me upstairs doing the actual labor, while he's somewhere else, seeing to his own needs. Oh well, too late now.

Compared to my pulsing head, I found early labor almost comforting in its orderliness. There was me, and there were the contractions — we made a team. Brian came and went with tea, back rubs, the stopwatch, and a reassuringly normal ability to fall asleep beside me. I cat-napped, kept a bag of frozen peas on the back of my neck, and let the migraine take its course.

Around 7:30 in the morning we called our doctor, who met us at the hospital. Like every other first-time mother, I imagined I was daringly close to delivery when I arrived. My doctor examined me and tactfully changed the subject. A pencil-sized baby could get out of me, maybe.

By luck we scored a "birthing room" — a regular room with a woolly wall-hanging and no visible machines. We puffed and joked and labored away. But by five in the afternoon, the novelty of "managing labor" nicely had worn off. How come, I said to anyone passing through the room, we have twist-offs for beer and it takes me twelve hours to open up? But the loss of control that characterizes the Flume Ride of family life begins with the experience of birth — indeed, it is epitomized by birth. Labor turned out to be long, surprisingly painful, and most illuminating.

Toward evening I was stalled in a five-hour transition — a typically protracted "elderly primipara" birth. The baby's head was slowly revolving inside me, as they often do, from face down to face up. I thought of those scenes in *Das Boot*, where the torpedoes rotate in the torpedo tubes.

All the time, Brian was right there, grafted to my hand. At one point, as he went to close the door, I felt one of those tidal-wave contractions coming on. I put out my hand and have this image of him literally sprinting to my side. No dilly-dallying or ambivalence now. He held nothing back, and his eyes gave me the steady anchor I needed. I began to think of him as one of those hydraulic lifts they use in garages for greasing cars. Employing a complicated system of grips and holds, I made it through the contractions while reducing him to a pulp.

Whoever looks into your eyes has to match that seismic energy inside. I remember looking up into the incredibly blue eyes of my doctor, above her paper mask. They blazed with strength and empathy, hooks suspending me a long way beneath her.

But the baby was not budging, a state of events that had me on exceptionally warm terms with the anesthesiologist, who had finally been summoned. We were trundled off to the O.R. But just as that darling man was topping up a needle and drawing circles on my spine, the doctor detected a new inflection to my yelps. I had one foot propped up on the overhead light, another clue that things were moving along. She examined me and saw that the baby had come round. No time for drugs now.

Back in the birthing room, Brian forlornly stripped the bed, assuming that things were now out of his control. I rolled back in, eyes popping, and we were in full-tilt delivery stage which —

if I hadn't been so closely involved — I would have found slapstick. On one side was a nurse, on the other was Brian, supporting me in a primitive squat, while my doctor and someone I had never seen before cheered me on like fans rooting for the Lakers. I wished everyone would settle down and let me get the knack of this delicate maneuver, getting the baby down and out.

I felt like an insect extruding an egg — a large, fleshy insect with a very tiny brain. I was as close to a beast as I had ever felt, and it was, all things considered, an amazing feeling. The job at hand — getting a baby out of the bottom of my body — seemed absurd. What a joke! Surely, they would find a better way soon. I wanted a cup of tea and a nap. But it also occurred to me that my body might become good at this sort of thing, given half a chance.

At the moment of birth, I felt myself drown in a dark tunnel; as ego flickered out, something else sustained me. I felt both accomplished and exquisitely passive, a collaborator in something that was going to happen with or without my consent. A baby was placed on my chest, a baby with wildly rolling eyes. He clamped on to the nearest breast, a tug I could feel right down to my womb. Meanwhile, there was the nuisance of delivering the placenta, a chore that ended in a grateful gush. They showed me the liver-looking thing, and I couldn't have cared less, although the silvery blue cord was otherworldly and beautiful.

They wrapped him up, and Brian carried him around the room, singing a song to him. He took him over to the wall-hanging. "See?" he said. "That's art, but you don't have to worry about that yet." The teaching milk was already flowing.

I inspected my son. A swirl of dark hair. A high, wrinkled brow, which I immediately attributed to tension rather than his protracted stay in the birth canal. Strong features, wide hands, abominable-snowman feet. While I craned my neck to look at him, a total stranger stitched me up. My body, I had learned, was an unsung genius. It was in cahoots with something bigger. This was sobering — a loss of conscious control, and a gaining of some deeper allegiances.

*   *   *

We were left alone. The bottom of my body felt dramatically reorganized, and I was dismayed by the dishevelled mound of my belly, like an unmade bed. But I was happy, soaringly happy, and Brian had obviously been inhaling helium, too. We sat staring at our slightly yellowish son, across whose face uncensored dreams flickered, in giddy silence. After we called everyone, Brian went home to get some rest.

That night, one by one, the mothers and their babies went to sleep. It was almost midnight. My son was still awake, sucking away. I felt a tiny panic at the fact that the rest of the ward was dark and still, while we were up making noise. A nurse came in and said she would help settle him down. Away he went for the night. I didn't think twice about this, I was used to sleeping with an adult, not a baby, and it seemed natural for him to go away. But for the longest time, his small cry trailed in my mind. A new channel had opened in my ear, the baby channel. It stayed on all the time like an intercom. Some part of me was now permanently awake and on alert.

lost

in

the

mother

zone

5.   Breast

LAST WEEK I noticed the family photo albums were out on the coffee table. Casey had been showing them to Irene. Casey is eight now; Irene, our neighbor and his favorite baby sitter, is sixteen.

I remembered a certain photo near the front of the album, of me with my breast-feeding breasts, sprawled half-naked on a cottage couch in the heat of summer. On my lap is Casey, at two months, eyeing my huge nipples. For the first time, I felt some embarrassment about these and other innocently half-clad post-natal photographs. I wasn't sure I wanted the young and lovely Irene casually leafing through pictures of my blue-veined, pragmatic breasts. Another picture featured a newborn Casey, his mouth open in the shape of a door knocker, about to clamp onto a large unidentified eggplant-object which is — was — my breast.

How could I have pasted my bare self into the family photo album in this manner? It could only be that I was proud of this accomplishment and that whenever I looked at a picture of myself and my new son, I could only see the baby. My disappearing had begun. I was the appendage.

I am amazed at how the power of photographs changes in this way. At a certain point, the soul exits from a cherished photograph, because we have come to the end of our loving projection into that moment. Someone new eclipses the old image.

We have another picture of Casey at three months, smiling a beatific smile — three months is the Age of the Beatitudes — with every molecule of his chubby self. I couldn't take my eyes off the picture for weeks afterwards. Every time I looked at it, framed on the mantle, I thought, This is the strongest, gentlest, kindest smile I've ever seen. Is it just this photograph, I asked Brian, or have we lucked into a baby with such a fund of sweetness that it pours out of him like honey?

In due time, the acrylic frame on the picture was dropped, and it cracked; one corner of the photo was somehow ripped. I picked it up the other day. Were his cheeks always that fat? I thought, incidentally impressed by the undimmed virility of the smile. His one hand was waving and blurred. The background colors were slightly washed out. Who gave me that corny blanket? I noted the imperfections in the photo, and in my own nearly perfect son. It occurred to me that I was no longer strung on that silver chain between the eye and the face of the beloved. I was separate now.

I flipped through the photo album and looked at other photos through Irene's sixteen-year-old eyes. In one shot, Casey is two months old or so. He is bare except for a red-and-white-striped T-shirt and tiny loop-covered white socks. It was our first trip away from home with him; he's lying on a towel on a deserted little curve of sand in front of a friend's cottage. I have my back turned to the lake and am crouched over him, full breasts dangling like a she-wolf, alert for sunburn, black flies, or sudden, baby-snatching waves. My belly is still rippled, my hair dark and unbrushed. My face looks as open to gusts of feeling and fear as Casey's face, which could careen from ecstasy to consternation. His gaze at the camera is calm and profound, the soul full-strength and uncensored. I am clearly oblivious to the fact that I am crouching naked on the beach. It is all I can do to meet that gaze, for the time being. My bare breasts might as well be a sensible flannel shirt.

During the cracking-open of birth and the streaming out of

milk and emotion, physical modesty becomes dimly remembered etiquette, like using the proper spoon. You remember to pull your nightgown down and spare hospital visitors the sight of too much thigh, but the gesture is for them, not you. Your body has just done this great and rather public thing: the beast of birth launched a baby into the hands of a team cheering your every animal grunt. You have been naked and split open like a papaya, without a second's embarrassment. After that, it's hard to remember, as you shift the baby from one side to the other, that a wet breast sticking out of your robe may unnerve the acquaintance from work who stops by with flowers.

When Casey was well past the breast-feeding age, I remember visiting a friend in the hospital who had just had her third child. As I opened the door, I walked into the smell of milk, clean sweat, and the faint brininess of the mother's bleeding — all of it sweet and intimate, a smell like a lover's bed. I was dressed up for an interview and felt the oily gloss of lipstick on my mouth. My friend's eyes flickered quickly from my face back to the face of her purplish son, who squirmed through his dreams in a see-through plastic bin beside her bed. She looked pale, but supremely relaxed and pleased. I could still remember how having a two-day-old baby makes you feel faintly sorry for everyone else, stuck in their wan unmiraculous lives.

We chatted and she even remembered to ask, without a smidgen of genuine interest, about some magazine matter that was obsessing our mutual friends. The pupils of her eyes were dilated with drinking in the sight of her new son. He began to cry, turning an even deeper shade of red, scowl-faced in his white flannel cocoon. She unwrapped him, bathing him in a musical stream of words with unselfconscious tenderness. Soon we could see that the scowl was related to a great dark explosive shit. As she held his two feet up, like cigars between her fingers, I took away the diaper, which smelled like earth, or something clean, and brought back a damp cloth.

"Now, let's see if I remember how to do this," she said to the baby, swabbing away. Newborns have plump, conspicuous genitals. A brand new boy seems to have two equal poles: the small, twisting face and the surprisingly strong, expressive contours of the genitals. Unwrapped, his arms trembled in the unfamiliar air.

As soon as he was dry, his crying ceased and his mouth popped open in a yawn. His skin was all sorts of shades at once — red, bluish, whitish, a tinge of yellow. The color seemed to change with every pump of the heart. The tiny nail beds on his fingers were a deep purple. Everything about him was as abruptly changeable as a film of clouds scudding across the sky. She reached into her robe like someone fumbling for a wallet and lobbed out one breast. As soon as the baby's cheek touched her breast, his mouth stood open in a crested wave, seeking out the nipple. His jaws closed around it as if he were trying to stuff the whole breast in his mouth. Two round, clean nostrils, through which we could see bright orange light, flared above the perfect suction he had achieved.

"Yikes," she said, "he doesn't fool around." The baby's head was the same size as her breast, two curves joined at the mouth. I felt the events of my day blow away, like old newspapers. Being in the room was like sitting on the porch of a cabin, realizing what a relief it is to look out across an empty lake. The falling away of everything else always comes as a surprise. We sat there listening to the pulling and swallowing, pulling and swallowing, a dialogue that comfortably eclipsed ours. After awhile, I propped open the cards on her windowsill, made small talk to break the spell, and left to do my interview. As I walked out of the hospital, I felt the headlong momentum of my day stagger a little, and then proceed.

*   *   *

Day two in the hospital. The first fews days after birth, the breasts produce colostrum, and Casey sucked away on that. The feeling goes all the way down to the floor of the body, where it plucks at the empty womb, drawing it tight again. The nourishing is mutual — the baby is grooming the mother's body from the inside out, the way bears lick their newborn cubs into shape. So far, so good, I thought.

But on the third or fourth day, my breasts turned stony hard and swollen with milk that wouldn't flow. My "letdown reflex" was apparently not letting down. In my susceptible postnatal state, hormones careening, I found this miserably in character with everything I had ever done in my life — going to the edge and then stopping. Going as far as Casablanca, but not Marrakesh. Stuffing my computer with words and never getting to hard copy. *Of course* I wouldn't let down — I was a hoarder, a coward, an up-tight white girl with useless round Jell-O molds for breasts. The more I thought these thoughts, the less I flowed.

I wasn't sure how this next thing was supposed to go. Birth had happened; the baby was thriving. Surely more passivity on my part would do the trick! So I waited. My breasts rose like ceramic teapots underneath my gown.

It was a Sunday, and the regular hospital staff were gone. Three strangers, a woman and two men in white coats, breezed in. They said hello and flipped back the sheets. "Oh, oh, trouble," the resident said. They palpated my rock-hard breasts. "Jump in a hot shower, massage them like crazy, and if nothing happens, we'll have to get you on a pump." Work on them, they said, and left.

Needs more work, I sniffled. The same old marginalia!

Tears flowed, but not the milk. I phoned Brian and whimpered like a caged animal about my maternal failure. This was just fatigue and hormones, he reassured me. I dissolved in a cascade of tears, liquid flowed out of me at every orifice, but my breasts stood firm. It felt like some horrible new version of writer's block.

This was also the day I looked at the intravenous pricks on the back of my hand, which still throbbed, and *knew* that they would become infected, and that I would die, leaving my newborn son motherless. Mortality washed over me and I mourned myself wholeheartedly. I was surely going to die, as surely as my son was born! My feet ached, with a residue of labor pain. My breasts ached. When I walked to the bathroom, I had the distinct sensation that most of my organs were going to slide out of me and onto the floor.

In the shower, I stood and kneaded away at the sides and tops of my breasts, weeping like a little girl. A drop or two of bluish milk hung off my nipple, but nothing more. The trick was to give in, now. I took my stony breasts in my hands and shuffled back to bed.

By 11 p.m., nothing had happened. It's not a good feeling to lie in bed and imagine what it might be like to blow up. "Yes, the baby's adorable, but unfortunately the mother exploded. . . ." A new nurse came into the room and said she would give me a session with the breast pump, to gets things moving. I noted that this nurse was one of those strong middle-aged women with large, girdled, cone-shaped breasts. She had a heavy German accent, and I'm not making that part up.

Once again, the rest of the ward was quiet and dark. I seemed to be the only one awake, the only one not yet functioning as a mother. The nurse sat me down at a white porcelain table, under a big wall clock. She rummaged in a storeroom and came back with a medieval-looking machine with rubber hosing, suction cups, and a motor.

"You can't let this sort of thing go," she said, "or else you'll end up like I did." Then she popped open her uniform, hauled up her industrial-strength brassiere, and revealed to me a great brown scar on the side of one enormous breast.

"Mastitis," she said, with a downward twitch of her mouth. "I had a blocked duct, it became abscessed, and they had to operate. I was in the hospital for three weeks."

I obediently placed one uncooperative breast in the cup of the contraption. This must be how men feel, I thought, when they have to come up with a sperm sample on demand. Or perhaps it was closer to a reverse form of impotence — I could get it up, but I couldn't get it down. The nurse glanced at the clock, turned on the machine, and left me to the infernal succor of the pump. Soon enough thick yellow liquid, like the old top-cream that rose to the surface of a glass bottle of milk, inched through the hose. The nurse came back and looked approvingly at the rich stuff in the cup. I reflected on the fact that I was more responsive to a machine under a clock than to the expert suction of my own baby: Robomom.

I hadn't figured out yet that giving birth is not a discrete event — in fact, it is just the beginning. Once the baby is born, the breasts labor on, gushing at the sound of the baby's cries or even in response to the image of an infant on TV. The baby's new connection to the breast heals the umbilical disruption, over and over. The mother-and-baby symbiosis is not severed suddenly, but stutters and fades, slowly. Once again, I had thought that my will, or skill, had something to do with all of this. But all it did was get in the way of what the body already knows.

*　　　*　　　*

It was time to take the baby home. As a nurse watched the two of us dress Casey for the trip home, I worried that if we couldn't get his little stretch-suit on the right limbs, we might be detained as unfit parents. Another nurse with a tiny, lopsided smile, who must have accompanied many anxious couples transporting their first babies home, walked us down to the exit.

"Have fun!" she sang as the door hissed shut.

It was noon on a summer day, white-hot and, to my room-dulled eyes, glittering with perilous shapes and surfaces ill-suited to a baby's perception. I flipped the undyed, unbleached, unsynthetic, elf-woven blanket over Casey's face as I waited in the heat for Brian to bring the car around. I was now in charge of another human being for the next sixteen years, at least.

Brian pulled up in the aged Volvo. With exquisite caution and smoothness, we drove home, as I marveled at the cruelty of car grilles, the plumes of truck exhaust, the offensive blankness on the faces of pedestrians. The brutal, insensate, ordinary world was an insult to my unsheathed nerves and feelings, which were now wired to another far more vulnerable human. It was searingly clear to me that no baby could make it across town during lunch hour on his own. My eyes sought the big trees in Queen's Park for consolation, the dusty tulips along Hoskin Avenue, the howling faces of the gargoyles on Trinity College. Any countenance, any growing thing. Cars especially seemed a nasty and alien invention. Everything ought to be measured against its imagined impact on a new baby, I thought, in my new demagoguery. The world was a comical breast pump, manned by a scarred nurse in a uniform.

*   *   *

Ten days later, I kept an appointment I had previously made with a dermatologist, to have a mole removed. I had never met the woman before. I took my newborn son, traveling there like a teacup in a taxicab. The doctor was friendly, glib, and too jocular for my taste; I was still in a weird hormonal mood. She looked at the mole, a black speck on my left breast, always the troublemaker. "Oh yes, that should come off," she said, turning back to pick out a little plunger that she used, without further ado, to excise the mole. Out in the waiting room, where the receptionist was holding him, my son started to cry. I looked down at the neat red circle where the mole had been, which the doctor was now bandaging. What she did with that little bit of me I have no idea. The doctor (did I hallucinate this?) was now asking me where I bought my underwear. All of a sudden, the invasion and casual snatching of various parts of my person and privacy came down on me, and I swerved into a passing but compelling madness. I hated the doctor, who told me I might have a "slight scar, which can also be removed." I remember feeling mutilated, and sadly misshapen, when in fact I had just had a tiny, benign mole plucked off. I mumbled something, got dressed, and retrieved my son as quickly as possible. The restoring of him to my arms was the beginning of a feeling of security I would return to every day.

On the way home in the cab, weeping those almost meaningless new-mother tears, I also cried for some other loss — of privacy, of certainty, of my old body — some indistinct, unrecoverable piece of myself.

When a mother comes home with her new baby, she will find her abstractions are all concrete now. "Freedom" now means being able to take a shower. "Mobility" means being able to reach the glass of water on the dresser while not breaking the baby's suction on the breast. "Flexibility" means being able to push the Record function on the VCR without dropping the baby.

Childless, I think I imagined that while breast-feeding, I would read, or even write a little, and "use my time" productively. I fantasized breast-feeding as a cozy way to sit there doing nothing. Then I discovered that while breast-feeding, I only wanted to drink him in, too — to gaze at my son's face, contemplate the genius curl of his exploring hand, and fall into his candid eyes. It was "doing nothing" in the same way that looking into a lover's face is doing nothing; it becomes the whole world. It didn't occur to me that this tiny human had captured my attention with just his mouth, his eyes, and the smell of the top of his head.

Falling in love is deeply preoccupying. When my son turned eight, I remember the day that he first fell for a girl in his class, the redoubtable Charlotte. I had picked him up from school. He spotted her going by, in her mother's car. "There's Charlotte," he said, and for perhaps the first time ever, he fell silent. All the way home, he was silent, turned in to himself. It was evidently a full-time job, to think about Charlotte. So it was with breast-feeding — a form of "doing nothing" that was as mysterious as love, or sex.

The flow of milk through that powerful little mouth clamped on to your breast is a demand that is easily fulfilled. It ceases to be a demand. There is no power struggle in this coupling.

Between the small and fiercely focused baby and the large, still mother, there is balance. Her giving adjusts physiologically to the baby's taking. No one in this embrace is guilty. The baby does not fantasize about Dolly Parton instead of his mother. The mother does not imagine a different or better baby. The infamous "erotic" quotient of breast-feeding is not so much the physical stimulation as the still, calm, sumptuous feeling of being conjoined with another. It is not lofty or cerebral, but simple, rich, and physical. It is enough.

Breast-feeding is part of the female sexual continuum. It is not "like" adult sex in the sense of being stimulated, or of stirring orgasmic feelings, even though breast-feeding can make the uterus contract. It is its own pleasure, a new chapter of erotic magnanimity.

A woman with her baby at the breast does not feel like a pastel, asexual mother sitting there doing something for the good of the baby. If she's not too tired and it's not the eighteenth go-round for the day, she feels powerfully, physically sufficient unto another. Oddly enough, although the mother appears to be large and "in charge," the feeling of breast-feeding is not of this tiny, helpless little thing clinging to your queenly self — you feel equivalent to the baby, and that the two of you exist in delicate equilibrium. This is physiologically true; the flow of milk is calibrated to the baby's needs and desires. The more he nurses, the more milk the breasts produce. When the baby nurses less, the flow slows down. There are no hurt feelings. The mother does not control the baby's appetite, and the baby does not control the mother, although she is kept sedentary and still for long stretches of the day.

Breast-feeding feeds your desire for communication and connection, takes the edge off your hunger and conveniently stupefies you with hormones. There is that deep preoccupation — not the pregnancy fog, but more a self-sufficient cocoon — that keeps you from being engaged too deeply or injuriously with the rest of the world. It is out there, beyond the more or less perfect economic contract between you and the baby, a warless, unblemished state of supply and demand. (Cracked nipples are another chapter. . . .)

People are loath to admit to the power of hormones in women's lives because we still feel that any sexual distinction will be used against us — but the hormones that accompany breast-feeding are like a shield warding off unnecessary stress. This doing-of-nothing changes her relationship to her partner, and even the rest of the world.

Her mate is over there, outside the bubble of mother and baby. She misses him. Or she doesn't miss him at all and feels twinges of guilt. Or she doesn't miss him and doesn't feel guilty. She wonders at this state of events. The rest of the world seems benignly chaotic, a hodgepodge of aggressions and suffering that suggest the whole planet has been orphaned and unbreasted. But the mother is no longer hooked, snagged, by the news. It goes by, outside her shield.

Her ability to fill the simple needs of this one baby gives her a kind of strength that the unquenchable demands of the world cannot drain away from her. The complacency of the mother-baby bubble has a useful sequel — namely, that the mother knows succor begins simply, directly, and that it is within her power to dispense life and nourishment. Before the baby, for so many years, giving or not giving was the result of cogitated decisions, the weighings of pros and cons. The ease with which one can give to a baby strengthens the intellectual courage to give. You sat there for hours, flowing into the mouth of an apparently insatiable baby who had no thought for your sleep or self-preservation. And the giving was in the end a gift to you.

Breast-feeding is an unsentimental metaphor for how love works, in a way. You don't decide how much or how deeply to love — you respond to the beloved and give with joy exactly as much as they want. In all our efforts to de-mystify motherhood and to free women from their identification with the life force, we risk overlooking the amazing integrity of the female body and its powers.

As usual, pedagogy has brought us to the point where new mothers view breast-feeding as a skill, a schedule, a kindly kingdom of motherly feelings. It will surprise her to find that breast-feeding is above all a relationship, and that it occupies the mind in a way you don't even realize until you step outside that tired, dreamy bubble.

6.   Mother Country

CASEY WAS six weeks old. I would get dents in my knees from the texture of the living-room rug, as I knelt watching him sleep in his basket. This gazing was a full-time job. Brian was busy listening to every song ever recorded by Sting, whom he was about to go and interview. I discovered a new meaning in "Every Breath You Take." Every breath you take, I'll be watching you.

In every other way, life was turning out differently than I had imagined, but here was this large, silk-skinned, clever-mouthed baby who triggered such straightforward love. All he did was eat, sleep, and screw his face up in uncivilized ways, and yet to my eyes he was mesmerizing in every detail, from the wide, square hands with their shocking newborn strength, to his creased, articulate feet, unblunted by shoes. Each movement fascinated, like the undulation of a snake or the slowed-down flight of a bird — I never ran out of wonder. The complexity of the adult he would become, the most convoluted thought he would ever think seemed to be already there in his expression, clear and abbreviated. I understood what it meant to feast on the sight of someone.

We would often both watch him sleep, like two people around a campfire. Perhaps this is a necessary sort of holding, too — a prayerful canopy of attention that somehow nourishes. We could see dreams move under his skin, through which the faintly visible blue and red blood pulsed. Even the delicate bone plates of his head were still shifting, knitting together. And yet when I held him, wrapped in flannel, he felt surprisingly muscular, warm, and alive. He was as busy shaping himself in my arms as I was in learning how to hold him.

So he slept and filled us up, and every song we listened to acquired a whole new meaning. It's amazing how much you can love when there is no inhibition or fear.

I was awash in this flow of bittersweet emotion — the fleetingness of babyhood shadows every feeling — when Brian went off to Montreal to write his profile of Sting. It was the first of many trips to come that would whisk him off to foreign cities and the ether of celebrity, while I stayed home with Casey. Of course resentment was nothing new — writing and envy seem to go together, like coal mining and emphysema. The competition between us is always fairly open and good-natured. But after Casey was born, our professional lives began to diverge.

Brian's rather eclectic assignments during Casey's first year included a story on chuck-wagon racing and a week of helicopter skiing. When he cracked some ribs on the chuck-wagon story, it was hard to muster up sympathy for him. He was managing to incorporate some travel and adventure into the job of supporting his new family. Meanwhile, I was free-lancing up in the bedroom and collaborating on a stage show with three women, a trio of lip-sync satirical performers known as The Clichettes. We were working on a show, a comedy about the future of gender, set in Niagara Falls. A few days after Casey was born, the Clichettes showed up at the hospital in their lounge-singer drag, wearing powder-blue tuxedos. They plugged in the ghetto blaster and performed Paul Anka's "You're Having My Baby," much to the amusement of the nursing staff.

The writing process went like this. One of them would have an idea involving two choruses of "Delilah" by Tom Jones. I would then try to dream up a narrative context for the scene. It was found narrative — rather like motherhood, when you think about it. Improvising both at the same time, however, was tricky.

Every once in a while, I would try to think of a scene that would explain the three of them in nude male body-suits, performing "Go To Hell" by Motorhead. Nothing would come to mind. I did my best to work, but it was clear the writing would have to wait a while.

*　　*　　*

Brian had been gone a few days. There were still a few breast-feeding kinks to work out, but otherwise I was under the illusion that I was deeply, comprehensively happy at home with my new son. I didn't even like Sting that much. I'd been to Montreal. Besides, Brian couldn't breast-feed, which was mostly what I was doing. Everything was going smoothly. Then the phone rang.

"Hi!" Animated, out-of-town voice.

"Hi." Instant flat mother monotone.

"How's Casey?"

"He's fine, although I can't get him to stay on the left breast. It keeps getting blocked. *But enough about that.* So — how was Sting?"

"Very articulate, down to earth. We got on quite well." *To make a long story short.*

"How's the hotel?"

"My room is great. They leave these amazing Belgian truffles on the pillows at night."

"So when do you think you'll be coming home." *Question as statement.*

"Well . . . I thought it would be good for the piece to see the concert tonight."

"But you saw the same concert in Toronto last week."

"This is a *club*, in Montreal — there'll be a whole different feel. . . ."

"I bet."

"What's that supposed to mean?"

"Nothing." *Silence.*

"So, how are you doing?"

"Fine. The usual, tired."

"Have you talked to anyone?"

"Judith. My mother called."

"Well, I miss you both." *Palpably untrue, to judge by the lilt in his voice; ah, the joy of missing your loved ones in pleasant bars in foreign cities!*

"We miss you, too. Let me know when you're getting in. Have fun tonight." *Palpably insincere, spoken in the tinny bright voice of the stoical wife.*

We hung up. I was standing in the kitchen, looking out the side window down into the tangled garden of the Chinese woman who lived next door. Huge marrow-looking vegetables grew under a canopy of thick, twisting stems. It was about four in the afternoon. There was not quite enough time to lie down and grab a nap before the baby woke up. He and I were still generic — I mothered, he babied.

A long narrow hall led to the small front room, where the TV and its blue breath lived. Upstairs was my cluttered desk, with lapsed work. In the middle of the apartment was the baby's yellow room, his motorized mobile, the quilted altar of the change table. The kitchen had a wooden parquet counter, where food crept into the crevices. A table sat under a back window with a green shade, overlooking the lane, a coach house where an unseen baby often cried, and the wild, overgrown yard.

As it happened, my friends either had no babies or older children, so I didn't have enough of the lifesaving company of parents with kids going through the same stage. My mother called often, which helped. We carried on wonderfully detailed discussions about herniated navels and iron supplements. But the days were long. I missed the world, and tea with stars. At the same time, this new loneliness coexisted with a voluptuous feeling of completion and arrival. I was here, where I had been so restless to be for the past five years. I didn't miss "work" at all. But I felt at an inexplicable remove from the rest of the world, and that I hadn't anticipated. It seemed as if fewer and fewer people understood what I was going through, and one of them was not, alas, the baby's father.

The things I did all day and all night with my new baby were changing me, with or without my consent. Brian held the baby, changed the diapers, tried to imagine, keep up, but his focus was on work, and earning money. It pretty well had to be. He was cleaving to the visible, to the worldly, to Sting. And I was disappearing.

*   *   *

Not that I was going to be a candidate for postnatal depression. As far as I was concerned, apart from a single bad day in the hospital I had skipped that one. Then, when I was least expecting it, it ambushed me when Casey was five months old.

Brian was going to take part in a publishing workshop, in Banff, Alberta, a town for which I felt a strong attachment ever since I worked there as a summer student, a town I had once written about. I always felt better in the mountains, and so I had great hopes for this trip, our first as a family. I imagined that while Brian worked, I would go cross-country skiing with Casey tucked in a back pack, wearing a little nordic tuque. (This is one of the more poignant things about new motherhood, the way you persist in these escape fantasies that involve the whole family.)

What actually happened was that Brian spent long days with the students, feeling attractive and professional. The town was in the grip of an unusual cold snap, way below zero, so tramping about with a baby was out of the question. Instead I read, and breast-fed, and spent the days alone. By 3 p.m., I was stir crazy; I would bundle the two of us up, call a cab, wait forty minutes sweating and peeling off scarves, then ride a quarter-mile down the main street lined with snowbanks to a coffee shop in the basement of a tiny mall. There I would prop Casey up in his pack and unwrap him and me so I could eat a bran muffin and drink a cup of tea under fluorescent lights, in the company of other adult humans.

One day the weather let up a little. It was sunny and windless. I packed Casey in thermal layers and inserted him into his back pack. The exhaust of cars was billowing white, a sign of intense cold. We walked over the bridge and up the road to Sulphur Mountain. I remembered that when I was three months pregnant, I had skied down a mountain this size. But now I was ecstatic just to be out, and Casey crooned happily. I turned around to check him often, mindful — as my mother certainly would be — of that rural legend in which a woman goes cross-country skiing with her baby in a back pack. When she gets back home, she discovers that the baby has died from hypothermia.

We returned without incident. I felt the blood rejoice a little in my veins. But as I undressed Casey, I noticed a white patch on his cheek. Frostbite. I touched it. It felt cold, almost wooden. I waited for the white circle to go pink as I played with him and blew on his face. He was happy and laughing, as usual. The patch wouldn't go away. My selfish desire to get out and walk had branded him with my restlessness — a tattoo of frozen feeling that is still visible whenever he goes out in the cold and comes back red-cheeked with just that disk of white.

I had counted on Banff to reconnect me to my past. Instead, I ended up bunkered inside an apartment, reading magazines and looking out sorrowfully at the mute, snow-covered mountains. I was pressed up against my past, but it was too cold to reinhabit it. Brian was baffled by my blackness, as was I. As far as I was concerned, I was in advanced motherhood — postnatal depression wasn't supposed to happen now. I couldn't even recognize how in the middle of everything I still was — "the overwhelmingness of the dominant," as Tillie Olsen calls it — or how completely breast-feeding still structured my days. Just the look of ego-fed extroversion on Brian's face when he walked in at the end of the day was enough to make me furious. Our cozy little threesome turned out to be a busy, absent guy, a bored, depressed mother, and a happy, frostbitten baby, immune to all of this.

At the end of the week in Banff, I was relieved to get home, to my rocker, to unambitious stroller-journeys up to the store or the café, and to all the routines I hadn't even noticed I had established. Banff reminded me of freedom, physical vigor and dreams, just at a time when an entirely different sort of intensity had me in its grip.

*　　*　　*

When I came home, I went foraging in the bookstores again. I needed new answers, but the more how-to-parent books I read, the worse I felt. They speak in small paragraphs of an "adjustment phase" for the father, or "baby blues" for the mother. Their advice didn't seem addressed to the mothers I overheard in the park.

It was dawning on me instead that family, like sex, is insoluble — it's a work-in-progress, a never-ending renovation job that begins with tidy blueprints and ends in plaster dust and daily chaos. Someone in the family is always a little bit in trouble, a little bit in the shadows. This natural imbalance is not the problem — it's part of the ecology of family, the way roots find a way to creep under every fence we put up. The main problem may be that we don't like to confront the reality of motherhood, or what children really need from us. Motherhood is like Albania — you can't trust the descriptions in the books, you have to go there.

While morosely scanning the shelves, looking for the section on Maternal Failure, I came upon the work of D.W. Winnicott, the British psychoanalyst who began as a pediatrician and went on to write a number of classic books on childhood development. I remembered him from my psychoanalytic reading — he was Mr. Object-Relations. But anyone who reads Spock and Brazelton is also reading *through* to Winnicott. "Neither the mother nor the baby needs advice," he wrote in 1968, in *Babies and Their Mothers.* "Instead of advice what they need is an environmental provision which fosters the mother's belief in herself."

Old-fashioned though he may be (he published mainly in the fifties and sixties, and his books tend to relegate the father to a largely supportive role), Winnicott's books remain timely and wise. He learned from ordinary mothers, he didn't impose learning on them. And in addition to being a charming and accessible writer, he even sees the bright side of "maternal failure."

In a lecture on the communication between mother and child, he said, "Human beings fail and fail, and in the course of ordinary failure a mother is all the time mending her failures. These relative failures with immediate remedy undoubtedly add up eventually to a communication, so that the baby comes to know about success . . . about having been loved." A mother adapts to the baby's needs simply and brilliantly, by holding — and this crucial time of holding "allows the baby to be able to feel real." But after a while, Winnicott explains, the baby begins to need the mother to "fail to adapt." All the time she adapted, the baby learned confidence. Then, as the baby grows and she "fails" to adapt to his demands, the baby is freed to exercise this new confidence.

Winnicott attributes the mother's complex response not to maternal instinct, but to memory. "When she was a baby, she had just these same needs. She does not remember but nothing of experience is ever lost, and somehow it happens that the mother meets the new baby's dependence by a highly sensitive personal understanding that makes her able to adapt to real need."

Gee. What a switch. He makes mothering sound neither tricky nor difficult, but valuable. At the same time, he deflects the mantle of paternal authority himself. Mothering, he writes, "cannot be done by trying hard, or by a study of books." The thing that sets Winnicott apart from the less insightful "parenting" experts is the fact that he was fascinated by motherhood not as a set of rules or a strategy, but as a dynamic *relationship* with the baby. He saw how vitally important it was to be held. In other words, he understood the importance of mothering, without transforming it into an area of authority or expertise. His focus was on babies and their parents as human beings engaged in delicate interaction. Benjamin Spock is in many ways a kindred spirit, telling new mothers to trust their own instinct. But Winnicott is worth reading in his own words.

Eventually, however, I fled the parenting shelves entirely and took refuge in other unfashionable visions. Rereading *To the Lighthouse* by Virginia Woolf was a revelation. Her portrait of Mrs. Ramsay remains clairvoyantly modern in its portrayal of maternal ambivalence.

"No, she thought, putting together some of the pictures he had cut out — a refrigerator, a mowing machine, a gentleman in evening dress — children never forget. For this reason, it was so important what one said, and what one did, and it was a relief when they went to bed. For now she need not think about anybody. She could be herself, by herself."

And this consoling fragment of a letter from writer Katherine Mansfield to her friend Ida Baker, quoted in Tillie Olsen's book *Silences* : "Jack can never realize what I have to do. He helps me all he can but he can't help me really and the result is I spend all my energy, every bit, in keeping going, I have none left for work. All my work is behindhand and I can't do it. I simply stare at the sky. I am too tired even to think. What makes me tired? Getting up, seeing about everything, arranging everything, *sparing him*, and so on."

I was hungry for any rogue theory or fragment of a novel that would reflect back to me my curious sense of being surprised by so much of motherhood. *Why* did it come as a surprise — it amounted to a conspiracy of silence around the true nature of child-rearing. At first, I blamed my own mild shock on my late-mother ego, fat on fifteen years of uninterrupted independence. Then another book by another maverick psychoanalyst came to my rescue — Alice Miller's *Thou Shalt Not Be Aware — Society's Betrayal of the Child.*

Published more than twenty years ago, Miller's book was one of the first to seriously address the roots and consequences of child abuse. She has since become something of a cult figure in the self-help field, but this hasn't obscured the brilliance with which she has dismantled our pedagogical prejudices.

When Miller was a practicing psychoanalyst (she now writes full-time), her most radical act was to believe what her patients told her. They convinced her that therapists are only human and tend to side with the "parent," or an authority figure such as another therapist, rather than accepting the truth of childhood memories. Freud had found the idea of adults sexually abusing children too preposterous to absorb; but by postulating his Drive Theory of sexual development, he was able to interpret his patients' accounts of childhood abuse as evidence of "normal" Oedipal yearnings, or hysteria, instead. Miller doesn't waste time chastising Freud, who went as far into the psyche as he could, in his time. Her point is that adults have a powerful investment in hiding some of the more painful truths buried in childhood.

If a child suffers at the hand of an adult, the memory of abuse may go underground but it persists into adulthood. It can cause not only pain but puzzling distortions of behavior, especially violence, in Miller's opinion. The recent flood of abuse and incest victims trying to repair the damage of the past seems to bear out what Miller says — when bad things happen to children, amnesia is the rule, not the exception. Hence the commandment, Thou Shalt Not Be Aware. But the self never forgets. Sooner or later, childhood will present its bill.

I think Miller's theory applies even to happy, "normal" families — the struggles that accompany growth itself, the strangely urgent battles with the two-year-old, the new mother's disorientation, the new father's melancholy sense of exclusion — all the strong and painful emotions that accompany the business of child-raising are eventually suppressed or "forgotten." Only mothers or fathers in the thick of it, or day-care workers putting in long days, are close enough to recognize the power of it all.

In other words, denial of the truths surrounding family is not an accident. It is *the way things work*. Mothers assume it is "just them," feeling divided between motherhood and self, home and work, husband and baby. They no longer see how the culture as a whole works hard to keep the world of childhood (and the mothers lost in it) at a safe distance.

But there is a hopeful side to this, too. As mothers, we try to empathize with our children. And as the products of a generation that has made a lifelong project of "growing up," we sometimes empathize more than is strictly necessary. Perhaps our anxieties around motherhood are not just the result of a spoiled generation discovering what the rest of the world has done so stoically for centuries. It may be something more encouraging — that modern parents, through their own confusion and refusal to "grow up," are able to side with their own children and to help them be seen and heard clearly, in an adult-oriented world. They don't accept the role of the parent who must retrain children in their own image. Despite our new impatience with "child-centered" education and permissiveness, we tend to heed the crying baby and pick him up, even when someone tells us to close the door and let him cry.

The idea that babies have emotional lives, that they are born with resilient personalities of their own, is very recent. Before this century, children were sent off to work or raised as little dolls, vessels into which schooling and self-discipline were poured. The discovery of childhood has also tempted many parents my age to remain unfinished selves. We prefer to empathize with children — indeed, we can go so far as to compete with them. But there are perils involved in this new fascination with childhood. To truly identify with a child, we make ourselves vulnerable again. For women who have spent the last twenty years trying to muster a little control and power, this new vulnerability as a mother can feel treacherous indeed.

7.   Rage

ONCE casually asked my mother if there was any job she would have liked. "Not really," she said, "I enjoyed staying at home and raising you kids." Then she added, "Although I did think at one point that I might have made a good geneticist."

I'm sure my mother would have excelled in any number of professions — medicine, journalism, painting. Instead she practices all these things and more, covertly, within the parameters of the family. She has a thousand skills, and my father and her three children and three grandchildren have been the happy beneficiaries of all of them. It's not quite accurate to say she "just" stayed home.

My father is a civil engineer and so, in a way, is she. He worked hard to earn the money to pay for what she then engineered, using all the science and ingenuity that running a household — making a world out of it — requires. Not having her own income was the only thing I ever heard her regret about this arrangement. She probably wanted to give more of it away and felt bad about doling out someone else's wages.

Growing up, home was a given, not a construct. There was the separate realm of school and friends, but not that looming, modern sense we have of a parallel reality beyond family. For the most part, the whole world took place within the walls of our split-level house. I didn't see my mother and father as having undernourished "selves" in conflict with their roles as parents.

I remember one night when my mother was down in the basement sewing yet another couturier prom dress for me, a lined black crepe sheath, with hand-stitched spaghetti straps. It was late, and as I sat on the stairs I made some callow remark, such as "Gee, it's a good thing you like to sew." Without looking up from the sleeve-shaped ironing board where she was flattening a seam, she said quite mildly, "I hate sewing. I've never liked it. It's too fiddly." It was a rare admission that everything she did as a mother was not, innately, her. For us she had created the reassuring illusion that she was all mother.

During my hippie phase, when I was living in a cave on the island of Crete, I wrote sprightly letters home. I assured my mother that it was a "very nice" cave, probably the best on the mountain. She sent back clippings on the white-slave trade and a recipe for non-rising skillet bread, suitable for cave life. I have no doubt she was appalled and worried but she opted for the recipe and skipped the lecture.

I continue to carry around this totem of maternity inside, even though everything has changed since then. It's no longer possible to live my mother's life. My parents were able to live very well on my father's salary, but the one-income family is now the minority. It has been the pressure of economic factors, not bored women looking for fulfillment in a job, that has altered the architecture of the family. Comparing my life to my mother's is beside the point now.

Nevertheless, comparisons will be made. For instance, my mother only lost her temper with us once in a blue moon. But in the first year that I spent at home with my son, I found that tantrums were remarkably easy. Birth pries the heart open, and it's amazing what can pour out along with love.

A friend who had a wakeful, colicky daughter said that she wanted to write a book about becoming a mother and call it *The Birth of Rage*. New-mother snappishness is often just the normal result of broken sleep and being at somebody else's beck and call twenty-four hours a day. But sometimes motherhood taps into something deeper.

My first memories of getting angry start with the helplessness of being pinned to the rocking chair in Casey's room. I was into my fifth or my ninth month of breast-feeding, I don't recall which. I rocked and rocked, restless and edgy, like someone in the vicinity of an orgasm that never arrives.

The honeymoon for the Nursing Couple was definitely over, but I didn't want to wean him yet. I suppose I could have encouraged a less debilitating "routine," but two things legislated against this: I couldn't bear to let him cry, and we lived in a thin-walled apartment with *no real door* — the staircase up to our hall was open. Jerry, the tenant below us, was a bachelor who liked to croon folk songs on his guitar while entertaining potential sexual conquests. We could hear everything he did, from taking a shower to clicking his cigarette lighter, to skillfully bringing yet another girl to a flamboyant orgasm. When you are a carefree, childless couple, this sort of antiphonal sex under the same roof is mildly amusing. But when you're breast-feeding, the sound of some woman panting a floor below you is infuriating, a double invasion of privacy. The baby's cooing, the woman is groaning, and all you can think about is whether or not to have another Oreo.

One evening, I was in Casey's room, staring dully at the ripped corner of the plastic crib-bumper. Brian was out of town on a writing assignment. I was holding my increasingly heavy son in my arms as he guzzled away, gazing, patting, letting the milk pool in the corners of his mouth, stopping for a sudden look at the knobs on the bureau drawers, then back to the breast. Renewed gobbling. As usual, I had put my glass of water just out of reach, on the dresser.

The window was open and the neighbors were out in their garden, talking and laughing. They had a two-year-old daughter going through toilet training and I could hear her mother saying

"Oh no you don't, not in the pool!" We lived in the lower Annex, a dense and nicely eccentric warren of actors, students, academics, and other families. A man down the street liked to stand in the back lane and play the bagpipes on overcast days. Every night at 1 a.m., the Brunswick House tavern closed and drunks came down the block, pounding on car hoods and singing "The Green, Green Grass of Home." Before the baby, all of this felt cozily urban and communal. Sitting in a rocking chair for the fifth time that day, it felt like being trapped in an overcrowded beaver lodge.

I suppose I wished I were out enjoying the dusk, strolling up the street to the outdoor cafés. I suppose I knew there was no coffee left for breakfast, and there was no one to stay with Casey while I went out to buy some. All these pinned-down thoughts occurred to me, as I sat there with my T-shirt pulled up.

Jerry was unbelievably leaden-footed, like a mastodon. At 7:30 I heard him hurtle through the front door, take three steps, then remember to go back and slam it shut. Small objects actually stirred on my third-floor desk when he came home each night. Then I would hear his briefcase crash to the floor, followed by the plop of accumulated mail tossed onto a table.

It drove me crazy to have to visualize everything Jerry did before he got out of the house. "Ah, I hear his change falling on the floor . . . the toilet lid banging down . . . he's undressing for the shower now." He sang loudly and badly in the shower, songs with complicated lyrics like "El Paso."

But on this particular night, he sat down only eight feet below me and sang "Scarlet Ribbons," sliding in and out of key, belting it out with totally unwarranted confidence. "Ifff I live to be a hun-dred . . . I will never know from where . . . came those ribbons . . . scarlet ribbons . . . scarlet ribbons . . . for . . . her . . . HAIR."

I snapped. The quasi-sexual tickle at my breast, the egomaniacal croon from below collided in my nervous system, and I began to stomp my feet up and down. I drummed my slippered feet, as Casey's gyroscopic mouth adjusted to this strange turbulence. The strumming stopped. I froze, unable to scream the words, "Go away, everyone." But he had heard. How could he not? The message of those petulant little stamps was unmistakable. He began to pluck the guitar again with something akin to self-consciousness, a whole new sensation for Jerry.

Pleased with my childish display, I pried Casey's sleepy mouth off my breast and took him up to my bed. Ten minutes later, Jerry exited, the house shuddered, and all was calm again. I was alone with the rest of the city audibly pulsing outside my window. The reddish aura from the neon lights a block away never left the sky, like a frozen sunset.

*   *   *

I took my son to be an ordinary baby, with ordinary demands. I refused to be a relativist, or to talk about my "active" baby who "never slept." This would be imposing on him, characterizing him unfairly. So I ignored the fact that he woke up four, five, six times each night and grazed all day, off and on, at the breast. I didn't hover; to the best of my recollection, I never leaned over, shook his tiny shoulder, and said, "Time to eat again!" I just responded to him.

He was happy. He was hungry, alert, and wakeful — all signs of an intelligent baby, friends would say. *And the sign of a demented, sleep-deprived mother*, I would think to myself. But what did I know? He was the first baby I had ever taken care of, so I didn't question or categorize his habits.

Now that I have seen other mothers with other babies, I see there is a huge variety — the nappers and sleepers and self-schedulers, the "good eaters," the fussy and the angelic, the inert and the turbo-driven. Now that my son's personality has not just jelled but carved itself in anthracite at the age of eight, I can venture to describe him as incredibly energetic, with a lusty appetite for food and life. Sometimes he talks in his sleep.

Recently he said, very clearly, "All the things that I want are so good."

As a baby, his demands were always good-natured and accompanied by a windmill of arm- and leg-churnings. But he never slept as much as other babies, or so I hissed to Brian in the night. We referred to it as "undersleeping."

He was always moving, too. One time he was on the changing table. I reached for a pin, and the next thing I knew he had arched himself right off the end of the table and had fallen headfirst into a big potted plant. Luckily, his head landed in the dirt. I caught him like a big pickerel, holding him upside down by his ankles. He wasn't hurt, but the days of not being able to physically contain his energy had begun.

His "twos" hit early, around sixteen months. I would try to put him down for a nap, but getting him to lie down was like trying to subdue a writhing Weimaraner, or one of those inflated, weighted, tip-over dolls. Whenever I put him down, he would bob right up again. Wrestle, bob; wrestle, bob. One afternoon a friend came to visit, someone who was about to have her first child. It was nap time. Casey had decided that nap time now signalled a derby up and down the hall, with me clutching at him until he mirthfully tore himself away. After too much of this — and a little on edge from being "observed" as a mother — I tackled him. Clinging to non-violence by my fingernails, I all but hurled him into the crib. My friend was impressed, or appalled.

"God," she said, "he's strong."

What she also meant was, his will is towering, absolutely adult-sized. She could see I was using all my patience and strength to contain him.

*　　*　　*

When I couldn't comfort him, and his crying began to unhinge me, my anger took a crazy self-censoring shape. I would do this thing of holding him tightly in my arms and running up the stairs to the deck, or even out the door and up the street, holding him close so I wouldn't shake him or hurt him, muttering under my breath, "Please, please, please, please stop crying." I was trying to escape the two of us at the same time as I kept him safe from my anger. I would rock him hard, a caricature of maternity.

It was usually before my period that I would lose it. There would come a point, inevitable as thunder after lightning, when the tension would break, and I would show my rage, whether it was by slamming a fist into a doorjamb to avoid doing anything worse, or by a single helpless slap on his two-year-old bum — especially if it was 10:45 p.m. and that bum was in the process of gleefully writhing out of his pajama bottoms. Then as a feisty four-year-old, when he accidentally hurt me with a flailing foot, it was sometimes all I could do not to strike back. Whenever I did lose control and give his bottom a whack, that was it, it was over. My anger would dissolve into the hateful sadness of having hurt him. Most of the time I could avoid this by the glowering and jaw-clenching that was the tip-off that Mommy was about to get seriously angry. The gargoyle spectacle was not nice, either. But sometimes his strength, his leviathan will, made me feel helpless in comparison. Children are small only in stature.

The rage arose in part from my own mysterious cauldrons of anger but also from being the one exposed to most of the frictions of child care — the day-long battles of will and the downright physical abuse that mothers at home absorb, especially with a two- or three-year-old who tests your ability to protect and love him at his most appalling. It's wonderfully chastening. Anyone who thinks they could do better I refuse to believe, unless they've been there.

Meanwhile, after a year of free-lancing at home, Brian was out of the house most of the day, working. His version of anger never went beyond a raised voice, or a mildly bullying, over-ra-tional argument with a child too young and tired to debate. He has truckloads more patience than I do — on the other hand, I had to be patient for longer periods of time. Losing it for five minutes wipes out the memory of sixteen hours of self-control.

When Casey and I were home alone, it was as if our combined intensity created a force field that we sometimes had to escape — the only problem being that we had to escape it together.

Our apartment had a rather decrepit third-floor deck that looked over the neighborhood roof tops. One night when I was at the end of my tether with Casey, because he wouldn't sleep, or he was getting a new tooth, I stomped upstairs with him to the deck. "Look at the moon," I begged, as I perched him on my shoulder and rocked. He gazed up and fell silent as the full moon absorbed him. I went on shifting my weight, from one leg to the other. The air was summery, the deck awash in blue moonlight. We could hear the sirens up on Bloor Street and a gust of back-yard-party laughter. "Moon" was one of his first words.

On overcast nights, I could also tune him in to the blinking light of the CN Tower, a slim needle at the base of the city. At night the tower blinked with red and white lights, giving off a distant, measured calm, like Mrs. Ramsay's lighthouse. It was less soothing than the moon, but the wink was hypnotic. The tower and the moon took us out of our enclosed world of damp shirts and sticky spoons. The cool air, and the restitution of the larger world, released the two of us from the tightening spiral of our bond.

One hot summer's day, as I negotiated the curbs with his stroller, I was preoccupied, feeling sad about something. I can't recall what. Around the age of two, Casey had begun to show the enormous tact children have for ordinary human sorrow. As I pushed the stroller toward some unpleasant chore, possibly calling up an empty bank account, he looked back at me, assessed the situation, and said, "Let's go home to see the hobo moon" or more childish words to that effect. We had been reading a book about hobos, and for some reason he put this together with our sessions up on the deck. The spectacle of my anger sometimes made him laugh, but sadness was different. Now he could comfort me as well.

8.   The Job of Gender

A COUPLE about to have a baby may agree beforehand to share the work equally. If the baby's nursing, the father, the Breastless One, will get more sleep at first, naturally. The rest they'll split right down the middle. Great idea. But that's not how it works.

The woman is already nine months ahead of the man in forging her bond with the baby. The father's physical connection begins when the baby is finally in his arms. So he's at a handicap, or an advantage, depending on how you look at it. Regardless of the chore-division lists, the mother and father have different roles to play at first. This pleasant little gender gap, which makes complete biological sense for a while, can end up causing trouble later on. By the time the gap narrows, roles and habits have been established. Mothers get locked into symbiosis, fathers into exclusion. A good rule of thumb is that whenever the family reaches a point of stability, it's time to change again.

The job of the mother is to separate her self from her baby. After birth, if she breast-feeds, that connection becomes an isthmus that keeps the bond from severing. Sooner or later, she has to extricate herself from the baby bubble. She can take her choice: it's leave, or be left. It's a shift in distance, not a dilution of love.

The task of the father is to create a relationship with the baby — to build it, like an engineer, day by day. It's a bridge that is constructed out of imagination, drudgery, and the daily practice of caring for the baby, noticing him in all the detailed ways that children insist on being noticed. This doesn't mean that men can't mother. Many do, and the day-to-day, hands-on presence of men in the lives of their children strikes me as the best thing that could ever happen to the world, politically. But fathers can't expect to replicate a mother's experience.

The mother is trying to keep her bond with the baby from overwhelming them both — she is busy skulking off and salvaging her self. Sometimes, she would much rather just stay inside the solar system of mother and baby, lost in its rich selflessness. When the baby cries, she picks him up and holds him, or puts him to the breast. Her ability to meet his needs is quite straightforward. Meanwhile, the father may be overwhelmed with his own emotions, but apart from working, he has no specific task. He can do as much or as little with the baby as he agrees to do — it is up to him. He has to ask.

Most men have been raised to be utterly passive to the female world of the home — the thought that men *make* a home is still, alas, a novel one. So the new father generally waits to see what will happen. And what happens at first is that mother and baby drift off in their own little boat. Apart from "remembering to include him" and other helpful hints from the child-care books (which put the onus on the woman to cure the father's sense of exclusion), the mother may feel this as yet another loss of control. She is lost in the mother zone, and her husband is waving to her, with a helpful smile, from the opposite shore. She can accept this for what it is, a temporary state of affairs, or else she can anxiously measure herself against the mother in her mind — the well-organized, upbeat mum who will have her baby sleeping through the night in six weeks, so that she can get "back to normal," or back to coupledom, as fast as possible.

How odd: they feel both lucky and bereft of each other. They must be doing something wrong; perhaps their love isn't as strong as they thought. The father may worry that he's not magically bonding with this squalling, alien infant in the bedclothes. The mother may feel exactly the same way. And all these doubts arise because nobody told us to put the baby first, which is the quickest route back to each other.

The point is not that babies interfere with romance (which is true). The more unsettling issue is that we've come to think of the total-immersion business of having kids as a kind of distraction, and that at some point — at six weeks, or three months, or two years — everyone will be "back to normal." "Well, I'm finally back to normal!" some new mother will report, meaning her weight, her brain, her energy. Friends with older children nod politely, knowing you are never truly out of the woods. Once you're beyond infancy, there is the battle-of-wills phase, and then, after a long breather when they go to school and you persuade yourself that you have finally achieved "normal," adolescence arrives. Adolescence is a different kind of infancy, in which the family is reborn yet again. By the time you are "back to normal," it's twenty years later, and you have turned into somebody else entirely.

The new mother may make another surprising discovery: it is easier to deal with her baby one on one, without the husband around. She wishes he would don an apron, take a vow of celibacy and silence, and serve her, schlepping drinks and diapers and then gently closing the bedroom door behind him as he leaves. For several weeks, or months, she feels guilty neglecting him and sad about her indifference to sex. She is touched out by the baby. Maybe she makes love anyway, as a form of consolation, or to feel an adult in her arms. At the same time, an unaccustomed tenderness creeps into her relationship with him, a distant appreciation of his face and his adult presence in her newly child-sized universe. Her days are utterly different in detail and mood from his, and there seems to be no way of turning this into an interesting difference. For the first time, perhaps, she feels that she is a woman, and he is a man. Just when they expected to feel closest, they may feel instead — with a curious sense of love and loss — that motherhood and fatherhood are worlds apart.

Single-child families have a unique chemistry. The three-person household soon resolves itself into a Bermuda Triangle in which someone is always in danger of going missing. First, when the baby is small, the dad disappears. He mopes around Shoppers Drug Mart, lugging Baby Wipes and nursing pads to the checkout, wondering if he will ever get his wife back. He likes the baby but it — he — cries and is inscrutable. The baby is impervious to his charm and fails to appreciate his "way with children." All in all, a baffling job, to find a place for himself in this new love affair developing before his very eyes — between his wife and the baby. His son amazes him, he moves him . . . but he doesn't know what to do with it, or rather him.

If he is the sulky sort, he may take this out on the mother, by withdrawing. He may even start sleeping in a fetal curl to get her attention. He doesn't actually howl, but his behavior cries, "Feed me!" This irks the new mother no end. Just when she needs an adult around, her partner turns into the baby's three-year-old sibling. Or, he may display an uncharacteristic new interest in sports on TV. (According to one recent survey, the larger the family, the more time the father spends watching sports on TV.) The TV he can plug into, work he can plug into, but family . . . it's not clear how he fits in.

If the baby is bottle-fed, if the father stays home and does everything while the mother goes back to work, things are different. The father mothers. But the house-husband isn't a movement that threatens to dislodge women from the house, and the idea of bottle-feeding just to "involve the father" is one more instance of preserving the status quo at a price to the baby.

The second person to disappear into the Bermuda Triangle is the mother. She may go kicking and screaming, but by the eighth week or the fifth month of this desert-island romance, she notices a strange sensation: she has shed her self. Her senses, her adrenalin, her imagination — now they all turn around the baby. In the middle of making love, she is thinking, "Should I introduce solids next week?" If she goes back to work, the old deadlines no longer strike terror. The work world, in fact, seems like a game played by other adults who get unbroken nights of sleep. If she's at home, she might accept a free-lance assignment and discover that her brain has been subtly rewired.

Instead of noticing the real work she is engaged in, she persists in judging herself by the outside world, where most people would never say "You're such a good mother" lest it be taken as a slight to her independence. So the mother worries about her ability to manage work and children — as well she might, because despite decades of feminism, women still do most of the work at home, in addition to holding down jobs. Even in enlightened households, it tends to be the mothers who oversee the management of the house, take on community roles, and give in to chores. It's *easier* to give in. According to *The Second Shift* by Arlie Hochschild, this extra work that women absorb adds up to fifteen extra hours of work a week — an additional month of twenty-four-hour days a year. It's called "the leisure gap." First, women couldn't vote. Then they couldn't work. Now they can't sit down and read the paper.

9.   Food & Grooming

WHEN CASEY was two months old, I noticed that I was crawling up to bed each night with a small but glowing pain in the gut. I ignored it, because I don't have stomach problems. Migraines, PMS, earwigs, dust mites, mitral valve prolapse — those are my things. So I gnawed on Rolaids and reduced my coffee from a mug the size of a beer stein to a succession of tiny cups. Then one night when Casey had finally succumbed to sleep at 11:20 p.m. and I was going up the stairs bent over the knot in my stomach, I decided to stop and think this thing through.

The diagnosis was simple: as a result of interrupted sleep, interrupted thoughts, and interrupted bodily functions ("I'll be right there! Just a minute!"), I was in fight-or-flight mode all the time. I wasn't used to having my days restructured in such a ravishingly unpredictable fashion, by a mere baby. Especially one as eager to party as mine.

My vigilance was never-ending. When I ate, I ate like a cornered animal. If Casey was asleep, it was still possible — probable, in fact — that just as I was sitting down to eat something, he would wake up hungry. Or if he was happily awake and beating the air with his fists as he sat there forming mouth-bubbles, he might see me putting objects, food, in my mouth, and demand to sit on my lap so that he could generously insert his fingers into my mouth as well. Babies have a radar for the few brief moments when a mother's desire veers elsewhere — if only to the plateless cheese sandwich before her.

I was bad at ignoring him, never could forget about him for a second. So around lunch time — or actually, any time at all — I would find myself standing at the wooden kitchen counter, prying solid chunks of tuna out of the can with a fork and eating them. Why make a tuna salad sandwich when you can get the stuff from can to mouth in seconds and be done with it? I fell victim to the snackin' mom syndrome; I would keep only styrofoam rice cakes around, or thin, dusty rye crackers. This meant I had to eat hundreds of rice cakes and cracker fragments to feel remotely satisfied. Such non-eating was taking up a great deal of my time. I also realized that much of my dining was being done while staring at wall outlets and the side of the toaster. These were my meals. Nobody forced me to do this. It was my own idea.

Restaurants were no better, really, although it was always a thrill to get out of the house. Sometimes I would scheme to have lunch at the corner café, to coincide with his nap. Inevitably, as soon as my sandwich arrived, his eyes would pop open like little hard-boiled eggs. They would see this wonderful edible airplane disappearing into his mother's mouth, and the competition would begin. Me! Me in mouth too! Hold me, feed me! The left-handed lunch is one of the mothering skills that no one thinks to practice.

This is why I found myself eliminating even the notion of "lunch" or "dinner;" if I went about making a meal for myself, my stomach would begin to tighten at the very real prospect that I would not get to eat it hot, or in my own good time. I would become pre-anxious about the potential for interruption. Even if Casey was in deep slumber, I was conditioned to sit down at the table, hunch over, and wolf my food, looking about me like someone picnicking among street urchins. I didn't even notice this until a week of indigestion made me reflect on my eating habits — although at least one friend had looked on in horrified silence as I clocked back my Thai noodles in less time than it took her to unfold her napkin.

When Casey began to eat real food, I would get carried away and make precious little meals for the two of us . . . labor-intensive chicken pot pies and casseroles that I imagined were emblematic of real family life. This is a truism of child-raising, of course — whatever you give special time and attention to cooking, your children will despise and reject, with annoying gagging sounds. One basic guideline is that food "all mixed up" (most casseroles and definitely bouillabaisse) is revolting to children. They want clear categories of unadorned food — macaroni in one corner of the plate, preferably with its own Kraft chemical-orange cheese sauce. Toast soldiers. Plain tomatoes. Pizza. Cereal and milk. Plain noodles, over and over and over. The few times I dared to venture into steamed quinoa or lentil pilafs, I had to get up and make him macaroni while my own meal cooled. My only victory in the food area has been his grudging acceptance of salads. But he is an eater, and always has been; I never had to do the circling-plane number.

Dinner continues to be deeply problematic. During the school year, it tends to happen in three haphazard stages. When Casey gets home from school, he stations himself in front of the TV to "relax," which is fine with me. Since Brian rarely gets home before 7 p.m., I often make Casey dinner first. Sometimes I eat with him, sitting at the kitchen table, a meal that lasts about three minutes before he rushes back to the plot line of "Star Trek — The Next Generation."

When Brian walks into the Media Cockpit we call home, he will either forage his own meal, or cook something for the two of us, or I may produce a dinner — my second or possibly third of the night. Usually just as we're sitting down at the kitchen table (the dining room table rendered unusable by the noise of the TV), Casey will mosey in.

"I'm sooooo bored," he'll say, kneeling on a chair and tipping it almost to the falling-over point. "Bored,bored,bored,bored,bored. What's that you're eating?"

These occasions cry out for a sibling, so the kids can fight, wrestle, or pull out the grates over the heating vents while their parents have twenty minutes of adult conversation — or knife-clicking silence, as the case may be.

I despair easily at 5:30 p.m. in the winter. A little shudder always passes through me when the disk of the December sun goes down. I am usually in the kitchen, listening to hyperagitated cartoon voices on the TV, wondering what both Casey and his father might conceivably eat that I can bring myself to cook. How did it get to be like this? I may ask myself, and then push that thought away. I may try to inaugurate new TV rules for a week, but they usually crumble. In part I blame the single-child syndrome for this dinner-time ennui. If we were ten people in a big household, food would appear on the table at 6:15, take it or leave it, if it's Thursday it must be fish fingers. None of this short-order microwaving.

When Casey was small, Brian began to have to go out of town on assignments, and I would spend days alone in the house. Loitering in the bathroom when Casey was awake and on the move became problematic. My already efficient peristalsis went into overdrive; I could be in and out of the bathroom before the yellow plastic giraffe on Casey's mobile made it through two revolutions. This tradition of long, leisurely sessions in the bathroom with the front section of the paper is historically male, I believe. I don't know any woman who takes the paper into the bathroom, unless it's to line the kitty-litter box.

I was also in awe of Brian's ability to go on taking long showers. Home alone with a wakeful newborn, I could shower so quickly that the mirror didn't fog and the backs of my knees stayed dry. The one-minute hair conditioner was too slow for me. When the noise of the shower drowned out everything else, I always hallucinated the sound of Casey crying. Dripping shampoo lather, I would turn off the taps and stand there, straining to hear. Nothing. The water would go back on, first the scalding hot, then the cold. It was a genuine discipline, an acquired skill, to put some of my own needs — basic hygiene among them — first, and for the longest time I wasn't able to.

After months of having her sleep sliced and diced, a new mother develops a kind of post-traumatic stress syndrome that means she never quite relaxes, because the Call might come. If she goes to a party and dares to unwind with a cocktail or three, the sound of the phone ringing will act on her like one of those choking collars that dog trainers use. Instantly, she will know that it is her sitter calling, to insist that she stop having fun and talking too loudly, in order to come home, get her breasts out, and find the digital thermometer. The nervous system of the new mother is a flayed and tender thing.

I'm convinced that the result of having all of a mother at a baby's disposal is not a "spoiled" baby. I would venture to say the result is a happy, confident baby, and a frazzled, overextended mother. You can't be too attentive to a baby, unless you start waking him up at night to play with him. It's not the baby's job to limit his demands on the mother — it's the mother's business to figure out how to keep herself sane and regularly showered.

With a second child, I'm sure you carve out necessary time for yourself. You have to, if only to have more of yourself left over for child number one. But I have never claimed to be sane when I was brand new at mothering. I was a love slave.

I'm not sure when the concept of relaxation came back into my life on a regular basis. He's eight now, and I think it happened about a year ago. There were mitigating factors, such as illness. I have seen relaxed mothers — smooth-browed, nicely groomed women with two children under four, out shopping — and whenever I do, I stop and stare at them. Are they on drugs, I wonder? Whence their sang-froid?

In most cases, the secret elixir is money, not temperament. Live-in nannies. Well-paid work that satisfies, instead of just using you up. Or else they don't have to work. Maybe they are blessed with hands-on, matched sets of grandparents. All these things will definitely make for a more relaxed mother.

I liked, craved, the time I spent with my son, but the in-between periods when I was supposed to be recovering a self and cutting my toenails were trickier. Going back and forth from the old me to the new one was often more trouble than just giving in completely to this tyrannical new affair.

Around the third month, I realized I was always subtly racing through whatever I was doing in order to Get To The Baby. Why was I rushing? He was evidently not going to go away. I was like a nervous hostess, and the baby was a house guest; his permanent status in my life had not yet sunk in. I waited for him to thank me and leave. Gradually his presence, his ability to drink in all of me, helped me capitulate. I learned that surrender was the more efficient route to independence, in the end. Trying to hoard myself was not the answer, indeed, it left me feeling more fractured than the moments when I gave up and gave in to him. It was only then that the retrieval of my self began.

10.   Sex, Writing & Sunday Nights: Salvaging the Self

AFTER THEY have children, women turn into two people — the mother, and the other. They begin to think like writers, whose job it is to record the dialogue between the two sides of themselves: the talker and the listener, the whiner and the judge, the drunk and the monk. The moral debate that hums along in the background of any interesting novel is a reflection of the writer loving and hating herself at the same time.

Writing is a form of nakedness, civilized nakedness; it represents you in detail, or should do. Despite the fact that most mothers wouldn't call themselves writers, to me the process of writing resembles the salvaging of the self that all mothers go through as their children grow up.

Naturally, real sex with human beings can interfere with this solipsistic little *tête-à-tête*. Sex incarnates, but writing disembodies. The distance between these two activities never gets any shorter, I find. The passage through to the writing state feels precipitous, like the edge before going over into orgasm. Just before the writing kicks in, the desire for sex can be strong and distracting. And just before embarking on sex, the desire to "write" — to erect that inviolate separate self — is strong, too. Each one represents a giving-over that, in the heavy traffic of family life, is never easy to accomplish.

Once launched, though, the writer lives inside the sentences happily. Then the connection to the words becomes more sustaining than the idea of crawling back inside the body and making love. Both writing and sexual intimacy have this breakthrough component that is arduous, each and every time, to confront. The main difference, of course, is that sex is usually — but not always — more fun. Both activities demand more of you than you ever imagine when you begin.

Making love, you give up the ghost, and at the farthest point of self-forgetting, the act of surrender gives you back your self. In writing, the same paradox applies, without the reassurance of the baby or the lover giving back. It becomes a process of imagining a listener, an ardent, nimble, frustrated listener hungry for certain words, your words. Like a masturbator fantasizing the presence of a lover, the writer feverishly wills herself into the moment. (Failing this, she prepares a snack.)

In our case, there are two writers feverishly willing themselves into the moment, all week long. Sometimes, in the commute between work and bed, the two of us get stuck in the domestic swamp of half-sex. Half-sex is nobody's fault and no doubt afflicts most couples with babies or small children on a regular basis. Half-sex is what parents are often reduced to — rushed, distracted couplings stifled by the presence of babies sleeping in the same room or restless children down the hall. Half-sex is when you're both too tired to put yourself across. The mornings after half-sex, I'm neither here nor there — neither a solitary writer, nor a nicely rounded-off, just-fucked mother. I've been opened, without closure. I have come, but I haven't gone anywhere. He feels the same, I think; goes off to work and finds the words jammed up, unable to flow. We haven't been able to give over to each other and get free.

But, if we manage to get to the bottom of our desire, then I wake up feeling lighter, freer. The next day's work won't necessarily be better, but it will feel more hopeful, because sex creates optimism. It seems to insinuate life in the future, even when procreation is not the point.

Sunday nights are always problematic. By 10 p.m., I detect

the pall of Monday already settling on Brian, and the little soldiers of language are beginning to drill away in my head, saying "I I I." I'm tempted to get a jump on that necessary separateness by crawling off into my own narrow bed, even if my body — or his — says otherwise. If I could, I would stay celibate writing this book. I would hole up in the spare-bedroom office, sleep on the futon, stay up in the driven ether of the writing mode.

But I live with my husband, and his physical presence works on me like gravity. When he's around, sooner or later I want him, I miss him. Longings — life — interfere. I have to give in, get through the bonds at work inside the family, and then salvage my self over and over.

This letting go doesn't come easily. Sometimes I try to resist sex and hoard myself, because I imagine that's what I should do to muster enough of me to write. Of course, I should be giving in more — out of love, not capitulation. Giving in and going through is always the answer. But married sex is mired in the daily stuff, and it takes *largesse* to transcend the daily stuff. (I make a note: work on *largesse*.)

Sunday nights cast their pall on everyone, apparently. I came across a survey claiming that only sixteen per cent of the couples polled make love on Sunday nights. The majority, boringly, choose Saturday night. Week nights lure a bare five per cent. By deduction then, the prime night for quarrels in the average household is Friday. I prefer week nights, myself, for their air of truancy. Or noonish on Saturday, as a pick-me-up between chores. Really, any time but Sunday night.

MONDAY morning. The strangest thing happened. I sat down to write, to try to tell the truth about domestic sex, and I lost my voice. First I idealized, then I demeaned. Sex, our real sex, seems impossible to document. I must make it up instead. So this is a story about sex after the baby. There may be certain things, tiny details, that carry over from our real life, but most of it is sheer fabrication. "Lies will flow from my lips," as Virginia Woolf wrote, "but there may perhaps be some truth mixed up with them."

Monica came home from the hospital with her new baby. Her body ached as she walked up the stairs to their bedroom. Blain brought her suitcase and an armful of all the cut flowers from the hospital up the stairs behind her. He poked her gently with the irises.

"I'm dyin' t' give ye a luvley screw, lass," he said in the thick burr she had fallen in love with long ago, in Aberdeen.

"Blain, I'm sorry, but that's over now. Nothing is ever coming in or out of that part of my body again."

"Oh, for the luv o' Christ, Monica, don't talk that way, ye make me want to pit a bewllet in me brain, I swear."

"It's not a joke, Blain. We have our baby now and my rear end feels like I've just given birth to an upright piano and you expect me to be in the mood. It's not fair."

"Not fair? And what about this, then?" Blain unzipped his thick corduroy pants and out peeped his cock, like a huge garden snail.

"Put that back and help me with the baby."

They went up to their big bed on the third floor, and all three got under the covers.

"Will ye lewk a' the size of yer breasts, woman!" Blain exclaimed as Monica prepared to feed their new daughter.

"They're for the baby," she murmured as smacking sounds filled the silence between them. Blain stroked her legs through the cotton nighty. What would happen to him now? He caressed his daughter's head. It was warm and smelled like bread rising. A pulse was visible under the skin and the swirl of fine gold hair. His daughter. He felt a flood of feeling that to Monica's irritation and his great embarrassment triggered a wagging erection.

"Blain, for God's sake, can't you see I'm busy?"

"I couldn't help myself, Monsie, the sight of the two of ye both so beautiful fills me up, it's just my way. . . ."

"Look, look, she's asleep. . . ." The baby had fallen away from the breast, the rosebud of her mouth was slack.

"Isn't she splendid?" he said. "She's brilliant, I think."

"Yes," said Monica, patting Blain's silky erection. Tired and sore as she was, she had a queer feeling, as if she wanted to take them both back up inside her body. . . .

But no, it wasn't right. Too Lawrentian. This gender thing could be taken too far. Surely there was a voice that wasn't taken yet, that fit. Monday morning went by. A solitary lunch. Defeated, she lay down on the futon, the Couch of Failure, fell asleep, and dreamed.

A woman comes home with a new baby, her body in rags. Love, blood leak out of her. She feels as if light streams out of her chest when she looks at the baby, which she does constantly. The times she is not looking at the baby are utilitarian and brief. Her husband's face sheds a discernible light, too, as he gazes on both of them and runs his hand over the warm and supernally round head of his daughter. The long-held-back tenderness in all of them seeps out, stains the air in the room, makes time swim.

Her ass is sore. She can't bear to look at the ruined and rumpled place where she tore at the last moment and had to be stitched up. She won't think about it at all. Her husband has lost a little weight, shed a thickness or two through the long hours of birth and the heavenly lightness afterward. They both move through an aqueous medium that is half fatigue, half euphoria.

They come home and go upstairs to their bed, a thick slab of foam on a cedar platform, wide enough for three. They place the wrapped-up baby in the middle, dwarfed by the huge bed. They can't even stay as far away from her as the edges of it. All three climb under the covers, the baby clamps onto her streaming breast, the father watches, amazed. The sun sets. He brings a tray of food up to the bedroom, time slides by sweetly, like a river. The baby sleeps, wakes, scowls, cries, rolls her eyes, is a creature they have never seen before, unshaped, utterly sincere.

She notices the man's new adult tenderness, the ability to calibrate his gestures to the baby's helplessness. His face softens each time he holds her. She wants to take them both back up inside her body. Birth and its aftermath feel like the center of sex — not the intricate, reasoning desire before, but the wide-open surrender. She wants to wrap the two of them up in her like a big coat. A yearning surfaces, to put all these puzzle pieces back together, to make love, but her slurred body can't, cringes like a cut worm at the thought of even trying. They hold each other and his emotional erection is warm and innocent as the baby's compact leg. She makes him come out of a curious urge to get inside him, or else to feed him like a baby.

When she heals, they make love again, but now it has less to do with the weighing of feelings and more to do with animal comfort. Plus her new indiscriminate openness. Come one, come all, is her philosophy now. Sex becomes more forgiving than it was before. The fatigue, this new carnal attachment to the baby doesn't entirely eclipse her need to measure herself against an adult body on some nights. It feels novel, to hold his long male back in her arms, after hefting ten pounds of baby all day long.

When they embark on sex, she no longer wonders who needs it or deserves it. She just goes ahead and does it anyway. Although the edge of desire is blunted, orgasms come more easily, they almost slip out of her like spare change. Does she like this new spendthrift sex better? It's impossible for her to say, it's all part of the new-baby blur.

A year later, the baby sleeps downstairs, in the room directly under them. She can hear the muffled flub of the flannel-covered plastic mattress as the baby stirs, and before her second cry, she's down the stairs. She is wired to her, even in sleep; the mother's brain waves stir two seconds before the baby's do. Her husband has a charmless ability to roll over and sleep through all this. The couple now make love gingerly, surreptitiously, as if the ghost of the baby sleeps on her chest between them. Which it does. Then one night, in the middle of sex, she finds herself thinking about dairy products. She really ought to take the baby off dairy products completely, she thinks, panting.

Two years later. Now she is more protective of herself. On certain days she can feel the pressure to write build up, but then sex takes the air out of it. Making love mollifies her, blurs a necessary fierceness. So with a new sense of betrayal, she begins to want to wall herself off from both her child and her husband. Now that she is beyond the swamp-of-feeling stage, motherhood has turned densely psychological — now she must negotiate two full-tilt physical, verbal relationships. The fantasies begin. She wants to be done to, sexually. She wants a sex servant. She feels greedy and selfish but isn't, can't be yet.

One afternoon, a friend calls to say that she is breaking up with her boyfriend. "I can't explain it," she says, "I just went off his cock, that's all." She decides this is a good and succinct way to judge whether a woman still wants a man. She thinks about it and decides she approves of her husband's cock, is aroused by even the thought of it. It seems a warm and concrete way to conjure him up in her mind. In bed, the way he curves in behind her with his rude erection irritates her sometimes, but is a sign she still wants him. It means he interferes with her, deeply, which is good.

Then she realizes that she has reduced her husband to nothing but sex, and concludes that this is part of the story, too, to spare some thought for the husband's undomesticated cock. Couples can't see pure sex for the forest of daily life. We don't often get that pure arousing glimpse of the other's separateness.

In the dream she comes into the bedroom and sees him lying on the covers of the bed, with a T-shirt on, paging through a magazine. She lies down beside him. The look, the soft horse-nosed feel, the amiability of his cock cheer her up. She is tired and the idea of sleep is seductive. The whole rigmarole of sex seems daunting, at ten past midnight. Still. They hear a cough, just one, from their daughter's room, and ignore it. As she takes him inside, the green of his eyes deepens. And when they look through their long years together, they see each other, really see into each other, again.

re-entry

12.   Angie

WHEN THE baby was eight months old, I went about finding a part-time baby sitter. I didn't use an agency. I had a superstition about the right person appearing at my doorstep and thought that professionals might be numb to such psychic stirrings. So I advertised in the newspaper for someone reliable, warm, and good-natured, with references. There were roughly twelve classified ads with the same wording — other parents casting a net for exceptional, affordable human beings.

The calls trickled in, followed by the cups of tea with candidates, none of whom seemed right. Then one morning when Casey, soggy-diapered, had all the dented pots out of the cupboard on the floor, and the bowls of half-eaten oatmeal stood hardening on the counter, a Jamaican woman named Angie came up our stairs and down the hall. Angie was not obsequious. Roughly translated, her demeanor was "Don't fuck with me, I won't fuck with you." Behind her was Ruddy, her sleepy-eyed husband. Angie came in, looked down at her charge-to-be, clapped her hands together, and said, "Uh huh, we like those pots better than any fancy toy, that's for sure." I liked that she addressed him first. She had presence. All my fine ideas notwithstanding, I'm afraid my first assumption was "Big Mama."

Angie was big and hard-packed, with a strong, smoldering gaze. She had four kids of her own, whom she left with her sister while she worked. Later that day I called one of her references. A man answered and said Angie had been great with his kids. "Just level with her, that's all," he said with a fairly affectionate chuckle. He seemed like a nice guy. I called Angie and asked if she was free to start the next day.

I was working on an article about my favorite subject, hormones, but Casey's cries colonized my brain. I had to get out of the house, but now there was nowhere for me to go; paying for Angie in order to work meant I couldn't afford to rent an office in which to do it.

Then a friend came to my rescue and gave me the key to her university office, which she wouldn't need until the fall. It was six blocks away, due east — I wouldn't even have to change latitudes! Suddenly, a wand had been waved over my life.

The empty university building was immeasurably arousing. I would get excited just walking down the buffed halls and into the book-lined office. The first morning I arrived, I closed the door, pulled a book down from the shelf, and lost myself in it for twenty minutes. Then I surfaced with a start: I had just left my only child in the care of a stranger. I called home. She took three rings to answer, I could hear the TV on in the background, but Casey was asleep, and everything was fine. I hung up and chewed on my thumb. Then, slowly I began to work.

Writing tumbled out of me, diffuse, urgent, and unmanageable. The sheer egotism of self-expression felt like a 180-degree shift. This is more like it, I thought, typing furiously away. But the euphoria was short-lived. After two hours, I was homesick for my son. I needed to feel his body, see his face. The craving was terribly real, like the panicky need you have for a lover after parting in mid-argument. On the way home, I saw someone I knew and crossed the street rather than waste thirty seconds saying hello. It was the most unswerving form of magnetism I've ever felt.

The key turned in the front door, I heard a happy crow from upstairs, and I was swamped with relief. Struggling to appear more detached than I felt, I raced upstairs, stood in the doorway, and said, "Well hell*o*!" to Casey, who was pushing over block towers and shrieking happily. He looked at me with undifferentiated delight and went on destroying. Angie sat on the couch, rebuilding the towers with one long arm. She was wearing turquoise leggings, a big black sweat shirt with embossed butterflies on it, and men's running shoes. Oh yes, we got along just fine, she said, no problem. A brilliant future began to twinkle ahead of me, and I peeled off some bills. Angie preferred cash.

A little routine began. I looked forward to the luxury of being able to miss Casey at the end of my work stint in the empty office. He was happy to see Angie arrive and chipper when I got back home, although he began to wake up more often in the night. And whenever I left him with Brian in the evening to race up to the store, he clung to me and cried.

Then one day I came home half an hour early. No Angie, no Casey. Usually she phoned to tell me if they were going on an outing. The stroller was gone, so I assumed they were at the park. Telling myself that this would give me a chance to tidy up, I went upstairs but all I did was shift things around. I couldn't concentrate.

Finally, I went out on the street again, shading my eyes to peer like a sailor up and down the sidewalk. There were two parks, both two blocks away. I walked down Brunswick Avenue until I got to the tiny parkette with the wrought-iron gates. My heart leaped at the sight of a blond head in the sandbox, but it wasn't Casey. No Angie here, although three brown-skinned women, nannies all, sat together on the bench while their charges played nearby. Why doesn't Angie have any friends? I thought with a stab of fear. How come she doesn't hang out with other nannies, anyway? Why these benches of Jamaicans, and other benches of Filipinas? I began to see her proud wariness as something else. Maybe she hated me; there were plenty of good reasons why she might. In any case, how much real love could you feel for the pampered white child of somebody who got money to write about her periods? Not that I rattled on to Angie about hormones. I began to feel a degree of paranoia about who Angie might be, beyond my shameful projection of Experienced Matriarch.

Up the street I pelted to "turtle park," so named for a big painted metal turtle. There were Andrew, and Caroline with Sirena, the neighbor's nanny. A Perego stroller like Casey's stood empty by the swings, but I could see by the knitted bag on the back that it belonged to someone else. It was now almost an hour past the time when Angie had expected me back and I was in the full grip of terror. Everything I didn't know about her turned into a trick, a trap. Either she had kidnapped my child outright, or she planned to torment me by lingering in Honest Ed's just long enough to have me gibbering on the porch. I was amazed at Angie's power over me, and the hugeness of her responsibility. She had my child.

I decided to go home, call Brian at his office, and wait. It was a hot day, she might have gone into some air-conditioned restaurant. Anne's nanny was forever ending up at the Eaton Centre — she roved all over the city. But I had specifically asked Angie not to go out of the neighborhood. Brian was in, thank God.

"Angie's not back," I said. "I'm worried."

"Where did they go?"

"I don't know. I checked both parks."

"She's just late, I wouldn't worry about it."

"But she knows I always feed him around now. My breasts are killing me." It felt saner to ascribe all this urgency to my breasts.

"She just lost track of time, take it easy."

"I can't. I'm going out to look for them."

"Call me, let me know what happens."

I went down the street and ran into a neighbor. I asked her if she had seen Casey and Angie and then stalked past her without another word. I went two blocks over, heading for another park. I made several attractive deals with God. It was swelteringly hot, and the streets were sensibly deserted. She's visiting, I thought, she's left him out on somebody's porch in the sun and he's dehydrated. She's taken him to Buffalo, to shop.

Then far down the street, I saw a blue and brown block: blue stroller, brown person. I kept walking. The stroller block was moving very slowly. The baby wore a tiny Blue Jays cap, a cap I recognized. With indescribable relief, I saw that it was indeed Angie and that Casey's capped head bobbed in sleep. His arms were covered in a T-shirt of mine, to keep off the sun. Angie was wearing a rakish straw hat. She moved no more quickly when she saw that the overheated woman heading her way was me. I think she pretended not to notice my alarm, or my carefully mild chastisement about being late. She wanted to take him to a park with a wading pool, she said, it was so hot. He loved the water, she said, he went all the way in. Oh I know, I gushed, he's absolutely fearless, isn't he?

Unlike his mother.

*   *   *

One day Angie was late. At 11 a.m., she came rolling up the stairs with a flat, angry face. I was poking a felt puppet in and out of its cone for Casey, who had spent breakfast ripping paper towels into strips.

"I phoned, but the line was busy," she said by way of apology. "I had to go get Ruddy out."

"Where was he?"

"They had him down at the police station, for impaired."

"Oh dear."

"My sister paid." Angie went to Casey, put him on her lap and began absent-mindedly dandling him.

"Is he okay — was there an accident?"

"No, nobody hurt. It was late at night, he was drunk, and the police stop him. Nobody on the road that hour but the police."

"Oh dear."

There didn't seem to be anything more to say, and so I left. It was half a year since Ruddy had had a job, I knew. The next week, Angie phoned to say that her daughter had split her lip on the swing set and had to go to hospital for stitches. The way she said it made me think maybe it was Ruddy again, but I didn't ask. Her troubled life was becoming a part of mine. We were developing certain silences, like a family.

One week I left a leather belt draped over the towel rack in the bathroom for a couple of days and then lost track of it. After a time, Angie showed up in a big flowered skirt anchored with the belt. I supposed she thought I was through with it; or maybe she didn't. Her audacity silenced me. I let it go. I felt so guilty asking her to take care of my kid while her four stayed home with her sister that I practically wanted to send her home with all my furniture in a U-Haul. More silences developed.

Then one morning I came back for a notebook I had left behind and saw Ruddy's big old silver Buick outside. Their two younger boys sat in the front. I ran upstairs where Angie was zipping Casey into his blue snowsuit with the stars.

"Where are you going?" I said, my voice up an octave.

"Oh, Ruddy want to take the boys to the museum this morning."

I was afraid to stand up to Angie — because she was older and tougher, because her life was unimaginably harder, because she was black and I was white, because I was obscurely ashamed of the intricate, protective relationship I had with my one child. But I couldn't let Casey disappear in Ruddy's dented boat of a car, even if he was stone sober at the curb with his boys beside him. It was an awful moment.

"Please," I said, "he's already been to the museum." It was true, I had been wheeling him around the dusty dioramas since he was four months old.

"He's just a baby, what does he remember?" She had a point.

"I don't want him in the car. I'm sorry."

Angie's back became more solid as I said this. She said nothing and began to unzip the snowsuit. It was an exchange she must have been through many times, when she had to pack down her own words, pour cement over them, go on anyway.

She finally spoke.

"He's careful when he's not drinking."

"I'm sure he is."

Angie lifted Casey, who was uncharacteristically subdued by the subtle electricity in the room, and carried him with one arm down the hall.

"I'll get his lunch," she said. "You tell Ruddy."

When I had found my notebook and gone outside, I leaned into the car window and told Ruddy that I thought Casey had the beginnings of a cold and ought to stay home. But Ruddy knew. The boys were dressed in new flannel shirts, with suspenders. They didn't say a word as Ruddy put the car in gear and drove up the street.

*   *   *

The following Monday, 9 o'clock came and went. It was no great surprise when 10 o'clock went by and still Angie hadn't arrived. I sat in the living room on the window seat, with Casey on his feet doing a jig, bending his knees, pounding the glass of the window dangerously, as I gazed up the street waiting for Angie's glowering figure to appear. I felt myself fall once again down the slippery slope of my work. I would have to drop the thread again, give it up, because my baby sitter was trapped in her own circular life and this seemed to have something to do with me. I felt responsible, and at the same time helpless, because the two of us were left alone to lavish our bitterness on each other, where it didn't belong. She had no choice but to fire me. Even on Friday afternoon, I could tell it was coming, in the way she had slowly, coldly counted the cash I gave her.

She wouldn't forgive me. She wouldn't call on Monday. It would give her a brief thrill when she stood me up and let me go through one morning like her mornings, sitting in limbo, falling back down the slope.

13.　　　Whining

AN UNMAILED letter to an out-of-town husband.
Sunday, Remembrance Day, 1984
Dear Brian,

A minute of silence, a moment of thanks for our Glorious Dead, the mother at home alone in gray November all week long, except for Casey's delightful but limited charm.

Basically, I am haunted by the fact that never, never, never will you experience what it is like to do this . . . when I go away, as I surely will some day for a few days or a week, and it's your turn to stay home, (a) Casey will be older and therefore more company and (b) you drive a car. Through no fault of yours, as a result of being car-less I can't go anywhere without lugging him up or down the subway stairs — and after commuting on subway and streetcar every day to Riverdale to the sitter's, I hardly feel like negotiating the subway, so we end up going nowhere, except along our tedious strip of Bloor Street West. So you will never know the joy of lugging heavy bags of milk and juice, hooked onto the stroller handles so that when I unbuckle Casey in a store because he is writhing with frustration, the stroller falls over with all the groceries. This happens, of course, in The Silver Spoon, where I am buying bread and compensatory-cookies, because it is cold and Casey is restless in the stroller, and I still have to go to the Supersave (for groceries) and the drugstore (for vitamins and ointment, since Casey has a rash from diarrhea, and a cold), so I have no patience to go down to Harbord Street to the bakery for bread, so instead I go to the expensive Silver Spoon — this is why I end up spending more money when you're away, because I can't bear to watch the water drop down through the coffee filter any more, so I have to buy take-out coffee that somebody else has made, and then it spills all over Casey's hat as I try to hold the stroller and the coffee at the same time. Not exactly Eritrea, but. . . .

Every time we head off to the sitter's I end up in a sweat, both of us bundled up, lugging him here and there, all thirty-five pounds of him, removing mitts, hat, putting hat and mitts on — even if I break down and spend the money on a cab, it means standing in the wind on the corner, then I rush to get Casey, my bag, the collapsing stroller into the cab while holding up traffic. I'm keeping Casey from lurching all over in the cab, keeping cigarette butts out of his mouth, I remove his hat, mitts, keep him from falling out the window. I arrive, fumble for money, get Casey, bag, stroller out, reconstruct the stroller, catch Casey, who is running down the street, put his hat, mitts on, get bag, go to Anne's, carry stroller up onto the porch, remove his hat, mitts, my mitts, carry Casey, bag upstairs. Talk to Isobel, the nanny. Take his boots, coat off, pry him off me. He cries (only when you're away, he gets insecure, as do I), I walk to the corner, freeze, wait for the streetcar, ride home, walk along Bloor past the panhandlers, including the one with the slicked-back hair who sees me four times a day and never recognizes me, buy milk, eggs, the papers, go home, throw out breakfast garbage, throw out dirty diapers, wash bum rags out, wash frying pan, pick forty or fifty things off the floor, close the door on Casey's room and that mess, boil water, grind coffee, make coffee, heat milk, throw out junk mail, become angry at junk mail, go up to the bedroom, which is freezing because of the wind howling through the air conditioner which I can't remove on my own.

I make the bed, which needs changing, pick up Casey-litter from last night — jewelry, socks, ear plugs, pennies — sit down at my desk: it is 11 a.m.

No point going to exercise class at 12, then, with work barely begun. So skip exercise. Make the cuts to my book column. Worry about how to reach the landlord to fix the doorknob that has fallen off — fallen off! — the front door. Go downstairs, read the *Star*, eat compensatory-Camembert and cracker, wish something new was in the fridge. Hook up the almost-more-work-than-not portable dishwasher, put it on, and go upstairs. Write for an hour. Get incredibly sleepy and go to bed, read recipe book, sleep for an hour. Wake up, it's 2:30. Judith phones — my first real conversation of the day. Talk for twenty minutes, hang up, work for half an hour, then go downstairs, tidy Casey's room, take his laundry down to the basement (which means going outside, around the back, and into the basement), clean out vaporizer, throw out diaper box, stack up books, change crib sheets, tidy living room, leave to shop for dinner and pick up Casey.

Arrive back at 5:30. Casey insists on going up to the third floor, so I can't cook and watch him at the same time. We play on the bed, with my jewelry. Read books, go downstairs, set up Casey with paints at the table so I can cook. He spills water, wants down, is tired and hungry. Cook tofu, broccoli, cut up tomato. He doesn't want it. Who can blame him? I eat it all instead. Open a beer, drink it. Push Casey around in his little car, watch "Polka Dot Door," get him to eat yogurt, which he spills on self, couch, rug, me. Snot on my newspaper. Somehow, recently clean kitchen is now full of dirty pans, dishes, bowls, food scraps, but neither of us has eaten much. Casey drags all his dirty laundry out into the kitchen while I clean up, wash frying pan, unload dishwasher, put fresh water in tofu package, boil water for macaroni for Casey's lunch tomorrow. All out of bananas, but can't face suiting up to go buy some. Put Casey in bath, sit on toilet lid, drink beer, watch. Pajamas down in the laundry, but can't leave him alone to get them. Put too-small pajamas on him, decide back will get cold. Change him. He plays at the sink, gets pajamas wet. Change him again. We play ball down the hall.

Clean out his crib, find old pacifier, breast-feed him, read him two books, he wants more. Read him one more, tell him it's time for bed, he resists. I carry him around, turn down the lights, sing. He slowly gives in, I sit down, he slowly falls asleep. I put him down, cover him, turn lights down, clear path to the door, take vaporizer out, clean it, fill with water, plug it in, close his door. It is ten to nine. I scrub the highchair tray, pick peas off the floor, go into the living room, ignore the mess, watch TV, anything, on any channel. Want to exercise and read, but no energy to do either. Lie there flipping idly through *Vanity Fair*, watching TV, staring at junk on the floor. At 10:15, I lie down and do eight sit-ups and ten leg-lifts. Go to bed. Can't get corner of new fitted sheet on mattress. No new mags. Cold air whistles through the air conditioner. In the apartment below, Jerry picks up his guitar and starts singing "El Paso," badly. Voices out on the street. Suddenly awake.

14.   Weaning in Kenya

AN UNEXPECTED call: an assignment had fallen through, and a magazine needed a writer to go to Kenya, on a photo safari, in ten days. Was I interested?

As usual, half of me wanted to bang the phone down and go back to cupping stray Cheerios off the counter. But half of me was detectably homesick for the rest of the world. Before The Baby, I used to fly off to write about strange things in remote places at a moment's notice. Surely that person hadn't been run over by the rocking chair.

It was April, 1985. My son, born yesterday on the clock of my heart, was in truth twenty-two months old and not yet weaned. There was a nice little window around ten months when it could have happened, but then he got sick, and went back on the breast, where he remained. This fact had escaped my notice. "Are you still breast-feeding?" some woman might think to ask, noting the gray smudges under my eyes. "Not really," I would reply, "now and then." Like, when the sun came up and the sun went down.

Well, delusions are a wonderful thing, and they keep you company, too. It was only when the phone rang and the outside world spoke to me that morning that I realized my son was almost two and I had been away from him perhaps twice, overnight. It was Time. It would be Good for Everyone. Besides, as far as weaning went, it made more sense to take my entire self far away, rather than waking up one morning and cutting him off. How strange for the never-disappointed baby to one day have his mother smilingly, mysteriously, button up and take away his daily breast. Putting a little distance — say, ten thousand miles — between us would make it easier on both of us. It would also be difficult to change my mind and come back home if I was lurching around Kenya in a Land Rover. Difficult, I thought, but not impossible.

At this stage of motherhood, my idea of a thrill had withered to the prospect of buying take-out instead of cooking. Specials on apple juice actually perked me up and featured in phone conversations. Going to Africa — going east of the bank machine — was beyond the radius of even my fantasies. It was time to shake things up.

But on the phone, I dithered. What shots do I need? I asked. Cholera, typhoid, polio, tetanus, yellow fever, and malaria tablets. Why don't I just get the shots anyway, I said, and we can decide later. No harm in being immunized! Yellow fever is not unheard of in the Annex.

I hung up and burst into tears. Late mothers are intense mothers. On the other hand, I didn't want to be in my yellow dressing gown nine years down the road, wanly typing away as a brutish voice came up from the TV room: "*Ma, breast! Now.*"

I called some friends. Most of them were sick with envy and wondered why I would even hesitate. Only one dared to suggest that this wasn't an easy decision and that there would be no shame in not going.

Why would the word shame even arise? Because it is part of the pathologizing of all relationships that has crept into our vocabulary recently. Passionate bonds unnerve us, especially since most of the time we aren't blessed with them. I was . . . embarrassed by the depth of my attachment to my son, and my fear of leaving him.

On the other hand, I had no excuse not to go. His father would take good care of him, dress him (backward? in things too small? remember when he put him in the Snugli facing out, zipper up against his little chin?), feed him (titlessly), bathe him (death by shampoo!), sing to him, and do all the things mothers come to think that only they can do. His grandparents would shower him with meticulous attention on the weekend. My mother would assess the hue of his complexion, the width of his smile, the viscosity of his mucus, and the spring of his step, with her trained maternal eye. He was a lucky little Canadian boy with every need instantly met . . . he might not even notice one breast more or less.

Who was I kidding? The truth is, babies and small children go along with the world as it happens to them. They adjust, they accept, and sadness begins as nothing more than an indistinct bass note under the merry tune of their days.

Say I went. On the first day, he would wake up, and instead of being plugged into the morning at the breast, like a singing kettle, he would just keep waking up and up, moving out, feeling lighter and freer — adrift like a helium balloon. Euphoria, excitement, freedom. Then as the day progressed, an itch would begin, a subtle shattering inside. There would be no focused tantrum or obvious indignation. The first night, he would laugh a lot in the bath with Brian, then fall asleep abruptly, as if hungry to escape himself. But three or four times in the night, his eyes would open and he would mistake the full moon outside the window for his misplaced breast. A new wordless feeling, loss, would unfold its wings under his ribs, only it wouldn't have a name. Everything in his room would be irrevocably outside him. Or so I imagined.

I called my mother. I mentioned rather too casually that I was "thinking of going away to Kenya for a week" (nine days, door to door). "With him," she added quickly, meaning, of course, Casey and not Brian.

Daughter voice. "Well, no, I was thinking of going on my own, actually. I may never get another chance, and anyway, it would be good for Brian to spend some time alone with Casey."

"Oh, how could you leave him," she quickly murmured, in a spontaneous maternal outburst. This was most uncharacteristic.

She has never criticized, never passed judgment on my mothering. But this was a simple, sincere question, to which she did not have the answer — and I didn't either. How *could* I leave him? He had become the hub of my life. Then again, how could I not? "Sorry, I'm afraid I can't go, I have a lot of apple juice to pour this week."

Africa. Thinking like a writer, on safari. It was cruel bait.

I explained to my mother that Brian was perfectly capable of looking after Casey, who was, after all, nearly two years old. Everything would be fine. She regained her customary tact, and we changed the subject, to, I think, the ravages of cerebral malaria. Then I hung up the phone for the third time that morning and burst into tears again.

At this point Casey zoomed into the kitchen, looking remarkably grown up and capable. Mummy cry, he cackled, amused by this infantile behavior on my part. He pointed a stubby index finger at me. "Sad." Then he ran off, laughing.

I got my shots and with puffed-up arms began to make quarts and quarts of chicken stock in preparation for my departure. I left six pages of single-spaced typed notes for Brian, including the helpful reminder to "change his crib sheets when they're wet." I concealed small bags of new toys and — total disclosure is called for here — made a short cassette of my voice, reading a favorite bedtime story. Oh, I was indispensable.

Then I bought a level 39 sunblock and a crushable hat and left for Africa. Casey said good-bye without a backward look, eager to hit the sandbox next door. Brian was buoyantly unruffled, no doubt grateful for a chance to plant his flag on the home turf. Short-term male motherhood can be tender and novel. He would have a beginning, a middle, and an end to it.

The airport limo had gray plush seats and a mercifully silent driver. I wept steadily and unobtrusively as the electronic billboards along the way spelled out their autistic messages. The route to the terminal is appallingly gray under the best of circumstances. Staring at a wrinkled cone of green gum left in the door ashtray, I felt something like Velcro ripping in my chest. Then the tears stopped. Here I was, back on the road. An old familiar numbness began, like a drug moving through the veins. I would be early enough to get a good seat, I thought, a bulwark one by a window. By the time we reached the terminal, I was already in motion, light and heartless.

*   *   *

There was nothing unusual about what had happened to me. Sooner or later it afflicts anyone, of any gender, who stays home with a baby. One day you wake up and discover that you've become a dependent, mildly agoraphobic person, with a three-block range. You go to the zoo, watch the polar bear rocking back and forth on one packed-down patch of earth, and think: yes, I recognize that.

You leave the house for an afternoon off, feeling giddy and free. Then after three or four hours unmoored from the baby, the core of you starts to fray and unravel like the inside of a golf ball. The older and sturdier the baby grows, the more enmeshed the at-home mother becomes. He is going up on the seesaw; you are going down. He lives entirely in the present, leaving the future and the past to you. It's only when you go away, you reclaim the present tense.

*   *   *

I have a first-class ticket. The airline is paying the tab, to get some press about their new flights to Nairobi. At the end of my story, there would be a little squib about "how to get there" that would mention the carrier, and that would be the extent of my collusion. Still, it all goes along with a sense of my half-legitimate status — a mother disguised as a writer. A junketeer disguised as an explorer.

One flight attendant refers to the stranger on my right as "my husband." Another, harvesting pinstripe jackets from businessmen up and down the aisle, smiles at me. "On holiday, are you?" The only other female in first class is old and infirm.

I meet my safari-mates on the overnight stay in London. They are all travel writers or agents, old hands at package tours like this. Seasoned drinking and repartee are called for. Our group includes two tough old birds who chain-smoke and a racist, misogynist, even quaintly colonialist travel agent named Harold. Harold refers to breakfast as brekkie, eggs and bacon as "eggies and bakers," and so forth. A guffawer, quick to buy a round. I feel like the free-lancer, the interloper, and the sensitive plant who will turn green and ask them not to smoke in the mini-van: all true.

When we land in Nairobi, the air at six thousand feet is an elixir — intoxicatingly cool and fresh. Light, the indescribable African light, floods the airport. I feel skinned. Casey chirps and dances in my mind. The breasts — not mine, not his, the breasts — are hard and aching. When we reach the hotel, I express milk in ejaculatory squirts into the pink enamel sink, a laborious and uncharming task, especially when reflected back in the huge mirror. The room is a suite, with a locked, stocked mini-bar, perfect for the mini-person I was rapidly becoming.

On Pay-Per-View, there is a choice of *Death Wish* or *West Side Story.* Instead I turn on the TV and watch Toller Cranston ("Cranston . . . cerebral . . . artistic . . . mature!") in the World Professional Figureskating Championship. Sitting in Nairobi, with the smell of jacaranda trees drifting in from the balcony, my breasts filling up like wineskins, watching a Canadian skater on TV. . . . Unreality sets in quickly.

The next day our little group of junketeers is herded into a rental van by Eddy, a Kikuyu driver. At every pit stop, Harold claps him on the shoulder and says, "Well driven, Eddy!" To bartenders and cleaning women, he bellows, "Adios, my friend," followed by quiet racist quips to the person beside him. Harold does not address me directly until days later, when I happen to get out of my jeans and dress up for dinner. "Oh Marni, I didn't notice you were wearing high heels," he says jubilantly. I hate

Harold. He stands between me and Africa, me and the longed-for landscape outside our van. The distance between our kibbitzing group and the dark green hills whizzing by our tinted windows is the distance between me and Casey, between me and my true body.

Our first stop is the Ark, a tourist hotel shaped like a wooden ship, surrounded by wild animals. Each room has an "animal buzzer" that goes off in the night whenever there is a good batch of watchable creatures — rhino, elephants, baboons — gathered around the watering hole. Guests can then assemble in a submarine-like viewing room, where, beyond thick glass, the animals silently converge. Since all of us have jet lag, we don't need the buzzer to be awake at 4 a.m. In the carpeted gloom of the viewing vestibule, we sit with cups of tea and beers.

A baby elephant comes to lick salt. He has little toothpick tusks. A larger male trundles up to the mud puddle. The elephants are reddish and dusty, their ears delicate and lovely, like tattered petals, or fingered pieces of modeling clay. When they leave, they well and truly amble. Wart hogs, with Salvador Dali tusks curling out of their mouth, come close to eat the grass. A water buffalo bearing a distinct resemblance to Margaret Thatcher appears out of the theatrical curtain of the jungle at the edge of the watering hole.

Downstairs, in a darker room, there are no windows, just two slits in a kind of concrete parapet, through which you can hear — and smell — the animals. The smell is thick, pungent, and arousing. There is a continuous chuckling, bubbling sound, like a percolator, that comes from the jungle. Even as they stand there shitting, tails lifted, the animals have an unassailable beauty. They look like something I have been missing all the time, without realizing it.

The animals remind me, of course, of my divinely un-socialized, unblemished, earth-anchored son. But the presence of so much self-assured nature around the hotel seems to have made the rest of our group hypercivilized. Their clothes look even more creaseless, faint British accents have sprouted. Observing these soft pink bipeds around me nattering to each other about the size of the rooms or the cucumber sandwiches, I feel like one of the animals, almost. Encountered on their own turf, wild animals have an emotional power difficult to explain.

At night, in my room alone, I feel luxuriously idle. I think about the chain of tiny, repetitive tasks that make up my days at home, the way they leave you feeling both used-up and unaccomplished.

The next day we drive from the coolness of the mountains down to a lodge in the desert along the shores of the Samburu River. The Samburu is swift, opaque, mud-red, and wide — a strong brown god if ever there was one. Crocodiles laze in the middle, their eyes swiveling at water level. This time my bed is draped in mosquito netting and the room has a tiny cement balcony, across the river from a hunk of goat carcass hung in a tree. The guests aren't happy unless they see something rare, like a cheetah, and so the staff have to bait the jungle. At night tall, beautiful armed guards — local boys with real spears — escort us from the lodge to the rooms. Signs recommend that guests not stray from the lighted paths. Fear of nature, justified and formalized.

On a pre-breakfast game drive through the desert, we see a treeful of baboons in repose. They are elegantly spaced on the branches, like musical notes on a staff. We see impala, lock-kneed, loping giraffe, and circling vultures, all of whom ignore us. Whenever we come upon some wildlife, Eddy stops, and the van roof pops up. We all stand up with our heads and shoulders out of the van, snapping pictures. The animals look back at us like bored movie stars.

By now I have a crush on the physical face of this part of Africa. After two years of going up and down my carpeted hall, up and down the urban corridors of shops, all the while fingering the worry beads of my daily concerns, I feel put to the breast myself. A pretentious claim, based on a few days spent careening through a game park, but true. I am content with the least between me and the landscape and am miserable sitting down in some gloomy mock-Tudor dining room for an English-style dinner of overboiled veg and chops. Although my romance with the land is hokey — *"I had a farm in Africa. . . ."* — it still nourishes the soul.

The place where I feel most calm is in a camp in the Masai Mara, where we sleep under canvas. You can hear leopards cough at night. The main lodge is a thatched building open to the air. Breakfast is served at white tables on the lawn. The sky here is grander than the big sky over the prairies, a Pacific of a sky.

I am out of phone contact with home for six days. Then we move on to the Mount Kenya Safari Club, near Mount Kilimanjaro. Everyone else breathes a sigh of relief to be back in "civilization" — an outpost of hideously retrograde colonialism run by a manager in a chocolate leisure suit with the most fastidious manicure I've ever seen. By this point my distaste for everything except animals, birds, and Africans out of uniform is exquisitely honed. My breasts still keep making milk and have to be tended, like little beasts themselves. I want to keep the milk going until I get back . . . "just in case." (He might be sick, he might only be four months old, and so forth.)

I am not haunted by home at all — Casey and Brian are puppet memories, kept in my suitcase. Not a single thing echoes my other life, as I sit here in a parallel reality, drinking rye with the game warden's wife, who uses long holders for her Kent cigarettes. Outside my huge cottage are birds of paradise, Egyptian cranes, an ibis on the putting green. Inside is a note "to our esteemed guest" and a chocolate cake with "Welcome to our world" iced on the top. When I go to lunch in the main lodge, the heads of a lion and an oryx stare at us from the walls. There is something about taxidermy that makes me want to fall down on the floor laughing. The manager makes a show of giving orders *sotto voce* to the hovering servants. The luxury, the genteel racism, the way no waiter was supposed to smile or meet our eyes makes me feel as if I can't breathe.

After lunch, I snoop around behind the lodge and find myself in the "staff town," where people live and hang out. With great pleasure, I watch a man in his undershirt brushing his teeth at an outdoor tap — it is the most ordinary, intimate thing I have seen all day. I am homesick. That night after dinner, I excuse myself and go into the bathroom, where milk and tears are shed, down into the round gold sinks of the Mount Kenya Safari Club. With a finger, I taste the milk and it is slightly sour. Then a guest, a woman in a gold-brocade jacket walks in and looks at me as if I'm jacking off. Which I am, in a way.

Instead of going back to the table, I stalk through the corridors and find a phone booth, where I tumble through the wires and cables that lie between me and home. Many accents, beeps, and oceanic hisses and then I hear Brian's voice. It is calm and confident, not at all the tight, distracted voice of the single parent trapped at home. "Everything's fine," he says. "In fact, he's eating and sleeping better than usual."

"You don't have to lie to reassure me," I quaver.

"No, really, everything's great. I took him up the Tower."

"You took him up the Tower?" I imagine my small eager son leaning over the railing of the world's tallest freestanding structure. "Put him on."

"Hi, mom!" Loud, happy, casual. I describe the animals I have seen to Casey, who listens, breathing noisily into the mouthpiece. Then he drops the phone to go back to his TV program. I talk some more to Brian and hang up, awash in relief and longing. I also know that it is distance that allows me to feel what I am feeling. I am as separate as separate can be, and it feels good. It's as if after hours of trudging through forest, I've come to a clear point of land where I can look back over the ground I've covered.

Then I begin to want to squander all my separateness again. I fly back into who I was.

*   *   *

I skipped the last night in London and kept on flying, eager to get home. We were ticketed on the Concorde, along with Walter Cronkite and his wife. By now my unmothering was getting a little surreal. I was the only woman under sixty, and the only person not reading the pink airmail edition of the *Financial Times*. My gracious seatmate introduced himself as Reinhold Feldsbrunt, "a managerial whore for one of the multinationals." In his briefcase he kept on a silver chain a little whisk, which he used to whisk the bubbles out of his champagne.

It was Monday morning, and everyone on the Concorde was going to work in Washington. They were commuting. As I closed in on home, the image of Casey's rusted stroller, with the tiny white flowers on a dark blue background, slowly swam into focus.

The first thing I noticed when I got back was that Casey seemed no longer a baby but a walking, talking, excitable boy. His eyes were very blue and he was constantly in motion — two basic facts I had forgotten.

For a few minutes he wouldn't look at me. We were outside, on one of the first warm days of spring. He tactfully took my hand and led me over to his immediate concern, a red-hot Hibachi barbecue in the back yard. "Don't touch," he warned me. He lorded it over me like this for another hour or so. Then at bedtime, confusion set in: did he want me or Brian? A short nervous breakdown ensued during which — I imagined — he let his hair down and cried with the no-longer-threatening memory of our mysterious separation. I comforted him, intact inside for once.

His father was now an initiate into the concept of being "overtired," as in "Don't let him get overtired." "I usually have him in bed by now," he said in passing as I loitered in Casey's room. New code words — "pagoda" for a particular bedtime story — had to be explained to me. "He turns out to love brussels sprouts," Brian told me.

For a day or so, I was a visitor to my own home, able to gaze upon finger-smudged windows without any sense of responsibility at all. Casey went back to the breast for a day or two, just to make a point, and then we gave it up. There was no big day, the habit had died. The deadline for the show I was working on was coming up in the fall, so I started scouting around for a day care. I thought our separating was over. In truth, it had only begun. Inside me, the brief, tender light of Africa lingered, lingered, and then went out.

*   *   *

When you wean, the world flows back into you. It is like a prolonged Monday morning of remembering bills, letters, and the business of figuring out who you are or plan to be. The self comes staggering back, in need of repair, sulky, more demanding than the easily fulfilled baby. You become more vulnerable to real or threatened loss, because this final stage of birth has arrived, full of such potent emotion — and once again, not marked on any calendar. Weaning doesn't have a lot of public currency. (A change of name would definitely help — "weaning" sounds like some kind of college initiation.)

Even if she can't wait to have her body to her self again, a mother may be ambushed by this contradictory sadness. Once again, she is alone with her feelings. Even her friends with older children look upon her as potentially lucky, rather than in mourning. What they think is, How free she'll be. What she may be surprised to feel is the loss of a briefly perfect union.

15.   Day Care

OFF THE BREAST and into the world. Casey was two years old. After receiving an award for the theater's longest work-in-progress, our show was scheduled to open in November. Once again I felt like a maternal vagabond for having failed to enroll my son in a dozen day cares when he was still a zygote. But how could I sign him up before I had an inkling of who he was, or if he was a day-care kind of kid? How very autocratic; how *parental*. So I had let the issue slide. Now I forced myself to get out my tattered and long-neglected list of day cares and make some calls.

I still cannot fathom how mothers of more than one child manage to plan ahead. Many do. I've seen them wearing Snuglis and lipstick, pushing a carriage and signing up their four-year-olds for kickball. Perhaps it was peculiar to me, this postnatal dyslexia that made it difficult to hold the baby and put change in a parking meter at the same time. My "maternal preoccupation" left little margin for thinking ahead — or indeed for any thinking at all. This gave life with Casey an engaging existentialist tension. Each day was a series of improvisations, which kept pace with the impressive skin-sheddings he was going through. No bossy planning for me; I would let my son take his own shape.

Brian was now working as an arts reporter for *Maclean's*, Canada's newsmagazine. I had always planned to work at home with Casey for a year or two, then find a day care. But as I went about arranging it, it struck me that I had never spent five minutes imagining what day care would be *like* — for me or for him. Day care was such a fragile, necessary institution; it was something you didn't question.

A friend had just enrolled her daughter in a brand new day care on the second floor of a community center across town. I took Casey for a visit one day. A brisk ponytailed administrator took us around with a polished spiel and a distracted air. I noted the cubbies with their hand-lettered names, stuffed with hats and knapsacks. I read the neatly typed list of snack foods (Monday: celery and cream cheese. Tuesday: Ritz crackers and peanut butter. . . .) and fingered the crepe-paper butterflies taped on the wall. We admired the new water-play table, at which tidy little girls in vinyl aprons stood.

The floors were hardwood, with a high acrylic sheen. There was plenty of light and space. The day care's playground was on the roof of the building — a point of pride, since the children could go out all winter without leaving the premises. But the playground flooring was sparkling, hard, and gritty. I imagined the feel of that on bare hands or knees. Was it too much to wish for real trees and grass underfoot? It all seemed sadly modular and urban, a Filofax day care.

In the second room, I made eye contact with a boy who was bigger than the others in his group. He was lying under a low table swishing his legs against the shiny floor, with a look in his dark eyes older than I was prepared to meet. I wanted to take him home and watch TV with him in my lap. Most of the kids were happily engrossed in whatever activity had been set up before them, but it took just one lost child to unleash my anxieties. Why was I banishing my son, so briefly small, so that I could make a minimum wage doing ephemeral theater? Work was important, work was necessary . . . but was my heart in it, or was I just telling myself that my heart should be in it?

The internal debate continued. He was an only child — he couldn't be Baby Jesus forever. It would be good for him to be part of a group. It was time to put an end to my sniveling dependence on him . . . and so forth.

As I made polite noises about the many bins of Duplo blocks, the debate escalated in my mind to a rant. How did we end up with a society in which single mothers are so poor they have no real choice? Either they work and the kid goes to day care, or it's home alone on welfare. And for women who aren't economically forced to get a job, why does work still have so much more status than two or three years spent at home raising kids? Why isn't it the custom, the normal thing, for both parents to cut back to part-time for a few months, or years, out of a long working life? Where is the money, the legislation, the social support for the work of raising kids? Staying home or going to work is not the issue. The crime is that the whole question of child care, which ought to be right at the heart of the country's politics and business, has somehow devolved into these patchwork solutions and private agonies for individual women.

Technically, of course, I had a choice. I could go on working at home, with a brain like a colander, earning peanuts. I had a partner, who had a good job (although in Toronto it takes approximately seven incomes per household to even approximate working-class life in the average American sit-com). So there was no reason for me to get so worked up about this.

In the next playroom, each child was placed on a tiny square of sparkling green carpeting. These little islands of play also depressed me. But I rejected my instincts as retrograde maternalism, put on a brisk face, and hung up Casey's hat on a vacant hook. The director suggested I leave him for an hour or two to see how he took to it. I became breezier by the minute, to reassure her that I was not one of those clinging mothers who live through their children. I plonked Casey down on his bit of green carpet and became unrecognizably offhand with him.

"Okay, kiddo, you have fun now and I'll be back in a little while," I chirped, turning on my heel.

His face darkened, crumpled, and out came the beginnings

of a long, anguished cry. I hardened my heart and gave the director a dry, knowing smile. Typical baby! Mom just needs to click-clack right out of there on her work pumps and "in ten minutes he'll forget all about you." But of course — babies are peerless survivalists. They aren't going to cry forever and risk offending the smiling stranger left in charge of them. They know enough to clam up and play along, saving the tears and revenge for mom. Small children and their parents pay the emotional price of day care every evening, around 6 p.m.

However, Casey was no pushover. I strode out of the room without a backward look, my heart contracted to the size of a raisin. Casey wept hard and piteously. Some cries deconstruct the brain, destroy cells forever; those cells were withering as I walked away. Halfway down the stairs, I could still hear him, the cry wailing down the corridor. Well, I thought, I'll just wait in the stairwell until he settles down. Surely with me out of sight he would be distracted soon enough. He was just trying to reel me back in.

So I stood in the weak gray light of an overcast August morning and watched the grocer across the street pick over his pyramid of tomatoes and listened to Casey's ragged, never-ending howls. His cries moved through angry indignation to bawling, heartbroken despair. All babies cry and carry on, I told myself, it means nothing, I mustn't give in. It's just me, projecting my own loss onto his cries. Or perhaps I infected him with my own doubts about the place before I left. It's nothing, it's nothing. My heart raced on.

Whatever the emotional physics, I finally went back up the stairs, two at a time. My vanity, my desire to measure up as an independent mother had overridden my instinct. There was an institutional coolness here that I smelled right away and should have acted on.

When I reached the door, I saw one of the staff — not the director, who was back in her office writing checks — walking around with my purple-faced son, shushing him. His passion was beginning to unnerve even her. I came over and took him out of her arms and the frightened gratitude in his eyes was more than I could bear. I mumbled something about looking for somewhere closer to home and scurried out of there. It made the rest of the day with him infinitely tender.

*   *   *

I went back to a place in our neighborhood — a university campus cooperative day care that was "child-oriented," which was the polite description of my own approach. I would have to take shifts there myself, which would force me to see how the place worked. There were men as well as women on staff, which I liked. On the other hand, it had a tinge of that depressing shabbiness that all underfunded day cares have. The tired old rugs, the little gulley of scuff marks under the swing sets, all fed my resistance to this new stage of separation. The staff and kids seemed happy enough, but it felt like an entirely different country than the one ten minutes away, downtown, where grown-ups, mostly men, worked in canyons of glass and gold.

No matter how well-run a day care is, the lack of money hangs about it like the odor of ammonia. It can't disguise the fact that it still exists in the margins, in the shadows, in basements and portables. The few enlightened on-site corporate day cares somehow look like model farms. I couldn't help seeing committed day-care workers as heroes, authentic heroes — underpaid, overstressed, doing the most valuable work imaginable, for less than a street vendor in a good summer.

*   *   *

Then came the day in September when I did in fact have to leave him and get down to work. A space came available at the co-op day care, and I grabbed it.

First we visited for a few days to get acclimatized. The cook had short platinum hair and made impressive vegetarian lunches from scratch. Mary, the woman in charge of Casey's age group, was young, pretty, and exuded the gentle, slow-moving, (i.e., exhausted) air of a single mother, which she also was. All day long she looked after a roomful of kids and then she took her own two-year-old home to her basement apartment. She was too much a mother for too much of the day — but in this she was somewhat recognizable, and Casey took to her right away.

His first morning of day care remains woven into the strands of my DNA. I handed Casey over to Mary, and he clung to her neck like a koala. His whole face became a big red chasm. I walked through the heavy iron gate and clicked it shut. This time I didn't go back. I went down to the theater where we worked on the show. I fled back to the day care as soon as I could, propelled across town by those amazing rush-hour rockets of mother love.

When I got there, I had the experience of watching him through a side window as he pulled apart a wad of purple yarn. He looked completely happy. My heart swelled with the luxury of seeing him like this, separate and serene. Then I walked in and within two minutes he fell apart, as the memory of my going reawakened.

We convince ourselves that these first epic partings and reunions are routine — just a thin membrane that exists to be ruptured. Like childbirth, as soon as it's over we call the pain "sensations." Memory's flair for revision takes over, and life rolls on.

16.   Work

ONCE CASEY was settled in day care, the re-writes and rehearsals for our show, *She-Devils of Niagara,* closed in. Theater involves lots of fourteen-hour days shut away from the light of day in underheated rooms, drinking bad coffee. It is considered part of the magic. Theater is exquisitely ephemeral, which makes it sexier than almost anything else. But childhood is ephemeral, too. I raced from one to the other.

I typed a stack of rewrites for the show that now fill two large cardboard boxes in the basement, but I don't remember the process at all. Although we churned out ideas at a great clip, the focus required to structure it all was beyond me. I couldn't see the narrative forest for the trees — we were lost in the scene, wed to fragments. The writing mimicked my daily life; the trick was to take all these dissonant pieces and make them work together as a whole.

About five days before the show opened, I had a little epiphany as I sat in the empty theater watching the Clichettes rehearse. Their performances were hilarious, the costumes were works of art, there was no end of creativity on display. But the story — our clever fable about the "wax museum" of sex roles, the endangered species of men ("Bring Back Bob"), the cultural mutations of gender past and future — struck me as largely indecipherable.

It was not a good moment. On the way home, I tried to grasp the notion of a failure that would involve money, vast painted sets, and an audience sitting out there saying "I don't get it." I bought a paper, put my wallet on the paper box, and walked on in a daze. The next day I realized I had lost my wallet, along with all my ID. Another disappearing act! I was more of a mother than anything else, and certainly less of a writer than I wanted to be.

*　　*　　*

The show opened to kind if puzzled reviews, and the rewrites went on till the last wig went back in the box. It was not the flop that I imagined, but it never came into focus, either — it was an organic creature that kept sprouting new appendages, like Shiva. Family was turning out to be an endless, murky collaboration, too. I was longing to finish something for a change.

I decided it was time to retreat to my little fiefdom of the first-person singular. That I could control, I thought. For the past fifteen years or so, I had written stories about the things that happened to me, and people were willing to publish them. Now, I thought, all I had to do was write about what I knew — motherhood. So when the *Toronto Star* asked if I wanted to write the occasional guest column for their Saturday page, I proposed this notion to the editor. We met for lunch. I said there was a world of frazzled families out there dying for honest dispatches from the home front. He looked dubious. And, I hastily added, I would write about other things, too, funny lifestyle pieces, urban foibles, and so on. Fine, the editor said, as long as it's light and bright. People don't want to read bad news on the weekends.

Home I went to my typewriter. I would courier the columns down to the paper, and two or three weeks later, they would show up on the page. Some were good and some were thin, but I never heard from the editor again. In fact, no one ever called to say "Write some more" or "Please write less." It was spooky.

Finally, somewhat experimentally, I stopped writing them. And that was okay, too. No one called! I could have choked on a rice cake and been lying for days, rigid under the toy bins in Casey's room, and no one would have known! Except for Brian and Casey, and even then, they might have dismissed it as a sulk.

This was discouraging. Here I was, writing with a certain bitter humor about living in limbo as a mother, and the world of work was making it clear that I was right.

*　　　*　　　*

For a while, as a new mother, my body had made a great deal of sense. But now things were getting blurred again. With my only child packed off to day care, I was half in, half out of the mother zone. I wanted to have another child, but the days of the miracle conception were over now. Whenever we agreed to be reckless, I never got pregnant. My work was proving treacherous, Brian's career was flourishing, and I was nudging forty. For the first time since Casey was born, I began to fret about how I looked.

I have a photo of me writing a book review while Casey sits beside me like a pasha in his infant seat. For the first year, work involved nothing more than a typewriter, a notebook, and whatever presence of mind I could muster. It didn't call for firm muscle tone or a decent wardrobe. I still had ten pounds of the weight I gained during pregnancy to lose, but the weight didn't obsess me the way fatness normally does. My son accepted me the way I was and liked to grip this extra flesh with his fingers. I forgot about how I measured up physically, because on many days, I simply wasn't seen.

Casey and I would cruise up and down Bloor Street, and the man in the coffee bar or the girls in the Supersave cared not a whit if I put on lipstick, or washed my hair, or wore only pants with elastic waistbands. But I began to stew about this creeping obscurity and to compensate in strange new ways.

First, I dyed my hair. I had always gone in for demure little highlights, but one winter day I decided I wanted a total dye job in what I specifically described as a "brassy blonde, with dark roots." I didn't want the tasteful beige touch-up, suitable for the fortyish mother. I wanted to look a little crazy and fucked-up.

So the colorist dutifully churned up a muddy potion, and I came out a flat shade of orange, the sort that drains the color from your face and can be worn only with certain unbecoming greens and browns. I had to go to a party that evening, where I weathered the level stares of my friends, who maintained eye contact with great courage and said nothing at all. Can't they at least crack a few jokes? I hissed to Brian, who was kind and noncommittal ("It's fine, it'll grow out, it looks great") about this little gesture of self-mutilation.

Around this time, I was seized with a desire to change my glasses, too. I had always worn round wire-rim glasses. Now I wanted something different. First, I bought black horn-rims — no-nonsense, Buddy Holly frames, not the sort associated with maternity at all. But on second inspection, these frames were dull. Why not customize them, I thought, to assuage both my bottom-less need for some attention and my frustrated creativity? Why not indeed.

So I took a bottle of white-out — the stuff people used to erase typing mistakes before there were computers — and care-fully painted tiny white polka dots all over my black horn-rims. This was an amusing notion, I thought, and the combination of the shaky polka dots with the flat orange hair would certainly stand out in the morning light around the old sandbox.

Who would ever link polka dots to a wistful rage? But it was true, I was inching into bag-lady territory, all because I had sunk a little too deeply into motherhood.

I have another photograph of me, in this incarnation, sitting beside Casey at his lemonade stand. He had overpriced his lemonade and it was not moving quickly at all. I look thick-jawed and blankly ferocious.

Just about this time, the call came. CBC's "The Journal" was auditioning new reviewers for the arts segment of their national news program. Was I interested? I stared at the phone as if it were a water moccasin. This was like a call from some central Image Authority saying "We hear you're fat and out of it, and we'd like to know how bad it is." How should I look? Who was I now? Would they let me hold my son on my lap while reviewing movies? I knew the whole trick was confidence, to breeze in and just *allow* the camera to feast on you. Instead, I saw it as a merciless measure of how attractive, articulate, and hard-edged I could make myself in twenty-four hours. Plus, here was a chance to be a genuine wage-earner.

I raced out and got my hair cut again, giving me the painful fresh-haircut look, and threw items of clothing around the bedroom. As I tried to put myself together, I found Casey's antics and piercing monologues ever more irritating. I wanted to look like someone with outlines around the eyes and lips, edges, borders — the things I still lacked as I oozed around the house in my fleece-lined wardrobe.

If I passed the audition, I would be the opposite of a mother — I would be on national TV. The prospect was both irresistible and sickening. TV magnifies any hint of a hungry ego, not to mention puffiness. How could I account for myself? I couldn't very well gaze into the camera and sing "I'm a Little Teapot."

I remember little about the audition, except that my hands were shaking as I held my styrofoam cup of coffee. I hated that I cared so much. They clipped a mike to my sweater and pressed foundation to my face to tone down the orange hair. I had written a review of the David Cronenberg horror movie *The Fly*, which I liked. My script was fine. Then they had me read the thing with a Teleprompter, suggesting I "liven up my voice," take it slower, be more animated, look into the camera as if it were a friend, and so forth.

Having half a dozen professionals coolly scrutinize me was refreshing, at first. I thought I did all right. When it was over, I went home with a surprising gust of energy and made lasagna from scratch. Casey struck me as an adorable child, and I did educational things with him, just like a working mother would.

The next day went by, and then a week. No phone call. No

yes, no no. No nothing. Now, in the terrible world of auditions, this is normal; actors go through this flagellation all the time. But to put your face out there for the first time and experience only the routine callousness of the working world was depressing.

Many weeks later, another call came. It was "The Journal" again! Oh yes, as memory serves, the audition was very nice, and now they needed a reviewer to go to Montreal to see a new play and do a quick review. Could I leave in two days? But of course. The producer would accompany me. He would rustle up a crew in Montreal. Were they aware I hadn't done this kind of thing before, and that drama reviews were not my beat? No matter. I was free to go, that was the main thing.

The next day, I delivered Casey to day care and went barreling down Queen Street, looking for something to wear on this glamorous out-of-town assignment. I found a denim-blue knit thing, which covered me from calf to jaw and was not only a good TV color, I reasoned, but went as well as could be expected with the still-orange hair. The skirt was rather flowing and long. To tell the truth, it was as long as a ball gown, but I didn't care. I would wear boots. It didn't strike me that I looked like someone riding to the hounds until I opened my hotel room in Montreal and saw the look on the producer's face.

Overdressed! the look screamed. Who does she think she is, the face said, Diane Sawyer? The producer was wearing jeans and a ratty old sweater. He would do a stand-up later on, too. I felt like Miss Iowa getting ready for the talent portion of the beauty contest.

The night before, we had seen the play, which I thought was great. I stayed up late concocting an essay on my reasons for thinking this. Over breakfast, the producer suggested I run a few lines by him. I began to read. His eyes darted to his watch. Once again, his face could not conceal the certain knowledge that I didn't know the first thing about this craft. "It's far too long, for one thing," he began briskly. "It can't go over three minutes." I retreated to my room and slashed away at my overwrought copy. Then we left in cabs for the theater, where we would tape the review sitting in the empty seats. The timing was tight, because the cast was scheduled to rehearse.

When it came time to shoot my bit, I sat in the empty theater, unable to see into the darkness beyond the camera lights. Each time, I would get almost to the end, and then stumble. The crew was friendly. The producer was patient. I read my opinions this way and that, smiling, moving forward enthusiastically, and when I finally made it through, the darkness erupted with applause — the entire cast of the show had been sitting out there like a circle of wolves, waiting for the shoot to end so they could get on stage.

That day I flew home to the forgiving arms of my family and phoned my parents. I would appear on national television, I told them, this Friday evening, sharing my critical views on a piece of drama. They were thrilled. My father set up the VCR and bought fresh tape. Then the call came. The CBC had, unfortunately, lost the tape. It was nowhere to be found.

Please, I said, you don't have to lie to me, I can take it. No, no, the producer said, it's very embarrassing, but I really did lose it. Could you come in and do it over in the studio? So I sat in an airless little cubicle and recorded the thing over again, and in the end it never did run. I didn't hear why. Pre-empted by news, probably. Not soon after, a check arrived in the mail.

I knew there must be some latitude of work that fell between having no voice at all and being on the nightly news, but for a long time, it eluded me.

*   *   *

There was no time to brood, however, because once again Casey was out of day care and back home, this time with pneumonia. His second case. He was bursting with health, he was happy, he looked like he was being groomed for the L.A. Rams — why was he sick so often? I refused to admit that he was home almost as much as he was in day care. "Everybody goes through this at first," the day-care staff reassured me. "He'll get over it." Instead, he got worse and worse. Where other kids motored through colds and coughs and were back in action after a few days, everything seemed to go to his chest and stay there. He was on antibiotics almost constantly that winter, which I knew was wreaking havoc with his immunity. I tried homeopathy and diet strategies. I considered taking him out of day care. But if I took him out and kept him at home, I would risk "losing my place."

Our doctor sent us to a specialist who said all this illness might be related to bronchial asthma. This would make sense, since there was mild asthma on both sides of our families. I said I would try the drugs he gave us. But here was something else I was loath to confront. A wildly energetic three-year-old with a chronic, incurable disease? No thanks.

The drugs helped, a little. And then I went back to the novel I had abandoned when I got pregnant. Screw the media. Maybe art would rescue me. I took the last draft out of the shoe box in the hall closet and sat down to read.

Like all first novels, the book set out to include everything of any importance that has ever happened to anyone, since time began. Well, I thought, if I take out all the ideas it might work. For another six months, I revised. I invented a new and even more detached framework but it was too late, I couldn't get back inside the story again. I kept picking it up and putting it down, like a piece of soiled embroidery, until I admitted defeat. The person who had written it had fled.

It was time to give up, get a real job, and move on. Besides, Casey would stay healthier if he were out of the happy germ-pool of day care and home with a sitter. I had to earn some money, too — the one-and-a-half-salary family was no longer an option for us. I accepted the irony that if I wanted our family to function better, I had to get out of the house.

17.   Guilt

I TOOK a job as a reader and evaluator of film scripts at a government film-funding agency.

This meant I would get to sit in what, to me, seemed a huge and well-appointed office, with oodles of stationery, where I would read drafts of film scripts, write reports, and attend meetings. It was a job that would shrink writing from the black cloud over my head to a finite, if repetitive task. But first, I had to hire a nine-to-five nanny.

Once again I advertised for an extravagantly perfect woman to take my place for $5.50 an hour. The first person who came round for an interview was a skinny white teen-age girl who looked bored even during the interview. She picked up Casey as if he were a duck decoy — something between cute and horrifying. Her name was Carmen. She was a Healing Touch massage student who immediately asked if there was an ashtray she could use. Her eyes flicked around the apartment and dully registered disappointment. I was not her dream employer. I knew from the first glimpse of her sharp, sad face that I wouldn't hire her, although for the next twenty minutes we both pretended otherwise.

Casey, ever indiscriminate, fetched her small gifts and broken cookies, which she accepted with sing-songy thank-yous, sticking her lower lip out to blow smoke in a careful stream above his head. I let her use the phone, then she breezed out. I said we'd be in touch.

Three other candidates showed up, polite West Indian

women who either lived two hours away by bus or were looking for work only between 4 p.m. and 7:30 p.m., because they already worked part-time. One older woman seemed so profoundly tired she was like a walking ghost. Her name was Esther.

Esther worked nights as a cleaner and had seven children and grandchildren at home. Her swollen legs, wrapped in elastic bandages under brown stockings, were thick as small trees. Esther labored up my stairs one by one, sat in my kitchen, and said she needed to make more money. She had taken two buses and a streetcar just for the interview. I babbled on about the link between hypertension and phlebitis and insisted she eat lunch. By this I meant chicken salad sandwiches. She took the sandwich apart, ate the chicken, and left the bread — thin, mean, health-store bread. It struck me that Esther was preternaturally still, as if she might sit there forever. There seemed to be no energy whatsoever left in her, just a wordless, impacted, stoical going-on. I explained that we needed someone who lived nearby, who could sit the odd evening. I said I thought the commute would be too hard on her. I didn't tell her the truth, that I wanted someone not so used up.

Esther betrayed no reaction to this rejection and accepted the bus fare I gave her. Slowly, she made her way down the hall and the stairs, one at a time. I told her I would keep her name on my back-up list, for sure.

The job loomed closer. I was getting a little worried. Then the phone rang and I spoke to a woman with a loud, confident voice who said her name was Galo. She was working at the moment, but her "lady" was expecting another baby and planned to leave her job to stay home. So she was looking for another family — hopefully not with two children, she said with a merry, explosive laugh, because two children were too much work! She was a little nervous, but direct. She asked as many questions of me as I did of her.

"So I'll come and see you, then," Galo decided. Fine, I said, come now. I liked her good-natured pushiness and her buoyant voice.

I put a clean sweat shirt on Casey, took the pots out of the dish drainer, unwrapped a new soap for the bathroom, chipped the toothpaste splatters off the mirror with a fingernail, and brushed my hair. A good nanny is hard to find.

The doorbell rang right at the appointed hour. I went down the stairs to the front hall and opened the door to a short, smiling, round-faced woman who looked like a young girl, although she was in her mid-thirties.

She came upstairs and we talked. She told me she was from British Guyana and had worked as a nanny in Canada for the past ten years. She didn't "handle" me — she was open and confident. It was clear that her thoughts about me and this boy on the floor weighed as much as my thoughts about her. This helped dissolve some of my huge, gelatinous guilt.

Evidently not put off by the clutter of our apartment, she sat down with a cup of tea, remarking on the decor. "Book shelves in the kitchen, that's different!" She wore a blouse with pants and new sneakers, very tiny, with pink boomerangs on the side. She took "the boy" on her lap and did the requisite dandling, to Casey's delight. She laughed often and handled him easily.

"Soon as you open the door, I think, yes, this is my next lady," Galo told me much later on. And these things are rudimentary, it's true. I felt she liked my face, and I liked hers. After phoning to check out her references later that day, I called Galo and we struck a deal.

I went off to my job, where I read all day, purchased danishes, gained weight, and developed a brief but intense crush on a man down the hall. I was deeply impressed by the social skills of everyone around me and their witty banter in the meetings. Everywhere in the city, in offices like this, people were making wry jokes about their personal lives, lucky inhabitants of a zone of work that was neither superficial nor intimate. I felt like someone scuba diving for the first time, amazed at the variety and hues of fish.

Everything went smoothly for weeks. Casey and Galo hit it off, and his health improved. Then the call, every mother's nightmare, came.

"Hello, Mrs. Jackson?" I was sitting at my desk, reading an offbeat, low-budget Canadian coming-of-age script called "Hey, Mikey!"

"This is Sergeant Allan Merrick of the Metro Fire Department."

Down went the script. A curious calm descended.

"We've been taking care of a little fire at your apartment here but it's all under control now."

"A little fire?"

"I'll let you talk to your baby sitter."

"Hello, Marni?" said Galo, slightly louder than usual. "Everybody okay, but we call the firemen just in case."

"Where is Casey?"

"Here on my lap, the boy is fine. His bed caught fire."

"*His bed caught fire.*"

"Not flames, but, you know, black smoke — a lot, a lot. You know how the bed is right beside the wall? I just put him down for his nap, and he had his little tape recorder plug in and I guess he try to pull it out, you know, and it make a spark, and get into the mattress."

"You mean to say his bed caught fire, with him in it?" I said.

"I didn't want to bother you at work but the fireman had to get some information."

"You were absolutely right to call, Galo. *Whenever* there is a bed on fire, you must call me."

"Well, he was having his nap, you know, and I was just going to have a bite of lunch when Casey race out into the hall all excited, his eyes big, big and he shouts, 'I need a glass of water!' So I rush in and see smoke coming up beside the bed. I phone the fire department and fill up a pot with water, Casey sees me and he fill one too and the both of us are running around with pots of water. Oh boy, Marni, wait till you see the mess!"

What about Sergeant Merrick, I said stupidly, not knowing what else to say, or think.

"Oh he's fine, he's having a bite to eat."

I was beginning to be able to think, and what I was thinking was: my only child could have been burned to a crisp while I sat here reading about some guy with a learning disability who races Monster Trucks.

"How is Casey now — is he upset?"

"He thought we were going to get mad at him but I tell him not to worry." Galo laughed. "He love it when we threw the water on the bed and all the smoke came up."

"Galo," I said, "you did exactly the right thing, thank you. How are you? Are you all right?"

Big nervous explosion of laughter from Galo. "Well, what you think, I'm going to let him burn in his bed while I drink my coffee?"

"What's the damage, then?"

"The wall, the mattress, and the bottom part."

"The box spring, right. You sure you're okay, Galo? I could come home. . . ."

"Oh no, you have to do your work! The boy and I just going to heat up some Zoodles, then go to the corner and buy him some of those green grapes he love." Affirmative noises from Casey on her lap. "Yes, boy, grapes!"

"I don't mind, it's no big deal to leave."

"Mr. Merrick want to talk to you." Slightly flirtatious chuckle as she passes the phone to the fireman, who takes a minute to swallow whatever he is eating.

"Mrs. Jackson?"

"Yes."

"Everything's fine here. Your boy and your baby sitter handled the situation very well."

"What's for lunch?"

"Excuse me?"

"Nothing. Thank you. Thank you very much."

I hung up. I went into my boss's office and said my son was having a nap when his bed burst into flames. I exaggerated a little. My boss happened to be a mother herself, with three children. I often heard her talking slowly and clearly to her own nanny on the phone. She slammed her hand down on her desk.

"*What*! You must be joking. Is he okay?"

I replayed the story for her, to very satisfying effect. She urged me to go home. The shock could set in later, she said.

But I didn't. There was no fire, except at the back of my mind, for the rest of the day. There was nothing to do but try to pretend that it had never happened.

*　　　*　　　*

I expected to feel a bit displaced by a nanny, but there was no rivalry, and it was good to have another woman in the house. Depression, health, and haircuts were our favored topics.

"Oh, look how nice your mum look this morning," she would say to Casey as I came downstairs trailing file folders, dressed for work.

"Your hair look good up like that, Marni," she would say approvingly. "Make your face look thinner."

She and Casey had an affectionate but businesslike partnership, which was fine with me. He had all the obsessives he could handle. I don't believe she ever got angry at him. If I came home in a bad mood and even spoke sharply to him, I could feel Galo's uneasiness, although she said nothing. She could be bossy, but she didn't have meanness in her.

Close to Christmas, her first Christmas with her new husband, Abel, we invited them to dinner one night. Galo wore her new Nikes — a present from Abel — and a fluffy sweater. She was impressed that I had cooked not only dinner, but a dessert as well; Galo knew the inside of my fridge better than Brian, better than anyone. Abel brought some salsa tapes for Brian, and after dinner the men went into DJ mode, hunkered around the sound system. We danced, and Brian hauled his drums out of the basement. I gave Galo an overly sensible tuque and scarf, but apart from that the evening was a success.

Galo was with us for about three years, without a single mishap or argument, although we both went through our own dark days. The only complaint Casey ever registered was that she cut his nails too short. Whenever I groveled and called home at 6:10 p.m. to say I would be late, she reassured me.

"Take your time, no problem, the boy and I just having some nice noodles. Go, go, Marni, everything fine."

The more generous someone is, I found, the more you do your best to get home on time. Sometimes I got miffed if I heard from Casey that they sat around and watched "America's Most Wanted," but that was about it. I knew there were days when she sat at the kitchen table flipping through *People* magazine, instead of playing board games non-stop; so did I, when I was home with Casey all day. Whenever my work or the rest of my life was flagging, I reminded myself that at least this nanny hadn't fired me.

*   *   *

Guilt is one of the most pointless emotions available — if it is an emotion. I suspect it is a weed of an idea that sprouts out of the compost heap of shame, now fashionably thought to be at the heart of the twentieth-century psyche. Guiltily, I sat down to open a new file called "guilt" and was amazed to find that the word wasn't taken yet. But once embarked on the job-and-nanny phase, I saw that guilt of one sort or another was going to arise.

Glints of guilt have been there from birth, of course, running through my days like a vein of soft metal. It's as much a part of modern motherhood as broken sleep and apple juice. Guilt strikes first when you realize that you're not, and can never be, a mother like your own mother. Then, if you have only one child, sooner or later there is a second wave of guilt about not being a real mother until you have two children, or more. But the guilt that never goes away is that other mothers somehow manage much better than you do.

I have a kind of guilt-ridden awe for mothers at home with two or three or more preschool children. I feel something of the same guilty awe around primary teachers who haven't lost their spirit. Awe is fine, and totally appropriate. Guilt, on the other hand, is unnecessary. It's divisive and self-absorbed, guilt. Lop off its head immediately.

The not-my-mother guilt can be atomized historically. Every daughter measures herself against her own mother (whether in apposition or emulation) but true competition is out of the question — the territory of family has changed too much. For the first time, not only do most mothers have paying jobs, but the majority of them have no choice but to work. And for those who do stay home, TV and the media, like the Big Bad Wolf, have blown the walls down. There are no white picket fences to keep the nightmares out, as Anne Sexton (admittedly not a great mother, but a good poet) once wrote. The mother at home hears the hum of the world outside, whether she wants to or not. She may be relieved to have left it, but the way things stand, she has a sense of dropping out, not in.

The question is not whether to stay home or to go to work. One way or another, paid or not, most mothers cover both. But when my parents were parents, the roles were clear-cut, and there was a sense of stable identity that went along with the sacrifices of being a homemaker. Now there are as many kinds of mothers as there are channels with a dish. What this means is that there are more decisions to be made, without the option of genuine choice. For too many women, the only choice available is which style of poverty they prefer — home on welfare or barely earning enough to pay for day care. But no matter what mother-style a woman chooses, none will resemble the mother who raised her. New satisfactions, and new martyrdoms, await her instead.

*　　*　　*

By the time she left, when Casey started full days at school, he was up to her chest. The parting was amicable, and we kept on hiring her from time to time to baby-sit at night. On our way to school, I sometimes saw her sitting in the park with her new charge, a little girl about two.

Several years later, I went to an aerobics class at the community center in Casey's school. And there was Galo, in black tights and the familiar tiny running shoes. She was looking strong and limber.

The class went along at quite a clip. I hate aerobics and was soon feeling winded. When the group was ordered to lope around the gym, I caught up with Galo. She said she had a nice new family and had cut back to part-time, so she could do other things. "And little girls easier than boys, you know, Marni," she chuckled. "How about you," she said, "your work going along?"

I told her I was behind schedule and sort of frazzled.

"Oh yes, I can tell. I always know how your work is because I see it in your face." She drew her hand down her jaw. I had forgotten how intimately she knew me and how tactful she had been with this knowledge. We fell into step for a few minutes as we ran. But the gym had bad acoustics and the music made it difficult to talk. We circled the room together for a few more laps and then I dropped back and Galo ran on.

18.   Fun

Aт 2:30 A.M. on the first night of our holiday, off we went in our rented Topaz, to the Izaak Killam Hospital for Children in downtown Halifax, holding a map of the city on top of Casey's head as he rattled it with his cough.

We pulled up in front of a dark, deserted-looking building where the parking-lot attendant was sharing a cigarette with the cleaning lady.

"My Lord, that's a terrible cough," said the cleaning lady as our son hacked his way through the doors under his own steam. We sat at the empty admission desks, listening to children scream somewhere down the hall. Soon a weary nurse holding an infant in the crook of one arm appeared. With her finger in the baby's hungry mouth, she did all the paperwork for our admission, stopping twice to answer the phone.

"It's wild tonight," she sighed, and disappeared.

*   *   *

People who claim to have carefree, regenerative holidays accompanied by their small children are either lying or self-deluded. Family travel has rewards, but never the ones you expect. It's like going into one of those Mayan ruins to view the king's tomb; halfway down you wonder why you bothered coming at all. It's dark, and they made the stairs too steep. Then you arrive at the bottom and enter a room with a faint but potent human magic. So it is with the subtly perilous, subtly thrilling family vacation.

The paradox is that the family on vacation doesn't truly travel — it explores itself. Childless people are forced to climb rock faces with their bare hands to feel elation and terror. But parents don't even have to leave their rented car. Protected from strangeness, the family rolls through theme parks and down beaches, a country of its own with its own little weather system. Dissipated by city life, nannied out, split asunder, the family goes on vacation to become a family again.

Islands are ideal for this because they curtail ambition, not to mention long car rides. The point is to go somewhere new and do nothing together. With this in mind, we planned a quick tour of the Maritimes that would wind up somewhere already thoroughly domesticated and famous for a child it-self — Prince Edward Island, off the east coast of Canada. After all, Anne of Green Gables never really went anywhere, or did anything — she simply lived on P.E.I. and used her imagination. Surely our tiny, battered family could do the same. How could danger possibly lurk among the lawn orna-ments and regimented potato fields of Canada's tiniest, mild-est province? Well, the wilderness is where you find it, or where it finds you, at three in the morning.

The first axiom of the family vacation is that someone, possibly everyone, will get sick. I'm convinced that the Air Canada computer is hooked up in some way to Casey's inner ear, because ear infections inevitably strike two to three days before any scheduled flight — or possibly in the air, causing terrible pain. This is a rule. So, even when he boarded the plane with a nasty cough, I felt optimistic. We had just seen the doctor, and his ears were clear. His ears were clear! It was only when he threw up a carton of cranberry juice into a defective sick bag, causing the spines of everyone around us to visibly shrink, that I realized he was ill with something else.

* * *

"Just in Halifax for a visit, are you?" asked another nurse as she took a pipette of blood from Casey's finger.

"It's the first day of our vacation," we said with a wan smile.

"I must have heard five sets of parents say that tonight," she said. "Isn't that odd."

We were led into a curtained cubicle to wait for the resident. Right beside us a little girl who had stepped on a light bulb was being stitched up. Our son kept up his awful resonant bark. At the very least, he seemed to have croup. Another nurse came along and began rigging up a see-through plastic croup tent, which he regarded suspiciously. An intern examined him and urged him to spend a little time in this tent. The nurses fiddled a disconcerting length of time getting the oxygen levels right, and the pipe kept falling off the back of the thing. Casey wore the expression of someone being sold real estate in the Florida Everglades. We coaxed him into the tent wearing a too-small blue and white hospital nighty.

"It'll be fun," we lied.

Of course, it wasn't fun. It wasn't even remotely like a vacation. He pushed his arms through the zippered holes made for that purpose. Valves hissed and he lay breathing in the mist. Instead of looking better, he looked worse, dusky and lavender in the face. His cough didn't go away. Another nice nurse came and took a blood sample, offering him hand-knitted finger puppets as a reward.

"Could I have another for my friend," he wheezed, never one to let an opportunity slide by. Finally, when we couldn't bear looking at his mauve face through the plastic any longer, we took him out and decided that the cool night air, besotted with ocean, would be just as effective as a croup tent and much more pleasant.

His cough settled down on the way back to the house where we were staying with friends. It was a big old frame house, with a garden of hollyhocks, black pansies, ornamental cabbage, stern red dahlias, tall wild-looking daisies. Much nicer than a croup tent. I wrapped Casey in a quilt and we sat in the garden, breathing in bits of the ocean. He went to sleep. I felt the dew fall on me. Day one of our carefully planned, low-key, fail-safe family holiday was over.

He then fell into a pattern that would persist — nearly undiminished energy during the day, apart from the room-clearing cough, and then at night, the vampire attack: coughing, barking, throwing up. We abandoned our plan to "do" the Cabot Trail and pushed on to Prince Edward Island, conforming to the second axiom of the family vacation, the Code of Lowered Expectations. We would not be reading novels, getting into shape, making reckless love at odd hours, and rethinking our life, as it turned out. Instead, we would be sorting and rinsing seashells, visiting all-night pharmacies, inserting insects into empty yogurt containers, and looking for restaurants that serve hot dogs.

P.E.I. had all those things, as well as endless beaches with sand that ranged from pink to the color of the moon. The landscape was delicately, unaggressively beautiful — canvases of tender blue sky coming down to meet the changing, secretive curves of the dunes, out of which marram grass sprouted in tufts, like human hair. All along the coast, the Atlantic was modestly curtained from view by these dunes, which offered enticement, like the foothills of the Rockies. They add a little suspense to an island that is otherwise smooth and green as the baize on a pool table. All in all, it struck me as the kind of green, orderly place my father might have designed, using his hedge clippers.

I loved the lawn ornaments and (crass Easterner) wished they were for sale, instead of the dreary lobsterabilia in the gift shops. The whirligigs and windmills were like geysers of irrepressible fancy springing up out of the paramilitary grass.

We booked into an old white clapboard lodge on the north shore that had a dour, windswept charm — a listing ship on a curve of lawn above a bay with blue herons and wind-surfers. Two big white wooden swings sat in the middle of the lawn.

On the first afternoon, I went wind-surfing, sailing across the bay into the arms of freedom for about twenty minutes, until I fell afoul of a mussel bed and had to splash back into shore, eyed with some derision by the resident herons. But this was more like it, I thought — speed! solitude! weightlessness! I went back to our room refreshed and ready to tackle the next holiday crisis.

Casey had now worked up an interesting new symptom, namely a gagging sensitivity to various odors — perfumes, chocolate on the breath (embarrassing), and, alas, the smell of lobster. P.E.I. is famous for three things: potatoes, Anne of Green Gables, and lobster. Come dinner time, we would lure Casey up the steps to a seafood restaurant, walk in, and after a few minutes he would clamp his hand over his mouth, run around in circles and shriek, "Drink! Drink! Drink!" Nothing galvanizes a room like the possibility that a child in orbit might throw up. After several people had zipped over with ginger ale and water, he would mysteriously break through the odor barrier, take his seat, and wolf down fish and chips with raspberry pie.

We had decided to opt for the motel-style units at the lodge so as to have a private bathroom at our disposal — an excellent idea, except that Casey refused to enter the bathroom. He said it "smelled funny," although not like lobster. I assured him it didn't — the bathroom was spotlessly clean. He insisted. Finally he agreed to use the bathroom, but only if, while he held up the toilet lid, I held his nose.

But this was not my idea of a vacation. After a day of nose-holding, I stalked into the bathroom and said, "There is *nothing* that smells in here!" whipping back the shower curtain and heaving off the toilet-tank lid. And there, to my dismay, was a blue air freshener, giving off noxious fumes. I seized the thing and threw it out the bathroom window, onto the porch.

"You see? You see? You see? I was right!" Casey said about

fifteen times. I lay athwart the bed and called for Brian to take over.

That night was quite peaceful, at first. The Cough was quiescent. Father and son played Crazy Eights until Casey went to sleep, and then the two of us went to bed. After three nights of sleeping with Casey, it was fun to sleep with an adult for a change. A beautiful full moon spilled its light on the water of the bay and made the lawn swings gleam dully, like bones.

But family synchronicity was still at work. The little tumblers that fall into place when the mother sinks into profound sleep automatically trigger the Cough Reflex, and the child wakes up. The horrible hacking began.

I got up and swung into action. First, the shower-steam routine, until the pages of his book were rippled. Then I wrapped him in a blanket and we sat out in the cool night air, as he barked at the moon. I was hopeful — night air sometimes did the trick. But for some reason this time it didn't help. He coughed and coughed. How could such a racket issue from one tiny chest? Finally, his father whispered something through the window screen.

"The freshener," he said from his cocoon of sleep. "I think you're sitting on the freshener."

I reached down and there it was, where I had thrown it earlier. This time I flung it off the porch and down into the bay, where it could freshen up the blue herons. But the cough had locked in now, and his fever climbed. Points of moonlight gleamed in his bright eyes. In the tradition of mothers everywhere between 2 and 5 a.m., I fell prey to terrible thoughts.

The life force ebbs and flows with astonishing drama in small children. One minute they're jumping off the dresser, and the next they're languishing in your lap, eyelids bluey-white. And in the middle of the night there's time, plenty of time, to consider how the windpipe can close like a flower, how things can so quickly go wrong. I thought back to all those close calls when I used to travel in dangerous places — the flash of a knife in the Casablanca hostel, the border town in Peru where the police, with the face of vandals, broke into our room. They all seemed like a cozy night around the TV compared to sitting up with my feverish son, not knowing how to make him better. It was beginning to dawn on me that motherhood was now my Casbah, taking me through a maze of fears even as I rocked on a moonlit porch, on holiday.

We were just about to make the dash to the closest Emerg when a slippered man in a bathrobe came across the lawn, carrying what looked like a food processor with a face mask.

"I hear your son has a cough," he said rhetorically. "My wife thought this might help." He was another tourist, with an asthmatic two-year-old and a portable ventilator. "I don't know, but it sounds like asthma to me," he said. He demonstrated the mask for our son, making fighter-pilot sounds, and we decided to try it. After the croup tent, Casey was suspicious but he put on the mask. As he sat there breathing in Ventolin, the three adults began chatting about the Charlottetown hospital as if it were a great place to get scallops. The cough stopped. Casey's lids lowered and he fell asleep.

"We feel so much more relaxed since we bought this thing," said the Good Samaritan, wrapping up his machine and padding back to the lodge.

Well, that's it, I thought. Our son has asthma. But that's okay, all we need is this new appliance. We will buy this gizmo and seize control of our lives again. The whole lodge now went back to sleep.

The next day at the hospital, a doctor confirmed the diagnosis of the stranger in the bathrobe and gave us some additional asthma medication that made him speedy. Three days later, when he was on the mend, we ran into the man and his wife, both looking wan. It turned out that their son had such a bad attack of asthma the night after we met that they had spent the last two days with him in hospital. We extended our sympathy, and I made a mental note: never congratulate yourself. Parental hubris will get you every time.

But the crisis passed, and we had exactly five days left in which to have fun. We moved into a housekeeping cottage down the road, stocked up on Shreddies and the local raspberries, and went to the nearest beach to recuperate.

Beaches seem to bestow a vestigial dignity on the family — everything works better there. They provide a degree of torpor and privacy for the parents, while the children expend huge amounts of energy swimming, digging, and — oh, precious phrase — amusing themselves. They may get tired, or sunburnt, but they never seem to fight or cry. Someone should study this.

Soon our days had resolved themselves into a routine. Get up, make breakfast, or even better, drive five minutes to the nearby campsite canteen where we could order the children's breakfast — $1.29 for toast, egg, orange slices, and milk — while playing "The Power of Love" by Charley Pride on the juke box. Then to the beach, followed by take-out fish and chips. A stop at Cove Head Bay to buy fresh mackerel to cook for dinner. Then home for more Crazy Eights and bed. Our desire to drive two hours to visit the Malpeque Gardens (four hundred varieties of dahlia) or the Car Life Museum (with Elvis's 1959 pink Cadillac) gradually faded. However, we did make the trip to the real home of the imaginary Anne of Green Gables.

Axiom number three: after crises comes crankiness. As we drove along the coast toward our destination, the bland prettiness of the island began to grate on me. Casey kept asking for a certain kind of juice, in a certain kind of container. Then he announced he was feeling "just a little bit sick." The sky ahead of us darkened with the threat of rain. We drove on into noisy splatters of rain; Brian and I exchanged never-again looks. We read the book, we saw the series, do we really need to see the house? I said. Then, abruptly, the thundery sky cleared, and we rounded a corner to see the blue ocean curving up like a further hill of land, and the vast, bus-filled parking lots of Green Gables.

We lined up and, behind velvet ropes, shuffled through the house to look at the washbasin that this Canadian girl, who never existed, who was invented by Lucy Montgomery, might have used. One could be cynical but I was amazed. People have such a desire, a compulsion, to believe in stories. Even Casey, untutored in Anne lore, caught the scent quickly. "Where is the famous girl's room?" he asked. "Was that really her brush?"

The next day we paid a visit to a Toronto writer who spends every summer on the island. The coast we drove along this time had a stern minimalist beauty, as if we were caught in a Christopher Pratt painting. His frame house and a separate studio stood facing the ocean in the middle of a huge field. We drove up a long straight road through meadows of yellow tansy ragwort. Inside, the house was equally uncluttered: one rocker, a hooked rug in which woolly white smoke bulged out of a farmhouse chimney, a white iron bed facing glass doors where the nearly constant ocean breeze drew out the curtains.

A typewriter sat in the middle of a table under a window with a view deliberate as a sentence — the blue sky, the slightly convex ocean, the field of delicate, worthless flowers, and a gray hydro pole. Here was a vision of the orderly, childless writer's life. Casey raced about and poked into things, raising unspoken alarm like a cloud of dust.

In the oven was a blueberry pie, which the writer had baked in case his ex-wife showed up. She had phoned to say she would be on the island this week and might visit him. It was now 5 p.m. on the day she was expected, and she hadn't shown up. We eyed the pie silently.

"I think I'll keep the pie, just in case she comes tomorrow," he said, closing the oven door.

We drove on the next day, right to the eastern tip of the island, where we visited a lighthouse. The lighthouse keeper, Harris Harrison, had made the newspaper some years back for harboring an arctic owl. The yellowed clippings were on the wall. We gazed respectfully at the rod and reel that had caught the world's largest tuna nearby — 1,496 pounds. We went back outside and peered over the edge of the island, down onto the red rocks. Laundry flapped on Harris Harrison's clothesline. The great blind bulb of the lighthouse turned, and the Atlantic seethed away beneath us.

This was our last day on the island. In the back seat, as we headed for the ferry, the Sleep Robber was healthy at last, gazing out the window as he sang an aimless song. Out of the corner of my eye, I watched his handsome father drive, following the white line of a daydream. The three of us hadn't gone far in miles, but we had arrived somewhere: this weightless, brief togetherness.

When we left the ferry for the mainland, the landscape abruptly changed to bush. I felt the sprawl of the rest of Canada, its numbing bigness, and already missed the human scale — the childlike scale — of the island behind us.

childhood

19.   **Echo Has No Feet**

TOO MUCH IS made of the Terrible Twos and not enough of the Metaphysical Fours. Around four, Casey began to look at the world with such a pure and unfettered intelligence I felt as if I were in a philosophy exam every night. The fourth year is a wonderful, metaphysical age, when he began to tackle the meaning of life completely free from any system of thought or the social conformity that sets in when they go to school. Along came the Big Questions, the ones about sex and death.

*   *   *

The goldfish expired, as goldfish will. The bowl on the counter was empty for a day or two before he noticed. Coward that I am, I thought that if I kept the bowl there growing algae for a few days this might create a *goldfish fade-out* that would avoid a painful discussion. But he noticed. Where was the goldfish?

"The goldfish? Oh, well, you know how he was looking sick, and sort of hanging under the surface of the water a lot?"

"Yes," he said, impatiently.

"Well, the other day he got so sick he died."

"But he was my pet!" he wailed.

"I know. I'm sorry."

"Where did he go?"

The dreaded question. I had flushed him down the toilet. There's just no nice way to put that, really. I was afraid that "down the toilet" would toll in Casey's memory for the rest of his life, and I couldn't bring myself to say it. Then his own imagination saved me.

"Back to the ocean?"

Yes, in a way, I thought, that's true! If you consider the linkage of the waste system to the Great Lakes and thence to the Atlantic . . . ashes to ashes, water to water. . . .

"Yes," I said, "he's dead, and back in the ocean." A fib in the name of home theology. And in any case, the toilet interlude is just an adult chore not worth mentioning.

He accepted this, with more indignant mutterings about the untimely snatching of his Pet.

On the same day, we were in the back lane kicking a soccer ball around, when he came across the dull, furry remains of a flattened squirrel. The squirrel was at that point more ground than beast.

"He's dead," Casey observed. This flatness now had some dimension in his mind. Then we sauntered up the street, past the outdoor café where people sat spooning up chocolate mousse from little pots. Casey hung about the sidewalk railing.

"There's a dead squirrel in the lane," he informed a table of diners. "If you want to see him."

The next day, the squirrel still had not left the lane, or his imagination. I was bringing him home from day care, on the back of my bike.

"Where *did* the squirrel go? "

I gave him a wishy-washy, liberal explanation, with animistic touches, concerning the bodily demise of the squirrel and the possibility of a squirrel spirit who carried on, perhaps even digging up our tulip bulbs. What I said was unsatisfactory and came down to something like "Well, there's dead, and then there's dead." He was not fooled.

"And if there is no soul?" he asked.

"Then he's just dead."

"Part of the ground."

"Yes."

He digested this, and I changed the subject to dinner, namely barbecued hot dogs.

* * *

His second investigation of the unseen world concerned echoes. Again, we were in the lane. The lane was our cathedral. I noticed that the alley, lined with garages on either side and abutted by a brick wall at the far end, made a perfect echo chamber. I demon-. strated this by shouting his name. "*Casey*" came bouncing back to us like the ball.

Casey tried it out. He shouted over and over. Each time the sound yo-yoed back to him. His name went away and came back, like the putative squirrel spirit, disembodied. He summed up this phenomenon.

"Echo has no feet."

* * *

On a warm, foggy night, Casey lured me out of the house for a spin up the street on his tricycle. I was mulling over a rather silly book on reincarnation I had to review. It was one of those watered-down pop-spiritual books that pilfer ideas that have been around for a few thousand years and re-invent them as entrepre- neurial tonics, or bumper stickers. I don't like the cynicism these books inevitably induce. Up ahead of me, Casey pedaled madly into the fog. It was his first fog, I think.

"We're in the mist of time," he sang out.

"What?" I asked, assuming he was quoting some cartoon or other.

"We're in the heart of the mist of time, and when I spin my wheels, you can be a kid again."

He spun his tricycle wheels and cackled in the fog. I wondered what on earth he meant. It was the first time I'd purely wondered about something all day. He had taken me out of my own fog and put me back on Brunswick Avenue, in the mist of time — where, strictly speaking, I belonged.

*   *   *

Relativism crept in around the age of six. He found out about the world of microbes, another invisible realm.

"Microbes can't see us, right?" he asked. "Because we're too big." That's correct, I answered with confidence.

"Then maybe giants are real, and they're all around us, but they're so big we can't see them."

I had to admit he had a point. Maybe giants are all around us. I had a flash of those awful photographs of the microscopic beasts that live in your eyelashes. *We are as mites in the eyelashes of giants.* However, I had to get the car to the garage to put on the snow tires, winter almost being over, so I put aside the notion that I might be driving there through, say, the hairs on the big toes of a giant.

*   *   *

This was also the age when Brian's world information began to take on more authority than mine. Indeed, Brian now went off to more places, and came back from more parts of the world, than I did. Casey would dig away at this cache of knowledge in the car, on the drive to one grandparent or another. If he couldn't be physical, strapped into the car, at least he could be metaphysical.

Brian reported one dialogue that took place when the two of them were alone in the car. Casey was stockpiling information on how fast things go and how big things are. Finally, he asked his father where the world came from.

Brian gamely launched into a brief cosmological overview covering God, the creation myth, and the Big Bang Theory. But the young lawyer was not satisfied. Obviously, his father was grasping at straws here, if not talking through his hat. He sighed and looked toward the lake.

"I guess only the world knows where the world comes from."

*   *   *

This ability to go straight to the heart of a matter is a brief stage. When Casey was four, Brian's father died, after being bedridden by a stroke for a year. The three of us had visited him in the hospital. When he heard the news of his death, Casey understood it completely, and wept like an adult along with us. Brian talked to him a little later about it all.

"I hope I can be as good a father to you as he was to me," he said.

"What kind of father was he?"

"He was honest and fair, and generous and kind."

"You mean he was true?"

"Yes, he was true."

*   *   *

When Casey was eight and I was cleaning out a box of photos and mementos, I came across this conversation in some notes Brian had made for the memorial service. I tucked them away. Sensing something private, Casey bugged me to read it to him, so I did. It brought this first grief right back to him and he wept with surprising passion again, for the loss of his grandfather, and, I suspect, for the new knowledge that the conversation was coming true — his dad was a father like his father, which meant that he too was going to die someday. The pure grief of the four-year-old now had new echoes.

20.   Loot

I HAVE whittled down my list of answers to family problems to just one rule: it is not necessary to hire performers for birthday parties. In the years to come, when playing Twister no longer suffices, I will probably change my mind — after all, I've changed my mind about everything else so far. But for now, I try to toe the line on the birthday issue. Keep the parties low-key, no frills. Why, then, with a work deadline in the same week as Casey's birthday, was I consumed with loot bags?

Loot bags, as every parent knows, are plastic sacks full of wretched, pointless plastic toys that somehow add up to a surprising amount of money and are inevitably greeted with hoots of derision before the toys are lost, forgotten, or broken. Loot bags are a useful symbol of the daily humiliation of parents. Telling myself that this week I was a writer and not a mother pouring her ambition and imagination into trinkets for her son's friends, I took the birthday boy for a walk over to the nearest mall.

We strode into Zellers and over to the Party section, where you can buy cardboard packets of Party Favors worth approximately .006 cents each. But I couldn't do it. I couldn't buy kazoos that don't kazoo, water pistols that leak, key chains for kids with no keys. So Casey and I spent a long time picking out individual items for the loot bags, trying hard not to buy twenty-five dollars' worth of novelties for each guest. Our chosen loot included — this is important — a swirly high-bouncing rubber ball, a tiny palette of paints with brush, a rhinestone ring, a game involving a plastic paddle and a ball on a string, and some wrapped, clear candies. I did not go to the museum shop to buy star charts or glowing stegosauruses or other imaginative items. I went to Zellers and got the thing over with as fast as possible.

Then I came home and ordered a Baskin-Robbins cake, an overpriced mound of ice cream covered with shiny brown icing and a birthday message. Mother, who is writing about the importance of motherhood, does not actually have the *time* to bake her son's birthday cake — a fact that makes her not so much guilty as irritated. The pleasures of cake-baking would not be mine. I think back to the soaring, funny, delicious, unpredictable cakes my mother has baked throughout her life, for birthday after birthday. I *can* bake, I tell myself, but not today, when I must write about not baking instead.

So I do the cake, I phone in the cake, and that's done. Then I sit down with my son to discuss party games, and he goes off with a friend to fill up water balloons for a balloon-toss contest. The morning of the party, I give Brian a list, reminding him that he is picking up the buns and the pink lemonade, so his presence at the beginning of the party is vital.

"Remember, you have the drinks," I say darkly as he leaves for work. He also has to buy the small electronic keyboard we have decided to give our son as a present, instead of the Nintendo he really wants, which his generous grandmother will give him for Christmas anyway. The keyboard is expensive, but not, we rationalize, nearly as expensive as Nintendo and besides it may lead to piano lessons. Most toys for boys his age are hopeless, a cardboard promise around a piece of dreck, or some grotesque, steroid-inflated, weapon-toting mannekin called Razorheart or Fistula or MangleMind. Still, I worry that I should have opted for Razorheart instead of the earnest keyboard. Decisions, decisions.

Our baby sitter arrives, and they head off to the park. Casey carries a wineskin of water in case he gets thirsty. "So long, shish-ke-bob," he says as he leaves. For some reason he is calling me shish-ke-bob this week. Last week, it was "killer squid." I go upstairs to mull this over.

At 3:30 I stop work, an hour before the party. Many professional writers stop work at three or even earlier, I tell myself. But I'm feeling unsure about the loot bags, so I whip up to the corner and find the perfect hand buzzers, even though they only come four to the package so I have to buy too many. By now I realize that I am quite nervous, as if throwing a huge dinner party for a dozen critical strangers — which, in fact, is *exactly what I am doing.*

I come back and begin decorating — tacking up streamers on the deck, blowing up balloons, putting the Snoopy paper tablecloth on the table. Sixty dollars of paper and plastic products are ripped open and deployed. I tactfully encourage my son to change out of his too-tight Ghostbusters T-shirt for a more becoming forest green Aliosaurus T-shirt, with yellow surfer shorts. At 4:20, the first guests arrive early, the parents retreating down the porch stairs at a clip, delighted to be childless for several hours. More arrive, in waves. We work through our agenda of games. I am horrified to find that this takes exactly seventeen minutes.

The kids are drifting listlessly through the house, some upstairs rooting through Casey's toys, others sitting morosely outside in the heat. Casey is on the living-room floor ripping open his presents. I try to get him to read the cards. He opens everything and looks around for more. It is then I realize that it is almost six o'clock and the Bun Man, the guy with the lemonade and the keyboard, is not here. "I'm thirsty," says one child, clutching her throat. "So am I," chimes in another. My palms start sweating.

The phone rings. A hysterical voice, my husband's, comes over the line.

"It's the Shriners. I'm caught behind the Shriners' parade, I've got the cake, and it's melting. You didn't tell me it was an ice-cream cake. I've had to literally *tack* across town, up to

Davenport, down to Dundas. Then when I went to pick up the keyboard, I left the car parked in front of Consumers, I watched it every *second*, but I turned my back and got a forty-dollar ticket. It's been a nightmare."

"Do you have the drinks?"

"Yes."

"I'll give them water till you come."

Twenty minutes later, the pale urban warrior bursts through the door bearing the suppurating cake, the buns, the lemonade, the gift. I rush to the barbecue and begin cooking. Brian runs upstairs to wrap the present that will, in ten seconds, be torn apart. The children by now are all happily playing with all the presents and relieved that both parents are off their backs. Casey unwraps the keyboard and to our great relief he loves it. He especially likes the Sample Keyboard function, which allows him to record his own voice and then use it as a musical note. He records himself saying "The bird is the word" over and over again, in distorted modes. I realize that we have just made it possible for him to deepen, amplify, and quadruple his already penetrating voice.

Then comes dinner, and the food reviews. Every child has a clear idea of the acceptable hot dog, the right bun, the correct relish. But silence briefly descends as the guests in rakish pointed hats make their way through the hot dogs, corn on the cob, watermelon, vegetable sticks with packaged dip, the lemonade, the special "6" napkins, the red Snoopy plates, the dozens of sugar-laden condiments while entertained by "Tic Toc Rock" on the Fisher-Price tape recorder. I bring out the cake, with his name on top. The wind keeps blowing out the candles, and the lighter burns my finger as I relight the candles, in order for him to blow them out.

The ephemeral nature of all these tasks is beginning to haunt me. "The bird, the bird, the bird is the word" plays over and over on the keyboard, in flügelhorn mode. When the cake is eaten, the guests retire, with much giggling, to separate bedrooms to change for after-dinner leaps through the sprinkler. A kind of calm descends.

His father and I cook and eat two hot dogs, which taste wonderful and remind us of when we last ate. "So," I say, looking at him, taking him in, for the first time that day. "I had to go to three stores to find the pink lemonade," he said. Well, it may sound deviant, but this sort of thing makes a man attractive to me. We have done our best. We sit together boxing balloons at each other for a moment, until I notice the girls from Casey's class, who have high standards, peering into their loot bags. They sigh melodramatically and look at me with a kind of pity, for my hopeless sense of loot. "Brenda's mother gave out My Li'l Ponies," I hear another little girl say to them. *Well, I'm not Brenda's mother!* I want to announce, snatching away their ice cream. *I didn't major in birthday parties — what do you expect?* Instead, I merely reach up into my handy cupboard of junk and hand her a magic-slate tic-tac-toe. "Oh, I love these," she says, to my relief.

The parents begin to arrive, eating half-slices of the melting cake while their offspring locate socks, shoes, and in some cases underwear. The party is over. The birthday boy is recording burp sounds on the synthesizer. The blood has returned to his father's face. Even the Shriners have parked their tiny cars and gone back to their hotels. I could go upstairs to work, but I suddenly feel I have nothing whatsoever to say. I sit down with a heaping plate of untouched carrot sticks, turn on the TV, and watch "Jeopardy" instead.

21.   Après School

ARRIVE at my son's school at 4:30 p.m. on a Friday, the shank end of the week. He is in Grade Two this year, when work gets serious: reading, writing, and arithmetic. After the make-it-all-up magic kingdom of kindergarten, he is having to measure up to the adult world. It's beginning to sink in that he's not perfect at this adult stuff, not perfect at all. I am discovering this, too. He is ahead in math, but so far spelling confuses him. He hates to be confused.

It's been raining all day. This means indoor recess, loud, rancorous indoor lunch, and then indoor games after school. The after-school care is right beside the school. He loves it and so do I. The staff is young and full of good ideas. I always want to sit down and make earrings or tie-dye T-shirts or do whatever they're doing when I arrive. Needless to say, I am completely over my day-care qualms.

On the other hand . . . school is school, and day care is day care: many bodies in one room, loud, ricocheting voices, long waits for the glitter paint or computer time.

I arrived at his school feeling jangled myself. I have been in my own mental day care, at home, plugged into the computer, with my mind racing, a crossfire of noisy, uncooperative thoughts inside my head. I am in the middle of a piece, that is to say, I am confused, too. I hate to be confused. All day I've been writing fast, racing across the screen, holding my breath, as usual. I enter a mild cryonic state whenever I'm on the computer.

Telling myself to start breathing again, I splash water on my face and change. In my ritual bow to the household god, I open the fridge door and look in: half a cucumber, four jars of assorted mustard, a tub of conscientious scrap-simmered vegetable stock going bad, last night's ravioli, Sunday's rice, a red cabbage I've been sawing away at for a week now. Better shop.

The story unfinished, my mind ajar, I grab the car keys and head out the door. I drive now. On the way to school, I turn on the radio. Callers to a phone-in show debate whether or not to outlaw kosher slaughter. I think about the things I have to do before the weekend, such as buying yet another birthday gift and paying for yet another parking ticket. Then I think about the things I haven't been doing now for weeks, such as getting a pant-saver mat for the car or teaching illiterate adults to read. I feel jumpy, as I always do after too long at the computer.

As usual, I look forward to seeing Casey and bringing him back home so that I can re-enter the slower, calmer orbit of family life. At least, that is how I imagine it when I am not actually in it.

I pull up to the black iron fence beside the school playground. The rain has stopped now, and all the kids are playing outside. This is the year of fluorescent colors and high-top sneakers. I see him in his neon green biker's cap throwing a neon green tennis ball up against the school wall. He sees me and waves merrily. "Ma, watch me try to roof the ball!" He throws the ball up onto the roof, which has a slight rake. The ball comes back down slowly, erratically, like a pinball. He runs over, all smiles.

"I thought you said you'd pick me up early today."

"I didn't finish my work. Anyway, this is still early."

"No, it isn't." A faint cloud begins to settle on his face.

"Have you got your lunch box and everything?"

"No."

"Well, go get your things and let's head home."

The mouth takes a down-turn into a scowl as he retrieves his Wayne Gretzky lunch box, his jean jacket, and the usual sheaf of notes concerning field trips and head lice. He climbs into the car and buckles his seat belt. A formal sort of gloom settles on his features and he sighs.

"Mom, can I rent a video game?"

"Not tonight. We can't park on that side after four. Anyway, you just rented one a couple of days ago."

"But I really want a video tonight. Can't we check and see if Battle Toads is in?"

"It's always out, you know that. Let's just go home." I've got the turn signal on and we're waiting to nose into the right lane. Rush-hour drivers eye each other through rearview windows.

"Why can't we buy Mario 3? You said we could."

"I said we could buy a used one, and they can't sell the used one until they get new stock in."

"They said they would have it last week."

"Yes, well, they were wrong."

He looks out the car window in silence.

"How was school?"

"Good."

Pause.

"Except I kept on making the same mistake in spelling, I couldn't remember what the word said and I asked Miss Mitchell to read it for me, and she said, 'Sound it out, sound it out'" — a devastating parody of Miss Mitchell here. He bursts into tears. "I just get confused!" Great angry tears roll down his face. "And Arden hit me in the ear for nothing. Look, it still hurts." He flips his ear forward. "Right here."

"I can't look while I'm driving, sweetie."

"If we can't get Mario 3, can we stop by the toy store? Just to look?"

"Casey —"

"I'll use my own money. You owe me sixty-five dollars, remember? Alyssa lost my whoopee cushion. I just want to buy another whoopee cushion."

"You don't need a whoopee cushion, you just want to buy a toy so you'll feel better."

"Well, a toy *would* make me feel better." Gush of tears. "That's what they're for!"

I grip the steering wheel. Just four blocks from the sunny scene in the playground, rage and despair well up in me over this familiar hunger. Something's wrong, something's missing, and he is sure that Mario 3 or a remote-control car or a medium Slurpee will satisfy his hunger. How well I recognize this desire, only in my case I think a sixty-five-dollar Night-Repair cream or suede boots might be the answer. I hate it in me, and I hate it in him. Aren't I enough? I think, childishly. Here I am, patiently inquiring about his day, having banished my own private video game from my screen, and all he wants is something else, something electronic instead. I am furious, but I know that the end of the day near the end of the week is not the time to fight.

"Look, we've been through this. Please don't ask me for stuff at this time of day. At the beginning of the week, we can plan who can come over on what day, and when you can rent a video game, and then you'll know ahead of time. You can't hit me with this now, I just have to say no, no, no, and then you get mad, and I get mad. . . ."

"You don't have to say no. You could just do it."

Silence from me on this one. Why is every ride home a day in court? Why did I have to give birth to a labor negotiator?

More angry tears. "School is too hard, why can't it be more fun like it was in Room 101?"

The person in the car in front of me is short and driving with infinitesimal slowness. I swerve around him with an angry glare and squeeze past a delivery truck where men are throwing bloody goat carcasses to each other.

"It always seems hard at the beginning of the year. You said this last year, and then you ended up loving school. Lots of things are hard at first. That means they won't end up being boring."

"It just seems that getting older just isn't any fun."

Tell me about it, I think but do not say.

"Can we visit Jordan?"

Delicately. Patiently. "I'm afraid not. She lives all the way over on the other side of town, and it's too close to dinner now."

"Oh." No fresh tears. We're almost home now. I feel trapped in his emotional traffic at the same time as we navigate rush hour.

"Can Marie and Emma come over?"

"Yes, fine, all right, but remember, they might not want to." Because they're girls, and they're older, I think. More potential disappointment.

"And if they can't come, then Morgan."

"Fine. Just not all three. I have more calls to make."

"Can we play Top Gun? Jimmy lent it to me for the weekend."

Sigh.

"Yes, you can play Top Gun, until dinner."

"Great!"

*   *   *

At six o'clock, Marie, Emma, Morgan, and Casey are four inches from the TV screen playing Morgan's Mario 3. I am upstairs on the phone, making a call that should have been made a day and a half ago. Brian comes home.

"Hi, dad!" Casey trills, eyes never leaving the screen. He is in Warp World 8, higher than he's ever been.

"Hi, Casey. What's all this? I thought we'd agreed there wouldn't be any Nintendo before dinner."

"Mom said."

"Where is she?"

"Upstairs on the phone."

I hear Brian's tired Friday-night tread on the stairs. He comes to the door of my office. I look at him and hold up three fingers, meaning three minutes more. He cocks his head in the direction of the kids downstairs and raises one eyebrow. I wave him out. I know it looks as if I'm chatting on the phone while the entire neighborhood parties downstairs, because I can't be bothered to enforce the rules. I know I will not be able to adequately reconstruct for him the maze of heartbreak and head-banging the two of us have just run, that somehow made Nintendo before dinner the least of a dozen other evils. He doesn't yet understand that I have managed *not* to rent a new video game, another movie, or buy a die-cast metal stretch limo, or anything at all requiring double-A batteries. No Slurpees, no Gummibears, no Red-Hots have entered these premises today. Still, I gave in on the Nintendo front, and that's all he sees tonight.

A surge of defensiveness on my part. However, he doesn't criticize me, beyond that one arched eyebrow. But he also doesn't understand how this constant consumer craving can leave the one at home feeling triumphant if she wards off the worst of it: the mother ends up as the mean gatekeeper of this theme-park environment, a seductive palace that forces parents to say no all day long.

This no-saying is frustrating and irritating to all concerned — to the mother, who would dearly love to buy a Mazda Miata herself, and to the child, who can't understand why he should have to be surrounded all day long by things he can't have. His desire at the end of the week to buy something, to eat something, to consume something, is not just the result of toy hunger (which is real enough), but arises from the feeling that something is missing.

Something usually is: the mother and father all day long, or peace and quiet, or simple privacy. When the thing you miss is missing, you don't have a clear idea of what's wrong; you just feel a space, a restless craving.

In someone Casey's age, I suspect toy hunger arises from the frustration of being in a large group all week, along with the alternate boredom and pressure of the school day. He needs both more stimulation and less. He could use an ambitious project, as well as an unchallenging lap, a lounge on the couch, a morning of goofing around with his parents in earshot. The stresses and pressures on small kids are just as numerous and soul-flaying as the ones on parents.

Childhood itself sometimes seems to be under siege. When I go to pick him up, I try to remember this, but the neglected space inside me echoes the hunger in him. Instead of acting the grown-up, impervious to his childish moods, I feel a shattering inside when he cries. ("Weak ego boundaries," pipes up my Inner Analyst, with whom I am very much in touch.) To cover the emotion, I get angry because it is ridiculous, absurd, to want a toy that badly. I drive carefully and keep my voice even, but all the way home the two of us begin to tumble down, like block towers.

*   *   *

The anger passes. I hang up the phone. Brian gets the picture now. We both go downstairs to make some dinner. The pinball sounds of Nintendo emanate from the living room.

"It's almost ready," I call to Casey before we sit down at the table.

"But I'm farther than I've ever been. Just let me finish."

"I want you to eat with us."

"Can I put it on Pause?"

A parental eye-lock and capitulation.

"All right," says Brian. Casey sits down at the table and drinks most of his glass of milk.

"How was school today?" his father asks.

"Good." Mouth inches from the plate of spaghetti.

"Just good?"

"I made a tussy-mussy."

"What's that?"

"A thing out of herbs. Mine has lavender and mint, for good luck." Seconds later. "I'm finished. May I be excused?"

"Okay. Ten more minutes and that's it."

He leaves the kitchen, and his father and I look at each other.

"What if I just took an ax to the back of the TV?" I suggest. "He couldn't argue with that, could he?"

"No, he couldn't."

"Then I will."

"After the play-offs."

"Okay."

"More wine?"

"Please."

22.   Play

SATURDAY. Housebound all week myself, I was ready to take him to the Y, or the island, or Riverdale farm, but no, all Casey wanted to do was hang around the house, with his friend Ben or Morgan. He phoned them both. Ben was out. Morgan came up to the house, and they blazed through the house cooking up one bizarre activity after another.

He took some copper wire off a tomahawk he had made, and the two of them disappeared into the basement. I heard the exercise-bike running. Casey ran up and got a cereal bowl full of water, walk-running downstairs with it, trying not to spill. What are you doing? I asked. We're heating up the wire with the bike and then trying to boil the water, he said. I took a look and saw him holding the wire against the front wheel, while Morgan pedaled madly. The wire got hot, and then they plunged it into the bowl of water, exclaiming all the while "Wow, it's steaming, man, it's rilly, rilly hot this time, dude," and so forth.

A physics class, using material found in any disorganized home. This was followed by a solid hour of bow-and-arrow play in the yard, using leftover tomato stakes from the garden as arrows. They tried to get the arrows right over the roof, and two ended up sticking out of the eaves trough. Then they took the tool kit out onto the back deck and proceeded to dismantle and smash with hammers Casey's rusted-out bike-bell. Then he oiled all the moving parts on his bike, as well as the hinges of the front door. Next, he took the rawhide whip that I brought him back from Texas and whipped the NDP poster to smithereens on the front lawn. Then he drew and cut out a sign saying "Stop! Stop! And nock" for his bedroom door, using yellow birthday ribbon to hang it up.

He stayed in this dither of propulsive creativity all morning, completing each project, then dragging Morgan on to the next, deliriously happy. I felt he was using up all the interrupted and unexploited energy that public school, with each classroom bursting to the seams, can't accommodate. His teacher is hard-working and unusually creative. But by Friday, Casey has the sort of hair-trigger temper you would expect of someone who has to spend his week in a large group, where individual enterprise is a form of disruption. I sympathize — his projects throw the house into disarray and sabotage my own minimal sense of decorum. But in the class, sheer numbers reign. I see the results of this — restlessness, consumer cravings, a heightened sense of injustice — and wonder. His big phrase now is "It's just not fair being a kid!"

*　　*　　*

It should come as no surprise, then, that powerless little boys love to play with guns. I know what happened with toy guns in our own household. I went from a serene pre-child conviction that they would never cross our threshold to the ridiculous but amiable compromise Casey and I arrived at when he was seven.

Childish logic is impeccable. If you give him an innocent green water pistol for the bathtub, then why not the hideous kiddy M-16 in the back yard? If he can play High Noon with a Popsicle stick, why not a space laser? So he now owns a bow and arrow (my old one) and a non-combat rawhide whip (history? art?) but he knows I have a "thing" about realistic guns, so he doesn't ask for them. They still turn up around the house, of course, like orphan socks. Nerf guns, Ping-pong ball shooters, high-pressure water bazookas, historical flintlocks, balsa elastic-band shooters . . . all of these have made their inroads. See-through guns are okay too.

He watches too much TV, but after flat-out indoctrination on our part — moral interference in the name of what we can or cannot stand to overhear — he now flips past the more violent shows, of his own volition. It's become a kind of household courtesy not to impose soundtracks heavy on the shrieks of the beheaded and maimed. We draw arbitrary lines between "good" video games and the ones bent on mutilation. As for movies, he himself admits he doesn't care to see people falling into vats of acid and dissolving. Will he be any the poorer if he doesn't see a robot's arm turn into a dagger and pierce an eyeball? We have enough image-fatigue in our house as it is, without the indiscriminate bath of violent imagery available. Even so, our rental standards are pretty raunchy compared to other families', I notice. And as the world exceeds the Grimms' imaginings, our definitions of violence are continually being refined as he gets older.

Rules are one thing, but prescriptive opinions about what toys are good or bad have a way of backfiring on parents. There was a time, not so long ago, when Barbie dolls were considered the worst sort of sex-stereotype propaganda. Barbie, with her foot permanently arched in the shape of a high heel, with her long, sharp, scissoring legs and high, hard, de-nippled breasts. It's true that Barbie has unswervingly represented a blonde gadfly of no fixed career, a weak-chinned Caucasian princess, and a fashion flibbertigibbet — eleven-and-a-half inches of beige plastic that has been accused of encouraging eating disorders, mindless consumerism, and low self-esteem in little girls. (Not to mention little boys. Despite repeatedly marrying Ken, Barbie's relationship to him appears to be rather generic and coldly expedient — the "date," the "doctor," the "dad.") Although she has careers that come and go — stewardess, skating instructor, astronaut (briefly, until the *Challenger* exploded) — her real interests revolve around her girlfriends, cars, clothes, and furniture. Small wonder that to the Birkenstock generation, Barbie was bad.

But little girls are not pushovers. They know what they like, and they like Barbie. Now in her thirties (but ever ageless and firm of chin), Barbie has triumphed over pedagogy, to the tune of more than five hundred million dollars annually. This decade, Barbie sales are bigger than ever. Some ninety-eight per cent of Canadian girls aged four to ten have a Barbie — or four — in their bedrooms. Like Coca-Cola, Barbie has insinuated her skinny little Coke-shaped self into sixty-seven countries around the world. None of this will surprise parents with daughters, but it was news to me.

A while back, I went into several department stores to get a blast of Barbie, a feel for Barbie, and there she was — row upon row of her and her almost identical pals, including li'l sister Skipper, brown-skinned Christie, freckle-faced sporty Midge, Hispanic Nia, red-haired vixen Ashley. The packaging is a violent, quite indescribable pink. Furnishings feature a bookcase with no books and a pretty roll-top "secretary" desk with a flip-out computer. Her countless outfits include the tiny tubes of her pantihose, salsa dresses, purses that turn into skirts, and skirts that turn into hair bows. Her eminently losable accessories — teacups, toe paint, Ferraris, guitars, curling irons, running shoes — cover the indoor/outdoor, trad/glam, homey/whorish facets of Barbie's busy lifestyle. And now there's the Barbie Living Pretty House, which you buy unfurnished and then furnish, or rather interior-design. That sounds familiar, actually. Isn't that . . . a *doll house*?

Each and every doll, I discovered, has hand-painted eyelashes — sometimes six, sometimes four or seven, with occasional Asian-type slashes instead on the lower lid. Indeed, if you spend long enough looking at Barbie faces, they take on personalities. This is what girls do. They play with Barbie in the most intense, psychodramatic fashion. Recently reported to me from a Barbie session: "Two men are driving in a car. They find a dead woman by the road. They put her in the car and take her clothes off. I told you you wouldn't like this story." Agggh! Not what Mattel had in mind, I'm sure.

What *is* it about girls and dolls, anyway? Boys play with He-men and Ninja Turtle plastic dolls but the marriage between girls and their Barbies seems more intense and durable. Girls' sense of pink and blue-ness strikes me as more acute, more precocious, although I base this only on the fact that last year I bought my son some plain but *purplish* boots, which were not a success. They didn't bother him at all until he came home from school one day and announced he could no longer wear them because they were "girls' boots." Who had decreed this? "The girls in my room."

Are girls more proprietorial about identifiable girl-things because they've already detected an imbalance in the adult world between boy toys (tanks and guns) and female fun? Or is it something simpler — that at a certain age, children want to see their particular sex as part of who they are. They want to make that clear. Just because adults have bequeathed them a culture that offers only testosterone-poisoned orange He-men and anorexic beige Barbies, must we insist on snuffing out any sign of gender?

Barbie may be eighty per cent cultural cliché, but at least she's not part duck or mouse. She's a grown-up female, albeit one who walks on the balls of her feet. Barbies may even be less insidious than google-eyed, soft-bodied baby dolls, which come with only one script — feed me, bathe me. Barbie, as her wardrobe makes clear, goes everywhere and does everything. She jogs, she owns a surf shop, she does nuclear physics in a pink smock. She may have a few body-image problems, but then who doesn't?

An eight-year-old girl of my acquaintance recently lugged over her five Barbies, in two pink vehicles, for my inspection. While twirling and braiding the long blonde tresses on one of them, she explained that although she doesn't want to *be* Barbie, she really likes to play with her. "We make up stories that are like real life and then we make the Barbies act them out," she said with admirable succinctness. She works in an allusion to Barbie's tarnished reputation. "Her body isn't very realistic," she admits, pointing the ballistic bosom of one toward me. "In fact, the only realistic thing about her is her ears." If she were designing dolls, she would opt for more variation. "Like it would be neat to have a tattooed Barbie, or one with a bigger head," she said. "Her head is too small for her body." And Ken is definitely in a rut. "I wouldn't mind a bald Ken, for example."

The sad truth is that Barbie has left the bland, rug-haired Ken behind in a spangled cloud of dust. In fact, his shelf presence looks more like a ratio of ten Barbies to one Ken. His accessories are laughable (a slice of pizza, a kite, a basketball) and his weekend outfits are a bore (blue pinstriped smock and navy pants). The only thing you can do with him, apart from suicidal dives off the couch, is change his hair color from a fecal-mustard color to an obviously touched-up brown. While Barbie has a choice of five stylish wedding gowns, Ken's lone wedding tuxedo is deplorable, a *nylon unitard* with an ill-fitting white jacket and a shiny bow tie. His loafers are interchangeable little boats. No wonder Barbie seems to prefer the company of her on-the-go girlfriends. (Can we look forward to a Bi Barbie next?)

As I walked down the department store aisles and saw Ken strapped stiffly into the passenger seat of Barbie's huge new pink RV trailer, with plates that say "Barbie," I felt a stab of compassion for him. A couple wandered by me. "Oh, there's Ken," said the woman. "We were always so mean to Ken with our Barbies, we used to do terrible things to him. I don't know why." Laughing, they moved on to inspect a Baby Uh-Oh ("Give her a drink and . . . uh-oh! Time to change her diaper!").

However retrograde she appears to be, I sense Barbie is a survivor. Her maddeningly firm little bosom and fashion-victim personality, her fickle careers are all voodoo tricks to ward off parental approval. If we had given Barbie a social conscience and sensible shoes, she might have moldered away at the bottom of the toy bin. As it is, girls play with their uneducational Barbies as they always have, madly acting away, with no parent-pleasing values to inhibit them. Therapists may envy the Barbie blankness — she too can create a private, privileged space where any and every feeling is permitted. May Barbie be "bad" as long as she reigns, for it is her lack of redeeming social value that helps keep her true to a child's sense of play, instead of an adult's worst fears.

are

we

there

yet?

23.   Shoddy Time

IT IS MONDAY morning. I am supposed to be writing about family in a lucid, vaguely hopeful way, but instead I am in a kind of comical despair, over nothing at all. Well, not nothing. Brian just phoned from the doctor's to say that Casey, now seven, has impetigo, in his *nose*, which is actually wandering strep from his sore throat, which I improperly treated with antibiotics last week, negligent mother that I am, too busy writing about her kid to keep him healthy. The ironies abound.

This means that Brian will bring him home for another sick day together — shoddy time, the opposite of quality time. Once again, I find myself measuring our family against some ghost of an ideal, even the new ones I invent.

The idealization of the family, one's own family, seems almost to be an instinct. I slide into a way of writing about my bungling but lovable mate, my flawed but charming son, my anxious but really quite admirable mothering. The desire to put myself and others in a good light — out of ordinary vanity, and to protect us, too — is nearly irresistible. The more honesty I strive for, the more I construct a fictional family, a moat around feelings that cannot, will not be addressed. With each chapter, I stalk a little closer. Then I stop. I realize I will never be able to reveal more than I can reveal to myself, and what remains to feel and think often ambushes me on Monday morning, in the empty house.

Tolstoy, who was never made bleak by impetigo, who was a

terrible husband and father, did write a number of good books. He said that novels are about the heart of the individual, at war with society. In that case, being a mother is like working on an unpublished novel. The public life of work, achievement, and power is so much at odds with the private, passionate world of the mother. I steal like a spy between the secret world of motherhood and the public place where writing exists.

Today, however, I am neither here nor there. Casey will amuse himself, he's good at being sick. I like his company. I can't imagine a more effortless love than what I feel when he saunters into my office and informs me that slugs have only one nostril, located on the foot. Still, my thoughts are full of the pneumatic shooting sounds he makes going up and down the stairs and his questions stop me in my tracks. "Which is more popular," he has to ask me one day, "soup or watches?"

Why even try to write? But whatever you have to do to get back to yourself — smoking a cigarette over a magazine for ten minutes, keeping a diary, trading complaints with another mother in the park — is a necessary chapter. Writing is the retrieval of your voice.

I see that Casey has yet another doctor's appointment this afternoon, with an asthma specialist, made months ago. Almost no point in sitting down to work at all, I think glumly. Since Mondays are his slow work days, I ask Brian if by any chance he has time to do the chauffeuring today. Okay, he says, except he has to tape some pre-Oscar interview for TV. He will bring Casey home, do the taping, and come back. Yes! This is more like it. Why settle for obstructed-view seats when you can insist on the front row?

He drops Casey off, and the two of us settle down in front of our respective video screens for an hour. Then, faced with the frozen lentil stew that I am thawing out for our lunch, Casey decides he wants to make his own meal. He is happy, even manic, perhaps as a result of the hideous, fuchsia-colored Big Gulp Slurpee he extracted from his father on the way home. He proceeds to assemble the ingredients for a tuna-fish sandwich. The kitchen is thrown into chaos, but I admire his domestic enterprise and don't interfere.

He eats the sandwich. I remind him to unload the dishwasher, and he does so, singing, very merry, until suddenly he sits down and gets pale.

"I need air," he says, and moves carefully toward the front door. He opens it, takes a deep breath, and throws up his carefully made lunch onto the front porch. We are old hands at throwing up; I'm surprised he didn't find a more suitable receptacle than the welcome mat. "Sorry, mom," he says. I no longer think, "Poor him." I look at the stuff and am amazed at the effects of the velocity, the sunburst pattern, the quantity, the way it goes all the way up the brick wall — all kinds of thoughts occur to me, as well as an estimation of how much time it will take me to clean it up. And with what? Mop? Sponge? Garden hose? With heartless clarity, I see that the time it took for us to make lunch has now been doubled, even though lunch itself has been erased. It never existed at all. Another lost morning.

I don't blame my son. He feels bad for me anyway. He sits down inside and turns on "Wheel of Fortune," using a Kleenex to swab off his shoes. Staring aimlessly out the front door, I see Brian drive up.

He bounds up onto the porch, still slightly orange from the TV make-up. Watch out, I say, pointing down, before he steps in it. Oh dear, he says. I shield my eyes with one hand and lean against the doorjamb. I don't know what to use to clean this up, I say, truly at a loss.

He sees that I am in the danger zone. I'll do it, it doesn't bother me, he says, zooming into the house for implements. With ruthless, wifely bitterness, I reflect that he is up for this disgusting chore only because he's in no danger of drowning, domestically. He's just had people powdering his nose and asking his opinions, on TV. I dimly recognize this sensation. You come home energized from some little triumph in the adult world, and these menial tasks are nothing, a sideline. You blaze through them effortlessly. But when you're home all day, the repetition of housework starts to eat away at you. Delinquency becomes a form of self-expression. Why scour the pots, when ten thousand other chores await you?

Brian gets assorted vessels and sponges and cleans the porch, careful not to get any on his silk shirt. I am grateful, transparent though his magnanimity may be. Casey now feels wonderfully well, perfect, in fact. Brian drives him off to his next appointment.

It is 2 p.m. The house is finally quiet. The kitchen looks no better or worse than it did at 7 a.m., despite all the tidying and untidying. Alone, I read the paper, all of it. The news alarms and saddens me. Then I go upstairs and turn the computer on. I make some changes to the chapter about how I came to fall in love with my husband. It seems a long time ago, when I was someone different. The phone rings: it is Speedy Auto Glass, saying that our vandalized car is now ready to be picked up. Then the news channel phones to say that the Oscar slot Brian taped was pre-empted. Another chore erased! I wonder what Casey's doctor will think of his father's orange make-up. I turn the computer off and pick up a magazine.

AFTER A solid week of shoddy time, I came up against another wall. I looked over my pile of fragments and had a grievous revelation: was all this protest and clamor a roundabout way for me to say I didn't want to be in this family, or any family at all? Surely it must be possible to love a particular child, a particular man, and still have grave doubts about the institution.

Perhaps I was writing about family in order not to face my own — a devastating thought. What if . . . I just wasn't *cut out* for family life, even our diffuse city sort?

I felt stalked by my own unconscious, as if I might finish the book, look into it like a clean mirror, and see something terrible. Maybe I didn't love my husband and son enough to put them up to the light like this; maybe no one does. I felt like a treacherous wife, and a distracted mother, taking refuge in the little fiefdom of writing.

What was a family supposed to be these days . . . what would make us *feel* like a family, I wondered. I examined our life during the past week and found it rather empty at the center, and yet there was no one to blame. Everyone was doing their best, after a fashion. I walk down the street, I gaze into other living rooms after dinner, I see their televisions on. Is that it?

Both of us read with Casey every night. We get him to eat at a table, in our company, with some regularity. But he's growing up, and the only thing he wants to do with his mother is ride around the neighborhood on our bikes. So we do that. He plays on a few sports teams at school. Otherwise, my role has shriveled to that of cook and Administrator of TV. Board games have lost their appeal for the moment. What he most wants to do, this week, is to ride his bike up to the nearest 7 Eleven where a crowd of towering louts wait their turn to play the video arcade game.

Sometimes we go to the Y and swim, if he isn't heading into or out of some virus, which turns out to be fairly rare. We enrolled him in karate lessons too young, and he shudders at the very mention of it now. Basically, he likes to hang around the house, go to a friend's house, and have friends over. This is fine with me. I have no interest in back-to-back scheduling. Still, I keep trying to think of what we might do together that wouldn't feel like a summit meeting of the Three Solitudes.

Then a week arrived when Brian's work pressures eased up and he was able to spend more evenings at home. And what is it that a seven-year-old, a grown male, and an adult female can do together amiably? Watch TV, it turns out. One night I lay on the couch not moving, my eyes idly taking in the baseball game on TV. Brian watched the game, as did Casey, while lying on me like a walrus seal. I have to say, it made me feel better. It wasn't a lesson in clog dancing or conversational French, but it was a cozy hour spent in physical proximity, doing nothing.

Idle togetherness of this sort is much underrated — or perhaps it's just endangered, since fewer and fewer families have the time to experience it, let alone relish it. After our evening of mute togetherness, the process of coaxing Casey to bed was good-natured rather than short-tempered. He sang in the bathroom as he got ready. He was happy to have us both kicking around the house, and I realized I was happy to be there, and that I had missed Brian.

*   *   *

Still, I continue to fantasize that some day we will enjoy something called "leisure time" on the weekend, instead of doing boring chores or sprawling narcotized around the house. I imagine other families arising at 7 a.m. for bird-watching forays, or skating on Grenadier Pond. Instead, what usually happens is that we go out Friday night, or stay home doing laundry. Then we sleep in on Saturday while our son bathes in the glow of cartoons downstairs. We could go to the market and pore over the fresh herbs, lay in the bulk food. Sometimes we do. Mostly, though, we slump about in a sea of newspaper sections, occasionally saying "It's a beautiful day outside, turn it off," to Casey in the next room. Brian rather touchingly keeps looking forward to "relaxing" on the weekend too — a fifties' notion that the nineties seems to have forever trashed. I saw an item in the newspaper recently that said most families spend the majority of their weekends doing chores and wake up Monday morning more tired than they were on Friday.

At the end of Casey's sick week, I decided to make up for lost time by working on Saturday morning. I tapped away upstairs. I came downstairs to make coffee at 11 a.m., noting that everyone was still in their pajamas, myself included. What kind of lame family is this, I thought, why aren't we at some sugaring-off festival at a conservation park?

"How's it going?" Brian asked, carefully icing his toast with jam. His leisurely — that word! — weekend breakfasts, within his rights as a working guy, not to mention a human being, get my goat. "Family, schmamily," I grumbled, "why do it unless you have to."

"Oops," he said, "maybe you shouldn't be trying to write this morning."

"I found some stuff I was working on before I met you," I said accusingly. "It was so much more adventurous."

"So say that," he said, smiling. "Work it in somehow." My ruthlessness amuses him.

"But what's the point of that?"

"The point is that you don't have to defend everything about the family just because you're in one. Keep the edge. Be tough."

"You're right." I leaned against him. He smelled like toast. "I'll finish off this one bit and then we should go to a park or something."

Casey chimed in from the living room. "I don't want to go to a park."

"We're all going to go somewhere," I responded firmly, determined to have a fun family outing, just as soon as I finished writing treacherous things about us all upstairs.

Over lunch, I thought about what my family used to do on weekends, and recalled two activities — getting into the car to Look at the Leaves, or (at Christmas) to Look at the Lights. The trees are turning, I announced down the stairs, we should be out there. Your mother might enjoy an outing too, I added. So very shortly the extended family was strapped into the car, headed for the nearest countryside.

"It's practically one big suburb now," we marveled as we drove through one subdevelopment after another, occasionally exclaiming "There's a maple, isn't it gorgeous!" When we got to the Caledon Hills, it was thronged with other bored couples and desperate families, doing the weekend thing: jostling through crowded conservation areas, lining up for "country" ice cream cones, and taking jolly hikes with children too small to hike.

On this particular outing, Brian was wearing his LA Eyeworks sunglasses and looked like a producer out scouting locations. He tends to be overtaken by chain-yawning on these outings, which makes me wonder why I should ever expect four people separated in age by sixty-four years to enjoy doing the same thing together.

But it turned out we were in the vicinity of a certain railway trestle bridge that Brian used to visit as a boy, with his family, so we had a mission. He would show Casey his boyhood bridge. His mother, the only one of us sensibly shod for this outing, was game for anything, as usual. So we parked the car and walked along the edge of the road, squeezing past a solid line of other cars, out Looking at the Leaves.

And there it was, up the nearest hill — a bridge of black greasy ties that spanned the main road below. He and Casey cautiously made their way across it, hopping from tie to tie. In terms of mildly illicit thrills, this was probably much more fun than the signed nature paths in the groomed park, which was what I originally had in mind.

His mother and I hung back, making somewhat nervous jokes about whether the track was still in use, and what would happen if a train came along. Neither of us had the slightest desire to trestle-hop. When the boys came back unflattened, I decided that our next goal would be something out of my past, the Bruce Trail. So far, a day heady with family tradition. But by the time we walked to the turn-off that led to the gate that would take us to the Bruce Trail proper, we were too tired to hike, and so we turned back.

Back in the car, we queued up to pay to get into the conservation park. We parked, and observed a large crowd of people who stood rocking on a suspension bridge over a few dispirited ripples of water.

As part of the craven bribery that accompanies these outings, we had agreed to let Casey bring along his bike, which we now took out of the trunk. He insisted on riding it down a rocky footpath, with steps. We moved deeper into the woods where the trees were half bare and the leaves were slippery underfoot. At last we had to stash the bike by the trail, and then worry about someone stealing it, as we made our way further into Nature.

The aptly named Credit River flowed by, unperturbed. Brian's mother, robust but no fool, turned back when the path turned boggy, but the nuclear unit pressed on. When we eventually retraced our steps, we found her sitting on the saddle of Casey's bicycle, enjoying the weak sun that filtered through the leaves.

Having made our little sortie into the woods, we agreed it was okay to go. As we hastened back to the car, still warm in the parking lot, Casey got back on his bike and headed off to his preferred destination, the ice-cream store at the entrance to the park.

He left the bike outside, and I lined up for half an hour to get our Swiss mocha cones. These we ate while sitting in the car, with Aaron Neville on the radio, facing a stone wall held back by chicken wire and a sign that said "Danger! Do not climb."

It was good ice cream, and despite the absurdity of the entire outing, I was still glad we were out here rather than shambling around the house. We were lucky, we said several times, this is the last weekend for the leaves. Overrun and overorganized, the countryside in autumn still has beauty to squander.

We drove back toward the city, with the faint glow of achievement one feels at the end of such outings. Fatigue and a comfortable silence took over, and Springsteen's *Nebraska* played on the tape deck: more grim beauty.

"You did put the bike in the trunk, didn't you?" Brian suddenly said, swiveling his head toward me in the back. I hadn't. We didn't. All of us had left the brand-new expensive five-speed bike back there leaning against the stone wall in front of the ice-cream store. I launched into a monologue about the honesty of country folk. It would be there! I said, there's no point in turning around, it's fine, it's no big deal. Let's not ruin the day. We would just have to drive back the next weekend to retrieve the bike.

The relief we felt when we got home, phoned, and were assured that the bike would be kept stowed away until we could claim it didn't dispel the sense that we could try and try, but we would never get the family outing right.

25. Going Home

WENT HOME to Burlington to visit my parents on Saturday. First, the turmoil of simply getting out the front door. Brian waits till everyone is on the porch before he decides he must shave. I get in a micro-tizzy going anywhere, because it always seems to involve crating up the VCR or whatever utensils we must pack with us. Casey loves to *be* in Burlington, but can't bear to *go* anywhere, or to interrupt his present glory. I wish there were some sort of household cannon that could shoot us all out the door and into the car.

It is near the end of summer, near the end of all our ropes. Organized summer activities for some reason stop dead in mid-August, and I've spent the last two weeks riding herd over Casey and the neighborhood kids, who rocket in and out of our house, as I call things after them — "Close the sundeck door" or "Those chairs cannot go outside" or "Where are my good scissors?" Fall, school, the colder weather looms. In our garden, slugs and earwigs have won out over delphinium and tomatoes, and the white resin chairs on the deck are grimy with urban fallout. We have not entertained in a casual fashion in the back yard in the way we imagined we would. Unfinished summer things pile up in my mind like our clothes on the bedroom rocking chair.

We decide to go to the downtown Y on the way. We drive there through sluggish traffic. Brian is yawning. A reptilian sleepiness overcomes him on Saturdays, especially faced with the domestic vortex. He never complains, the spirit merely seeps out of his facial features and he yawns. In a conciliatory gesture, I slip a Rolling Stones tape into the deck, to perk him up.

We are in an instrumental section, with Jagger moaning and making black noises. "Dad, this song makes no sense," Casey observes from the back seat. "You can't hear the words or anything. It's getting on my nerves."

"Wait till this song is over," Brian says.

"Can't I hear C + C Factory? You've had your song now."

"It's getting on my nerves, too," I mutter, looking out the window at an herbalist's window full of twigs.

"God, moaners and complainers," Brian says, not without provocation. He punches in Casey's tape.

When we get to the Y, they head for the pool and I go up to the weight room where I stand in line for the LifeStep machine. There are five people ahead of me, so I give up and go into the warm-up room, padded with maroon mats, and lie down. I don't move.

Two men are doing the splits right up against the wall of mirrors. At least a dozen people are bent into strange and revealing positions, none of them making eye contact. I loll around and note how tight my neck muscles are, then go back to the weight room and push a few machines around. After ten minutes, I feel a thin red line of optimism moving through my veins. Yes, the trick is to stay in motion.

*   *   *

On the drive to Burlington, we head into the featureless gray sky that seems to loiter over this stretch of highway that runs along the lake. We have our usual in-car conversation. "What an asshole," Brian says, referring to a rabid lane-switcher with back spoilers ahead of us. I cluck agreement. Casey asks us why, since the bottom of the ocean is dirt, it doesn't soak up all the water and become a giant mud bath. We fake an answer.

Burlington is a forty-five minute drive from Toronto, a

prosperous commuter town on the snout of Lake Ontario. Most people passing through know it for the big bridge, the Skyway, that arcs over the bay near the steel mills of Hamilton. I grew up here down by the lake near Indian Point, where we used to find real arrowheads in the ravines. Then we moved into the subdivision where my parents, now in their eighties, still live.

We pull into the driveway of the ocher-colored split-level where I spent my teens. Although it's a big house for the two of them to keep up, it continues to be the place we go to celebrate holidays and birthdays with the entire family — my brother and his wife, my sister, her husband and two sons, us, and our parents. My mother seems to need thousands of house plants around her, and my father likes to keep the apple tree pruned to within an inch of its life.

No sooner are we inside the door than my mother hands me a sheaf of clippings on beta-agonists and other asthma drugs, which she says may interest me. Then she pulls out a new dip involving black olives, and we sit down to begin the steady consumption of things to eat with "nothing in them" — things with no cholesterol, no gluten, no sugar, no cream, no tartrazine. It must be true, because after eighty-seven thousand desserts my father is still trim and amazingly spruce. He admires her skills in these matters. "Oh, your mother's a smart one," he'll say at the dinner table, shaking his head and chuckling.

My mother has a near-professional knowledge of medicine and nutrition, and out on this limb of the family tree, she needs it. The list of food allergies, suspected, diagnosed, or imagined, at various times over the past few years includes chocolate, chicken, beef, shellfish, carrots, eggs — just about everything but parsley and bananas. My sister, thin and pretty, has the appetite of a dormouse. My father avoids garlic and fish. Brian and I roll our eyes at domestic wine and canned soup. My older brother insists on milk in the teacup before the tea is poured. My brother-in-law has an aversion to lamb, and my sister's little boy, Daniel, would prefer a heaping plate of jujubes instead of wild-rice pilaf. My sister-in-law is surprisingly normal and rolls with the punches. These get-togethers furnish my mother with the ultimate challenge — how to bake a cake without milk, eggs, flour, salt, or chocolate. She will pull it off. As for her, there are a thousand dietary things forbidden for this or that medical reason, but she's not above sitting down to a nice bowl of vanilla ice cream with just a drizzle of liqueur and some instant coffee sprinkled on the top. Food and wine, the mortar of families.

Before dinner, Casey retires to the den where my mother erects a tray for him, in the event of necessary snacks. Brian is encouraged to slip upstairs for a "quick nap," which he does. My father may watch a golf game on TV in the den, or go down and play Casey's version of pool on our old Sears pool table with the balding baize, a game that involves using one ball to blast all the others around the table. Three generations of toys are still up and running in the rec room, where the wet bar is stocked with train tracks.

My mother may have some little gift for Casey — a glider, some bloodshot slinky-eyes, a hand-buzzer, or a book from a yard sale. Her ability to anticipate whatever stage he's going to be in just before he hits it — the joke-book stage, or the sticker-collecting mania, the bug-jar phase — is uncanny. She thinks like an ally of his desires, not like someone seventy-four years older.

At some point, my father will list all the taxing chores he has completed around the yard and the house, pointing out the vines he took down from the trellis, or the branches he took off the tree, or the new border in the kitchen. He still oils the thirty-year-old clothes dryer to keep it going. "All it needs is a drop of oil and it's fine," he says. I silently compare their Depression values to my own "if-it-won't-work-throw-it-out" impatience. It would be nice to keep a good house, like this, I think. But we're too busy working and doing other things, I forget what.

It's not a huge yard, but my father always plans and executes his grounds keeping carefully. He puts on work pants, and gardening gloves, and a peaked cap for the sun. He sets the aluminum ladder up in a perfect inverted V. He is neat and meticulous, the owner of many fine-leaded automatic pencils and transparent rulers. When he is finished, he may retire to the den after lunch with a single hard-earned glass of beer. Work defines him still.

The central feature of his yard work is the trimming of one hundred and thirty feet of hedge. Indeed, his identification with the hedge is famous in the family. Last summer, my parents visited us at the cottage we rented. I suggested they stay on for an extra day or two, and my mother asked my father what he thought about this suggestion. "Well," he said, "we really should be getting back." He dusted his knees. "There's the lawn to cut, and the hedge needs trimming. . . ."

*　　*　　*

Dinner time. I check a casserole left warming in the oven, a complex edifice involving snow peas, broccoli, rigatoni, cheese, and possibly water chestnuts. The smoke detector in the hall goes off. My father likes to keep it sensitively tuned to any wisp of smoke rising up from the stove. He shuts it off with a broom handle. The sound of the smoke detector going off is one we have come to associate with dinner being almost ready.

My parent's dinner table is an extendable affair with extra leaves, which are all in place today. For birthdays or get-togethers, my mother always devises some kind of centerpiece — miniature narratives that change with the season and the occasion, made from things at hand, the nearly blown roses from the garden, some disguised Christmas cupid sprayed gold and then force-marched through pine cones and ivy. This time the centerpiece is strictly ikebana, a single plum branch half in blossom. I have detected evidence of the centerpiece gene in my sister's home too.

We also have a tasteless object that gets hauled out for birthdays — a wind-up musical Taiwan carousel with bobbing-chicken heads under a whirling pink umbrella with plastic balls. Over the years, the chickens have come unmoored and dropped back inside the base of the toy. The grandchildren have learned to overwind the thing so the chickens bob away madly inside, upside down, like pandemonium erupting in the hen house before the ax comes down. Dented and damaged, whirling with manic persistence, the thing is a reasonable icon of the family itself.

Each time I come home and have some reason to go to the hall closet, I see the boxes labeled in my mother's flowing, loopy writing: Christmas lights, candles, wreathes, tablecloths, decorations. Family theater. My father's annual cursing over the missing bulbs on the outdoor lights, the fussing with the infernal Christmas tree stand — it can all seem pointless at the time. But eventually it sinks in that families are made up of people of vastly different ages, with little in common. Tradition and domestic structure provide coherence. They're part of the art of family.

Ritual connects up the years. As the centrifugal force of history pulls the family this way and that, domestic ritual acquires more meaning. Lackadaisical Protestants, we were raised with a minimum of spiritual rituals — church amounted to a kind of pep talk, with gloves and hats. As graduates of the sixties, it was hard enough to accept shoulder pads, let alone formal celebrations or a ripping good wake.

I can understand grandparents who want to ditch it all and time-share a condo in Florida. But if setting the table, hiding Easter eggs, and decking the halls still gives them pleasure, it is an inestimable gift to the children of their children — who for the most part don't have mothers who make two hundred potato latkes at a toss, or construct gingerbread houses. We do know where to go to buy excellent gingerbread houses, though. We're nonpareil at shopping.

*　　　*　　　*

During dinner, we may enjoy a spirited discussion of mole formation or skin grafts, while the non-medically minded put down their forks. When dinner is over, my father serves dessert at the head of the table. He never fails to look at the dish my mother sets before him as if he's about to dissect a raccoon — he pokes it and tests the consistency before deciding how to attack it. This year my mother actually came around to where he sat, put her hand over his, and helped him press the knife down through the starfruit on top of the eggless cheesecake. "It's rich, people won't want a big piece."

"Oh, I never know what she's going to come up with," he mock-complains.

Before we leave, my parents give me something, too. It's an orange fluorescent sign that says CALL POLICE. Should I have a flat tire on the highway, I am to lock the doors, roll up the windows to within two inches of the top, and place this sign in my rear window. There have been "incidents" in the area lately.

"Truck drivers with CBs will see it and phone the police," my father says, with some animation. I thank them and say I wish I had two, so I could wear them as a kind of all-purpose sandwich board — taking the offensive with muggers and that sort of thing.

As we leave, the sky looks thundery. My father twitches the living-room curtains and peers out into the threatening weather. "Look at that wind," he says. "One good blow, and that big spruce out front could come crashing right down on the roof." The spruce is forty feet high, and it's true, it sways. My father lost his father at the age of twelve to TB. His mother taught piano and raised the family alone. When there were no engineering jobs, my father worked as an insurance salesman during the Depression, traveling by car through the Canadian prairies, while my mother stayed home with her first baby. I don't think the world has looked entirely trustworthy ever since.

26.   Hallowe'en

IDO HAVE SOME boxes in my hall closet —
ones with Hallowe'en costumes in them. It's the one holiday that
just is what it is — kid-centric, refreshingly pagan, and devoted
to the power of make-believe and candy. Kids lose their faith in
Santa faster than their faith in Hallowe'en, which appeals to their
modern greed and the urge to dress up and be somebody else (an
ageless desire). My faint but still detectable Hallowe'en excitement is rooted in memories of being out after dark, racing around
the neighborhood, through curbside mounds of leaves. I can still
pass certain houses near my parents' home and think, "They used
to give out chocolate bars."

One neighbor used to put on a sheet with eye-holes, park
himself in a lawn chair behind his big Buick, drink a case of beer,
and go "Boo! Gotcha! Haw haw haw!" to every new arrival. Back
then, scary drunken guys were just that — old drunk Mr. Hewett.
The dangers in our Hallowe'en rounds were all manageable,
delicious dangers.

After Casey came along, the first few years of Hallowe'en
costumes in our family were a cinch — cat's whiskers, a red nose,
a Borg tail pinned to the snowsuit. Then when he turned four,
movie culture took over. He wanted to be Roger Rabbit. I
calculated the effort involved: ears, red pants with suspenders,
fluffy tail — no big deal, I thought.

But as it turns out, there are physics involved in getting rabbit
ears to stand up on a human head. I bought milliner's wire. I

bought white and pink felt, for the ears. I picked up a plastic headband, thinking to wire it up with the ears like antennae. Nothing more than an evening's pleasant diversion.

I bought stuff to stuff the ears. I hand-sewed the ears, with the wire in them. They bent great. Attaching them to the headband was daunting but not impossible. Everything went along swimmingly until I put the headband on Casey. It had little teeth along the edge and was about three inches too narrow. The thing popped up off his head like a clothespin.

"I can't wear these! Mom, they hurt my head."

Unreasonable irritation and defensiveness rose up in me.

"Please, don't cry," I said. "I'll make another pair of ears."

More sewing of felt and bending of wire. The second pair of ears benefited from practice. This time I sewed them onto a hood. But when I snugged the hood over his head, the stuffed ears fell over backward from their own weight. Other mothers got their rabbit ears to stand up. What was my problem?

I put the ears aside. The red pants with the oversized buttons were a success, and luckily Casey's ability to see what he wished to see kept him thrilled with the finished product. On Hallowe'en, he carried the ears in a basket; if he encountered any puzzled faces, he pulled the ears out and explained who he was. It never occurred to him that he was swishing around the block in red pants and a big fluffy tail and no one had the faintest idea who he was supposed to be.

Next year, the choice was Mario, of SuperMario fame. No problem this time, I thought. Same red pants, no tail, black mustache, weird hat. Did he want those cretinous round ears? Ears could be fun, I thought. No, he didn't care. But the boots had to be brown. Fine. We got out his black rubber boots. I'll just spray them brown, I thought. With something.

Then began my tenacious journeying from hardware to hardware, from Sears to art supply stores, looking for a brown spray that would adhere to black rubber. There is very little call for this, it turns out. Finally, I caved in and bought gold lacquer.

The old Jackson standby, gold spray! Gold boots had, I thought, a certain mythic heft. I went home, spread out newspapers, and sprayed the black boots gold. They didn't look like anything an Italian cartoon plumber might wear, but they were splendid artifacts. Make a great centerpiece, too, with bonsai trees growing out of them.

Casey came home from school.

"Are my boots done?"

"Indeed they are," I said, "they're drying in the basement." He pelted down the stairs. Then came silence. He dragged his feet back up the stairs.

"Mom, they're *gold.* Mario doesn't wear gold boots."

"They'll look brown in the dark," I said without much conviction.

"I'm not wearing them. They look like fairy-tale boots."

The next day I went halfway across town to a Canadian Tire store where I found a reddish-brown car-body spray, for only eleven dollars. I resprayed the black/gold boots, all the while congratulating myself that I had picked an easy costume, again.

*   *   *

My mother made great costumes, using the old material and party shoes kept in the costume barrel in the basement. I remember the excellent silver scimitar my brother carried the year he was a pirate, wearing big gold satin pirate pants sewn out of a dress my mother wore to a dance in college. Another year he was a skeleton, each bone pasted separately to a black body-suit. Even my dog, a miniature pinscher with his own anxiety disorder, used to routinely wear leopard-skin coats that my mother made, not entirely with a straight face.

I have a sewing machine, which I can operate, but I tend to be torn between sewing and not sewing. Equal rights will certainly remain a farce until fathers feel compelled to sew mouse costumes. Or rather, feel guilty about not sewing them. But why buy a store costume for twenty dollars when you can spend thirty-six dollars on fabric, Velcro, buttons, bows, rickrack and other dressmaking items intended to save you money?

This year, Casey made a truly foolproof choice — Zorro. I rejoiced inwardly. Black shirt, black mask, hat, whip — he already had the whip — and sword. A fencing foil, as I recall. No ears, no tails, no devil's horns. A little reflecting tape on the cape and he wouldn't even get run over. I already had a black satin shirt with the requisite Spanish bloused effect. This year I had it made! For two solid weeks he didn't even change his mind about who he wanted to be.

Three days before Hallowe'en — a full three days — I went out to Sears and looked through the pawed-over section of ready-to-wear costumes for a suitable black hat. But Zorro's flat black *vaquero* hat is unlike any other hat — bowler, cowboy, pirate, or otherwise. Undaunted, I bought heavy black construction paper to construct my own hat. This involved many bendable tabs and white glue to assemble the three parts — crown, brim, and whatever you call the bit that stands up. I measured, cut, and glued. It looked great when it was done. But the bit that stands up was too tall — too unSpanish. I put the hat on Casey as he stood on the armchair to look into the hall mirror. Silence. Crestfallen silence.

"Mom," he said, struggling not to lose his composure, "I don't mean to be rude, but it looks like a top hat. It really does."

Something very akin to hysteria and panic welled up in my breast.

"No, no! It looks great, it looks Mexican. With a hatband and a mustache it'll work —"

"*Mom*, I'm not going to wear it. And it doesn't fit, it pops up, see?"

He was right. It was creeping up off his thick hair. I felt a childish sense of defeat. I was so sure I could make that hat, and have a good time making it, too. Now I was panicking — the next day was his class party, costumes required. He was heartbroken, as only an eight-year-old boy can be about his mother's failure to come up with a great costume.

He could see I was almost as upset as he was.

"It's okay, mom," he said dully. "I just won't wear any costume." He gripped me around my waist and stifled his sobs.

"Take it easy, take it easy, I'll give it another try."

Hallowe'en costume skills will pass with my mother's generation, I thought bleakly. And yet I refused to buy a costume, because . . . because so much of every day is homogeneous, and on Hallowe'en you can be whatever you want. Why should one-third of the school come dressed as Ninja Turtles?

I switched to the cape element. A cape is not difficult to make. You buy a hank of black material, make it cape-shaped, and add ties. Or you can even just knot the corners together around the neck. However, in penance for the hat, I hand-sewed the cape material to an old karate belt, then hemmed the cape all around because it was cheap satin and unraveled fast. Can't have a fringed Zorro. That took me through two sit-coms and the news.

Then I tackled the hat again. By using quantities of masking tape and tapering the diameter from head size to brim size, and making it rather more oval than round, and more or less discovering that milliners are sainted technicians and gifted artisans, I made the hat.

In the morning, Casey accepted the hat. He looked in the mirror and was satisfied. He loved his cape. But then, everyone loves a cape. I used my eye liner to paint on a nice thin Spanish mustache. I had to back the mask with tape to keep it from crumpling into his eyes. And off he went, speaking in a Zorro accent that was inexplicably Japanese.

27.   The Bad Patch

IT'S THURSDAY night. I've put Casey to bed. I have some reading to do, but I sit down and aimlessly click around the channels instead. I hear the door open and Brian's heavy briefcase thunk down in the hallway. Thursday is his late work night. He drops his coat on the banister of the stairs.

"Hi," he says.

"Hi."

"What are you watching?"

"Nothing."

"Is there anything to eat?"

"Not really. There's some of that chicken to heat up if you want. Casey and I had the rest for dinner."

"I'll just have some cereal or something."

"Did you get your piece through okay?"

"Yeah, it's done. I lost a column because of Yugoslavia."

He goes to the kitchen, gets a bowl of cereal, and I get up and stand against the counter while he sits at the table. His upper lip has that compressed look it gets when he's angry about something.

"The termite guy phoned today," I say.

"What did he say?"

"We need a six-inch wood-soil clearance, front and back. It involves ripping up part of the deck. I talked to Blake, he can do it for about four hundred dollars he thinks."

"Well, I guess we'll have to do it, then."

"There were these little beetles in my office again last night."

"Cockroaches?"

"I'm not sure."

"That's all we need." He is looking through the sea of newspaper sections for something to read while he eats.

"How's your chest?" Colds always go to his chest.

"The same. The usual."

He takes his cereal into the other room, I follow him, and we sit down in front of the TV. There's nothing on. We switch back and forth between Arsenio and Johnny, because Johnny won't be there much longer.

"Who is that?"

"Kirstie Alley. She's lost weight."

"Switch back to Patti LaBelle."

We watch in silence. I wish I were Patti LaBelle.

"Well," I say, "I'm ready to pass out. I've got to get up tomorrow."

"I've got an early screening, too."

Neither of us move.

"Okay, I'm going to go up. Try not to wake me up when you come," I say. "Good night."

"Good night."

*   *   *

How did Marianne Faithfull put it in that great, nasty song "Why'd You Do It?" — "Is this the end, or is it just a bad patch?" The great and mysterious thing about bad patches in marriages is the way you never notice the beginnings or the ends of them. Then one day, or one night, you're up to your knees in one, like a cranberry bog, but neither of you can figure out how you got there. No single scene or fight tipped the balance. It just . . . happened. There are two people in the room, but nobody's home. Or you're going somewhere together in the car, and the silence has gone from comfortable to empty. You find yourself lying in bed, turned away from him, hands folded under your body, wife as sarcophagus. Curious, how it happens.

Household hollowness comes around in irregular cycles, like meteor showers. But the true sign of a bad patch is that it never feels temporary or fixable. It has a shudder of the inevitable to it. The thought crosses your mind that when love goes it goes all at once, and forever.

It begins as one of marriage's little myths — the freedom to stop trying so hard and just coexist. You can trust that the love will be there even if you don't tell fascinating stories and wear lipstick, in fact, the love keeps chugging along even when you make *no effort whatsoever*. And so you stop. Or he stops. Then one notices that the other has stopped. Domestic details fill the gap.

When a couple turns domestic, for the first while having to talk about the need for aluminum eaves troughing and other matters only gets in the way of the relationship. Then, magically, these negotiations take the place of the relationship. But sooner or later, the endless house problems will ease up, and your child will shrink from the size of a sun that eclipses everything to just a normal, demanding child. He will go to bed too late, at 10 p.m. Along comes 10:30.

Do the parents leave the TV on, gazing upon anchorpeople instead of each other? Yes. Yes, they do, at first. Because nobody can be bothered to summon up the effort required to de-ice the lock and get the door open again. Each waits for the other to make the tender gesture, do the love work. They both sit there watching the news thinking, "I refuse to be the one to make the effort here." Nobody gets to be adored.

One of the first signs of a Bad Patch is the misleading calm, the pseudo-satisfaction. One day you are thinking that things are truly happy and stable for the first time in months. You congratulate yourself. The day after that day, you happen to see a couple in a restaurant relishing each other's presence, unmistakably in love. Not pre-sex infatuation, but solid, rich true-blue love. And it occurs to you that you have not behaved like that with your husband for longer than you want to admit. Strangely enough, your first response is to feel sorry for your husband, who ought to have someone looking at him like that. Then you realize that you miss it, too. The calm has turned comatose.

A marriage is supposed to accommodate these long, rolling grades, where you don't notice the uphill stretches until they're behind you. Marriage is the one place where there is enough room to take these rides through unexplored territory. But it's just as easy to get lost, and there are no degrees of that. Lost is lost.

*　　*　　*

When we first met, we fought a lot. Tick, tick, tick: I was too old to dilly-dally, I wanted things to fall into place fast. Then when I got pregnant, I stopped fighting. After all, the main issue was settled — we were having a baby. The rest would have to be negotiated bit by bit.

Which is what happened. Bit by bit, we worked out how to work things out. Our fights continue, but in new, subtle form, the result of years of sedimentation. Housework hassles go on, are never resolved, and will probably extend into the afterlife ("Why am I the one who takes the clouds to the dry cleaners?"). But warm or cold, in or out of arguments, we at least treat each other civilly in front of our son and, for the most part, in private.

The civility is his idea, I'm afraid. I like to set the glassware rattling from time to time; it's like getting the car out on the highway to burn the carbon off. But now, instead of staging fights (which have a paralyzing effect on Brian, like high beams), I have developed the dreadful wifely art of a thousand-tiny-cuts. Needling. Knowing where and when to strike. But did I say wifely? He's good at it too.

Usually he shops, but one night I come home with groceries, bags and bags of them. The other writer in the house is in a very shallow funk. "Did you buy Shredded Wheat?" he may inquire, meaning did I manage to spare a thought for him, instead of just buying only the Honey Groats and Cap'n Glucose that Casey wants. Or, conversely, I may greet him in the morning by saying, lightly, neutrally, "By the way, you left the milk out last night," meaning, you careless cur, if you can leave the milk out you could *walk out on me one fine day and never look back.*

He comes home from work, finds his son lolling on the carpet watching "Flayed Corpses from the Crime Files" and says, "I thought we agreed about Casey and TV." I say, "Well, we can agree on the rules, but it's still up to me to carry them out, isn't it, because I'm the one who's here most of the time, and anyway he just turned it on. They don't show the actual flaying."

Late at night, as we are getting into the XL promotional T-shirts that constitute our bed wear, he will put his hand on the light switch and ask, "Do you want to read?" Meaning, shall we dim the overhead light to Sex Mode or crank it up to *Vanity Fair* reading level? He has no objection to some nice, alienated sex at the end of our long and wildly differing days. The problem is I know him too well to have completely alienated sex, so I find myself wanting a few hours of the foreplay known as a relationship first — nothing too ambitious, a conversation over a meal, even an hour in the same room. I don't have to have baked polenta in a corner banquette or things in blue velvet boxes given to me or . . . but I digress.

To meet for the first time that day in the door of the bedroom and then proceed directly to sex calls for creativity, and some nights I just don't feel like getting out a bowler hat and a bentwood chair at midnight. Some nights, the best thing you can hope for in the way of coupling is chummy connubial sex, and for that you need friendship. Even friendship becomes elusive when you're both busy taking each other for granted. "Not trying" slips over, indetectably, into catatonia.

Our bad patches usually come round in the fall, when school begins, the film season goes into high gear, and Brian disappears into the work vortex. Suddenly I'm the only one home, and the family has flown apart. I brace myself for it, I tell myself that no one is to blame, I know very well the cracks and pressures that bring it on . . . but sooner or later I wake up, and there it is, all around me, the Bad Patch, once again.

In good years, it takes the form of a hearty kind of loathing — I loathe his socks on the chair, I loathe the snail-trail of honey left on the counter, I loathe the lingering light on his face when he comes in late at night. He's working hard, he's having too much fun, and it shows. Meanwhile, I'm on the stern deck watching for icebergs. We don't see each other for days on end, just each other's brush and comb and a shifting pile of clothing.

Brian is always surprised by my grouchiness, and this only makes things worse. I feel it is up to him to make the effort to stay in touch. He feels the same. I resent being at the mercy of his work schedule, and he quite sensibly resents my resentment. And so the frost creeps over the pumpkin until I become quite adept at doing without him. We fall into the waiting game, where each waits for the other to make the conciliatory, the emotional gesture.

The cure is always sex — not the considerate, better-have-sex sort but a genuine reunion. Getting over the hump, as it were, is the hard part. The work binge is over, he's home in bed, and I lie there, feeling cold and armored, resentful and needy, saying superficial, inane things. Whole continents of fire and ice get reduced to small talk.

"You know, we really should put some sealer on the basement wall, it's started to sweat in places," I say. Or "I think I prefer your hair longer."

I may even prop myself up on one elbow and absent-mindedly twist pin curls of hair on his chest while the interior monologue begins. "Yes, I could live very happily alone," I'm thinking, "Whitehorse, or Pond Inlet, although in that case shared custody would be a problem, luckily we have equity in the house, our families will be shocked but we can't live for them, Casey's old enough to weather a separation, in any case it can't be good for Brian either, this domestic fog, anyway everyone else we know has split up, divorce isn't the end of the world. . . ." But I'm just furnishing the bad patch. At the same time, I'm wondering what he's thinking as he takes off his glasses and turns off the light, I'm wondering who is on his mind, is he sad, is he waiting for me to make the move?

And if I do make the move, or if he does, if we fake it, that might let some light back in . . . and so we inch back together, both victims of our neglect, hoping for some genie to enter the room and move us into a friendlier position. These private thoughts inhabit the bedroom alongside two separate and on this night obdurately lonely halves of a couple asking themselves how long bad patches are supposed to last.

28.   Madame Ovary

SOON AFTER this, at dinner, I said I thought it might be a good idea for me to get out of town for a few days. Nobody moaned or clutched at my sleeve, I noticed. I took the train to visit a friend who lives in a house with no running water, a four-hour drive north of Toronto. She has concocted a luxurious life of austerity (or vice versa) — no shower or bathroom, but raspberries for breakfast. She wears thrift-shop cashmere to chop firewood for the wood stove. In the morning, she heads off to work, and I'm left alone in the house full of winter light and silence. It's heaven.

I had brought up work to do, but first of all I was seized by a desire to cut my hair. Normally I get this urge only before my period, when various forms of self-mutilation are high on my list of priorities. But my period wasn't due for some time, so I picked up the scissors with confidence. No harm in a little trim. My last cut had been an experiment — early Julie Christie. A bit of a bust. Maybe late Chrissie Hynde would be better.

So I took my friend's old mirror, with the cracked blue milk paint around the frame, which I remember from her first marriage, out onto the front steps of the house. It was nearly spring and mild, for North Bay. No black flies yet. She was outside, too, in a rakish fur hat with earflaps, sawing away at a slender tree just her size. I took up my shears. The two of us hacked away, me at my hair, her at her tree, several yards apart. At first, I intended only to thin out the sides, but a shape inside the hair called to me, and I slashed away boldly. My first job at sixteen was in a hairdresser's. My sister is an excellent hairdresser. Little doubts bubbled up, but I crushed them immediately. I can and will cut my hair, I thought, and it will be a good thing.

I always want to grow my hair, but never get past the collar stage. I hate hairdos, precision cuts, or shaved napes. "Make it look like hair," I beg whoever cuts it. The last conversation I had with my hairdresser, with whom I have a well-worked-out relationship, was about how I was completely over being neurotic about my hair. It turned out to be premature.

By setting up another mirror, I found I could layer the back. Tufts of hair wafted away on the breeze, like milkweed fluff. I put the scissors down and checked it out. The shape was okay, I hadn't ruined it by any means, but . . . it was short! Once again, I was a sensible mother in a cap cut with a boy in school and Reeboks on my feet. Fantasies of the leonine mane withdrew.

Perhaps, I thought, I have diminished myself again, the way I always do before my period. The hair-cutting urge is part of the general closet-cleaning and compulsive purging behavior that echoes exactly what the body does between ovulation and menstruation, when it rolls up the womb's red carpet and throws it out. The monthly rummage sale, the trim, the cut. But my period was at least twelve days away by my reckoning, so I went ahead and cut my hair.

Anyway, why have long hair? It only attracts men. Off with it. And why have a nice cozy, upholstered womb, awaiting the orphan egg? Out with the blood buffet. The obsession with excess, clutter, adornment, and softness always comes with the re-orientation of the body, away from the receptivity of ovulation, toward lean, mean self-sufficiency. So I cut my hair down to little ragged exclamation marks. It looked fine, but it wasn't long.

In the cruel northern night, I investigated my face in the mirror. The skin below the eyes showed a half-moon of faintly crosshatched lines. This half-moon crinkled finely when I smiled.

Only normal at forty-four. Normal at thirty-four, even. I decided that my skin is — was — my best feature and that now it was "going." I met these thoughts with a kind of turgid stoicism, as if they didn't depress me, which they did. This was unusual. My age hasn't bothered me for . . . well, for years now! I felt my oldest at thirty-six, just before having my son. I've felt younger, mostly, since that year. Until the haircut day.

*   *   *

The weekend. I am back in the city, and Brian is preparing to fly off and interview Madonna in L.A. On Sunday night, he is playing percussion as part of a big native benefit for the environment. A busy and rather schizoid schedule, but that's fine with me. I know that half an hour of making music can fuel many long, arid days of writing to deadline. When he phones during intermission to say he'll be home soon, I tell him not to rush. So there is no earthly reason why I should be in such a foul mood when he returns home near midnight. I could have gone to bed early, a prospect I usually relish. Instead I stayed up watching bad TV, eating a long row of buttered crackers.

"I was expecting you earlier," I say when he comes through the door, all smiles and baggy-eyed from the exertion of playing.

Bitch! "You didn't say that on the phone."

"You made it sound like you were on your way."

"The end of the concert was longer than I expected. Then I left. I didn't even stick around for a beer."

"I don't mind you staying late, I just like to know so I won't wait for you." These rational lines are delivered in a dark and sulky fashion. I am wearing the bottoms of a pair of rose-colored long underwear that I favor in winter, a yellow robe, my freshly cut hair, and a tiny bandage on my chin, covering a tampered-with blemish. In addition to my unbecoming anger. Absently swabbing away at the surface of the oven, I go on.

"I was looking forward to either having the evening to myself, or spending it with you — one or the other. Instead, I ended up half-expecting you all night. And now you have to pack."

"Okay, I apologize. Let's not go over the same ground again."

"I'm just so tired." I look up at the clock like a drowning woman. Twelve-thirty.

"Look, I told you, I left right after the concert was over."

My horrible need for him makes me cruel. "I think I'll sleep in the office," I say, flouncing up the stairs and into my office with its narrow futon, knowing this strategy is hopeless. I'm lonely and need to be with him. The need humiliates me, because I'm tired, and I also want to be intact and alone.

"Fine, good night," he calls after me evenly. He is dealing with me. I open a book but the print looks like Sanskrit. I briskly go back downstairs and say I've changed my mind, I can't possibly sleep with him rummaging around, getting packed.

I ask him how the concert was. He says it was good, the music was interesting. He has two reddish scratches on his neck. I finger them. What are these? I ask sarcastically. They're from the neck strap of the drum, he says, it cuts into the skin. He looks at me, insulted by my jealousy. "You think I'm going to tell you I'm playing the congas at the Royal Alex so I can sneak off with somebody else?"

"Well, look in the mirror."

He does. The marks look exactly like lipstick prints. "I can't believe you would think that of me."

I realize then that I am feeling bottomlessly paranoid, about everything: my age, my mother's tippy holding of her teacup during dinner, my shorn hair, even Brian's flying off to Madonna. I say he should ask Madonna about the state of her fallopian tubes, which is the only fact that remains to be revealed. Then I read some motherhood tome and wait for him to finish packing, irritated by the hysterical zippp! of his suitcase pockets as he stuffs in socks and a bathing suit — a bathing suit! While I rot here in the north.

"Do you realize we've been together thirteen years this winter?" he says, not without tenderness, when he finally gets into bed.

"I don't count the first three years," I reply.

Instead of closing my magazine and saying yes, isn't it amazing we've come this far, a ridiculous, bitch-powered argument ensues about whether we have been together for twelve or thirteen years. And finally, the punch line.

"If you hadn't taken so long to make your mind up, we could have had another child, or three, by now." Ah-ha! He wasn't just late home from the concert, he was deeply, profoundly, late in my life! Talk about an argument not worth having.

"Yes, and maybe we would be divorced by now."

"Anyway, it's eleven years, not thirteen."

"I have the poster in the basement to prove it," he says, meaning the poster for the dance he played at on our first date.

"So go get it," I say, with half a smile.

"This is ridiculous."

He gets up, puts on a robe, and descends into the basement. I lie there, truly amazed at my unchecked barbarism. He comes back triumphant.

"Nineteen seventy-eight. Thirteen years."

"Well, you didn't really think of yourself as being *with* me for at least two."

"But we were. It doesn't matter what we thought." This shuts me up. I want to reach him, but just this minute I can't. I'm ashamed at my lack of tenderness, but at the moment he exists beside me at a great remove. It's obvious that neither of us has the largess, the depth of soul to get past this. So, covered in self-pity, I slump out of bed and over to my pallet in the office. I am sorry not to be able to make love before he goes away. I'm not even particularly angry at him, since he hasn't done anything wrong. The sadness has an oceanic, impersonal tinge. I wonder what it's about.

The answer is banal, is biochemical, is lunar. The next morning I wake up and, ten days early, my period arrives.

Well, I think with huge relief, I'm not crazy after all! Or not every day of the year, at least. It was a fight worth having, but the reason I blamed, got angry, felt jealous, felt old, felt gypped on the maternal front was mostly because I was premenstrual. The blind, optimistic little one-ticket egg was in the process of exiting and taking the furniture along with it. My body was shifting from blinkered optimism — the lottery of ovulation — to groundless pessimism, that little death-space when the cycle moves through barrenness.

This shift of focus reverberates through the body and results in a generalized sense of fruitlessness that coats everything, like the fallout of ash from a volcanic eruption. PMS is a junky sensation of cosmic pointlessness and missed opportunities, of being in the wrong place at the wrong time.

But a bout of biological mourning is not to be confused with the perception of women as nothing more than breeders, failed or otherwise. As usual, two contradictory states are involved. While my mind goes about not getting pregnant, every month my body still plots for conception. When it doesn't happen, the body then goes through a mild, formal stage of grief. It won't get expressed that way. Ovum-grieving doesn't exactly have cultural currency. Premenstrual mood swings are viewed as a disorder, a lingering female defect, not a bout of mourning appropriate to the internal events in the female body.

Culture determines the valency of PMS, and the culture has never known what to do with the power of female procreativity, including the echoes of the reproductive cycle known as PMS. It's history, not biology, that cramps a woman's style. She vibrates at a pitch that fluctuates, the world pursues a monotone. PMS is just a useful little hallucination, a fragment of craziness that mirrors back the way the culture placates women but continues to find ways to suppress the heart of female nature, her sexuality. Maybe the antisocial side of PMS says more about the signals coming at her than the messages she sends back.

letting

go

29.   Going Out

SEE HIM on his bike, heading out, away, each day further and further. I remember my mother's mother, as I slid down the banister, tremulously saying, "Take care! Take care!" and I feel the same. But I let him go around the block, out of my sight.

I hope that the result of my holding him so close, to satisfy my own needs as well as his, has only been this confidence and eagerness to move out and away. He's had enough of me. My compulsion to rush home to him when he was little, my endless months of breast-feeding don't seem to have turned him into a clinging wimp after all. It may not be a crime to feel too much.

The other day I had a baby sitter lined up, but Casey didn't want me to go out that night. This was unusually clingy, but it was the first week of school, after a summer of togetherness. He begged and pleaded, he argued and cajoled, he worked away at me like a lawyer. He didn't approve of the B-list baby sitter I had managed to line up. He was working himself up into a lather. I was trying to coolly defend myself for going out like a normal human being as I microwaved a hot dog for him, because I knew hunger was the first problem here. But I over-microwaved it, and the bun turned to Kleenex, sticking to the shriveled-up little weiner.

As I picked at the bun and said soothing things to him, he started melodramatically pushing the guilt envelope: "This is the worst day of my life so far, why was I ever born," etc. Now, I am not a mother who goes out a lot at night. When I do, Brian often stays home. At this particular stage, the two of us going out together, at the same time, in the same car, happens roughly as often as a lunar eclipse.

He badgered on. "You're always going out. Do you have to? You're just doing this because you want to, not because you have to. I never get to see you . . ." The ruined hot dog approximated my soul at this moment. "Fine, okay, I won't go, I'll stay home," I yelled and flung the shriveled-up hot dog into the corner of the kitchen, where it bounced down the basement stairs and disappeared.

My son drooped silently at the table, both sorry and indignant. "You don't have to get so cooked up," he said. "It's not my fault." I stalked out of the kitchen before I threw anything else. I really wanted to go out that night. I spend the day in a tiny room with a paper blind and the high but not inaudible shriek of my Mesozoic-era computer. Surely it was not a sin to go out on a school night and leave your seven-year-old with a sitter who charges professional nanny rates even as he sleeps and she watches "Studs." I went out.

Two days later, I had reason to go out again. A function, a dress-up party. I had informed Casey of this the night before. Now it was 5 p.m., an hour before I was to exit, and I was standing in the bedroom flinging assorted items of black clothing around trying to assemble something that would stand in for decent evening wear. This took concentration, confidence, and creativity — three Cs incompatible with Casey in the room. I remembered that in a fit of anti-aging hysteria, I had had my one good black dress shortened to within hailing distance of my pubic hair. The dress was ruined. Casey came into the bedroom, looking for some shoes to throw up into the eaves trough or on some similar mission.

"What's that you've got on . . . hey! Are you *going out again?*"

"Yes," I said defensively, "I told you that last night."

"Ohhhhh no!!!" he said, collapsing on the bed. "Not again! You've been out every night!"

"That's not true. I went out two nights ago. I have to go out tonight. Irene's coming. You like Irene."

"*Why* do you have to?"

"Because it's dad's work party, and he wants me to go. I want to go with him. You get to go to Wonderland and the park and Ontario Place and movies. We get to go out sometimes."

I could feel us both crumbling, and I didn't want to leave him in mid-frenzy. So I took brisk initiative. "Listen, here's what I'll do. I know you've had a rough week, and you don't want me to go out. But I'm willing to pay. I will give you five dollars for spending tonight with Irene. I'll pay you just like a baby sitter."

Surely this was some kind of mothering nadir, never to be repeated. But it worked.

"Really? Five dollars?" His face shone like a saint's.

"That's right. That's fifteen Freezees. That's at least eight Slurpees. One thing, though. Don't tell Irene. Let me tell Brian. And I wouldn't mention it to your teacher, either."

"I won't. Great!" He ran out of the bedroom and down to his assortment of banks to add up his assets. I congratulated myself on my craven action and continued to put things on and take them off. I went into the bathroom to paw through my make-up. Casey stood in the doorway, the glow fading from his face.

"It's still not worth it, mom."

"Well, how much am I worth, then?" I replied jauntily. "Twenty-five? A hundred?"

"Six hundred dollars."

"So that's my price. Uh-huh." I put some concealer under my eyes. "Well, that's out of my league, I'm afraid."

"It's just not fair!" he said. This was strange, I thought, wondering if there was a problem at school. But I can't switch schools now, I thought, he'll be behind . . . My mind began to lurch along in this fashion about some of the deeper reasons behind these tears. Now where was that old silk purse . . .

"You're killing me!" He lay on the bed, sobbing into my clothes.

"No, I'm not. You always have a great time with Irene. The minute I leave, you'll be perfectly happy."

"No, I won't!" He stomped into his room, where he lay on the bed like a corpse with the duvet over his face. Wearing a black skirt, a black body stocking, a black jacket, and long earrings, apparently in mourning for both of us, I followed him into his room and sat down. I could feel myself falling over inside, like an old, mossy tree. I couldn't bear to see him, hear him cry. He was being manipulative, that much is clear, but he was also truly upset. I remembered being this upset. I remembered how this felt.

"If it is so very, very important to you tonight, then I will stay home," I said quietly. "I won't go to the party."

He raised his head from the pillows to look incredulously at me.

"Just don't expect me to be in a good mood, that's all." I left the room with uncharacteristic, tragic quietness and went into the bedroom, where I extricated myself from the dress and got back into my jeans. This was ruining my pre-party effervescence. He was splitting me in two, again. So I calmly settled into my evening martyrdom and picked up the phone to inform his father that I wouldn't be stepping out with him in my anti-mothering gear. Then Casey walked in, like Frank Perry on Death Row.

"All right," he said in a choked voice, his head drooping. "You can go." His face contorted with the effort of not crying. "This is the hardest decision of my life," he continued in a strangled voice, "but you can go." He had both hands over his heart. I should have been torn apart. On the contrary, I was delighted and impressed.

"You're sure?"

"I don't want to ruin your fun. You'll just be unhappy all the rest of the night, and I'll have a miserable time."

"That's right. You're being very brave. Thank you."

"Why is life so hard all the time?"

"I don't know. It's just a stupid party. I'm sorry it's causing all this trouble."

"Mom, don't call it stupid. You want to go."

"Okay. So, let's go downstairs." I took his hand and we left the bedroom.

"Will you phone at bedtime?"

"Yes."

"Promise?"

"Yes."

I did. I knew he would be fine, and he was. His voice was his usual voice, light, merry, animated. The strange anguish that had held us both captive had disappeared. It was hard work on both sides, but we got somewhere in the end.

*　　　*　　　*

Months, possibly years, go by. The phone rings. It's four in the afternoon on a Tuesday. Brian calls to say that an invitation has fallen into his lap for a night out, a reception, a party downtown. Could I possibly book a sitter and join him?

What complex, contradictory emotions this simple invitation unleashes! First, you think how nice it would be to dress up and go out, just like that with your husband, alone. Then you think that you are now down to one sitter, who can't stay late on week nights. You curse yourself for not researching new sitters. Then you feel a flash of irritation that your husband, so intimate with every cranny of your domestic life, somehow always forgets that "getting a sitter" in fact means "phoning Irene." He knows perfectly well who the sitter is and what her conditions are. Why this innocent query, this dangling invitation, this *problem* that you now must solve?

Minutes ago, you were looking forward to getting into bed with a book. Now you face bitter disappointment because the hurdle of the Sitter stands between you and a festive night out. Your husband has inadvertently resuscitated old versions of yourself, the person who would ride a bicycle at midnight to a bar. If he were truly romantic, you think, he would have researched a new sitter — test-driven by a close friend — and then picked up the phone. This would be the conversation.

"Darling! I hope your black dress isn't at the cleaners."

"Why?"

"Because we are going to Sanssouci tonight, with Jack Nicholson, Jodie Foster, and several of the Lakers, in a white stretch, thanks to a screw-up on Warner Brothers' part — "

"Hold it," I interrupt, "we don't have a sitter."

"Ah, but yes, we do, my dove. Gretel is on her way over. She's a pre-med student, she sits regularly for Carol, and Casey met her once at a birthday party."

"You found a sitter . . ." I whisper, feeling a kind of parental lust, some new hormone, course through my body. The black pumps, the dusty, neglected black suede will do.

"Yes," I say into the phone. "Yes I will yes in half an hour, yes, yes."

The Elk on the Stairs

THE MORNING AFTER our night out, I was able to ignore the household mess. It had no hold on me. But by mid-afternoon, I broke down and tidied up. I tidied, and tidied, and as I did, I thought. I admit that I sometimes think of formally testing the limits of oblivion in this household. In what decade will my son roll up his Howard Hughes penny collection? How many weeks will the flaccid, rotting cucumber languish at the back of the fridge? And how big a thing can I leave on the stairs and still be confident that no one will carry it up to the second floor? For instance, what if I left something very, very big on the stairs — a rotting elk carcass in a garment bag, say . . . would anyone notice?

First of all, I should say that I am not neat myself. The top of my dresser looks like a disturbed person's yard sale. The bottom of my shoulder bag could be used to sprout mung beans. I do not consider the eight broken-pointed eye liners on the back of the toilet as clutter. But I reason that no one has to walk over or through the top of the toilet tank, whereas communal space in the house should be everyone's responsibility. The problem is that both Casey and Brian show signs of gender-adaptive perceptual bias — that is, they can find a fishing lure in a crowded drawer, but they have a blind spot when it comes to generic clutter. They have no problem ignoring humidifiers, shoes, jackets, toys, and towering stacks of toilet paper pointedly left on the stairs, awaiting helpful couriers.

Is this target vision the last biological vestige of the ancestral hunter? While stepping over supermarket flyers and drifting baseball cards, they're able to spot casting rods, long-necked beers, bows and arrows, or channel changers without noticing a cantaloupe rind that has taken root on the coffee table. Because they do this so sweetly and with no malice aforethought, it occurs to me that this is not a moral defect, but a genuine disorder. Perhaps they suffer from a form of domestic dyslexia that causes them to read clutter backward, as *decor*. Perhaps their rods and cones just don't register junk mail, bath towels, old batteries, or vacuum cans of tennis balls. And what they can't see, I must pick up.

I suffer from the opposite. Like a fly with ten million eye facets, I see it all — the wads of gum left on lamp bases, the dented Ping-Pong balls hidden in the potpourri, last year's fur-balled tuque wedged behind the sideboard — but I can't act. I clearly see the jar of tomato sauce sprouting mold in the fridge, but a little voice says: Why me? Why should I throw it out? I have a son obsessed with molds and fungi, let him throw it out. I have a husband with a high level of personal hygiene that stops at the door of the fridge. Let him throw it out. (He is reading this now. "That's not fair," he calmly protests, "I clean up a lot." And he does, it's true. He shops, he cleans, he puts the foil things under the stove elements. In countless ways, he is an outstanding life partner. But, still, the mold falls to me. I tell myself that *tidying up* is trivial, but I know this is a lie. Parity stills begins at home.)

So one day, when I stumble over some toys pointedly left on the stairs, I snap, lapsing into a housework hallucination, a dream of revenge. I consult the personal ads of a local tabloid and find someone who will bring me a freshly killed elk, no questions asked. I zip the elk into a garment bag, and with the help of two FedEx men, I drape the carcass on the stairs, like dry cleaning on its way up to the closet. Then I wait.

"Hi, mom, what's the horrible smell?" Casey says when he comes in from school. He detours around the elk and bounds upstairs, shedding jacket, hat, lunch box, and gum wrappers. On the way back, he slides down the elk bag, whooping, and disappears out the front door. Later, Brian comes home zombie-faced from work. He has bought the dinner groceries on the way and my cleaning. I thank him. Then, with his long legs, he steps over the rotting elk and up the stairs. "Have you seen my shin pads?" he asks. (Last hockey game of the season coming up.) They're on the tool bench, I say. He carefully detours around the bag and goes to the basement. So far, my theory holds.

Two days pass. The elk bag has now ballooned grotesquely and is making awful percolating noises, but no one has noticed.

"Have you seen my blue silk tie?" Brian asks. "I have to go to a thing tonight." It's under our pile of clothes on the rocking chair, I reply. This pile, I freely admit, is perhaps fifty-nine per cent mine. My work at home demands frequent changes of promotional T-shirts, matte gold accessories, and bathrobes, after all. Both of us use the other person's uncloseted stuff as permission to add to the mound. He rummages around, finds the tie, and carefully replaces the compost heap of clothing.

"Are you cooking something?" he asks. "There's a smell in the house."

"Of course I'm not cooking," I reply. "What do you think this is, a home?"

I am determined not to crack, so I seal myself into the upstairs office with gaffer's tape and order in pizza. The bloated elk bag now blocks the stairs completely, cutting off access to bathroom and bedrooms. Father and son joke about the "stuff on the stairs," but until it is "taken care of," they are happily camped in the living room. They don't mind using the neighbor's bathroom, and with the doors open the stench isn't too bad.

Then, the unexpected — our paper boy turns out to be an animal rightist. The day he comes around to collect, he notices our hamster gasping on his treadmill, as the fug in the room intensifies. The paper boy calls the Humane Society, who arrive to investigate.

"Sir, you have a very sick hamster, and a rotting elk on your steps," the officer informs my husband, who is watching a Blue

Jays game with a tiny fan trained on his face. Casey, wearing his old asthma nebulizer mask, is watching with him.

"Oh nooo!" Brian cries out. "Nooo! Gruber, you idiot!" He smacks his brow.

"Still tied, is it?" the Humane Society officer says.

"Two-two going into the thirteenth, with two on base. Grab a seat."

The officer sits down and begins rummaging in the popcorn bowl.

"Mom!" Casey calls up the stairs. "It's tied! Two on base!" And just at that moment, the elk explodes, with a terrible ripping, splatting sound. There is silence, and then a great roar from the TV as the Jays win the game. I put on my Walkman and go back to work.

A short while later, I come down to find elk shreds on the curtains and a bit of hoof shrapnel imbedded in the walls. But the steps are clear, the rug is spotless, the floor gleams.

"Something blew up, mom," my son says, wringing out a sponge. "But we took care of it, don't worry."

I am about to gush with patronizing mom-type compliments ("Will you *look* at this place! You guys!"). I am about to wag my finger and say, yeah, well, just don't leave the dirty mop and bucket beside the sink. Instead I turn around and go back up to my office. I began to "let go, and let guys." It's up to them now.

31. Fishing

THE OLDER the child grows, the more lax and played-out the mother becomes. The father acquires a whole new relevance. After years of intensive one-on-one, the mother is busy carving out her autonomy, her uninterrupted phone calls, her life under the same roof as the love-tyrant. But home comes the father, who has a secret weakness for winning at Monopoly. Their one-on-oneness begins in earnest.

In our house, it's been creeping up over the last few years — the mysterious, powerful, low-key, father-son love affair. At four, Brian taught Casey chess and began a thriving game-centric relationship that continues. Board games, with a few exceptions, drive me mad. When playing Junior Trivial Pursuit, I furtively pick the easy questions for him so he will win faster. But Brian enters into the spirit of the game seriously. He likes to play.

When Casey was five, they began "throwing a ball around" outside. This was a revival of the sacred game of "catch" Brian remembers playing with his older brother, Howard, in his own childhood.

Last year he bought Casey a glove. I marveled at its fetishistic shape, a cozy leather canal. On the ritualistic pummeling and working-in of a leather catcher's mitt, I won't comment. But I did notice a new surge of initiative on Brian's part — the driving to Sears, the rejection of the inferior glove I had previously bought along with socks and underwear. "Catch" was serious business.

He and Casey would head off into the back field, an unkempt

triangle of city property, to toss the ball around. Then came the bat. From time to time I would join them, but the sly comments would begin. "I want dad to pitch." "Mom, you take the field." "Look at how mom stands, dad!" And so on. I stayed just long enough to counteract this totally uncalled-for sexism. Then I withdrew, swiftly and happily.

Next, they developed a fast and ruthless method of playing Monopoly. This involved rolling the dice at breakneck speed and tearing around the board as fast as possible, leaving younger children and non-readers in the dust. "It's less boring this way," Brian explained. They established a rhythm and plunked down hotels the way dominoes players slam down their dominoes. They were doing the Monopoly dance. They also played to the bitter end — bankruptcy, and mercilessness and gloating on the winner's part. The amassing of property and triumph over the weak seemed to come naturally to my son. I thought back to Brian's extensive rock collection in his youth and pondered whether acquisitiveness could be a genetic trait. (I do not consider the halter tops that date back to 1957 in my closets hoarding in the same sense.)

After years of my being the number-one parent, paged in the middle of the night or in sickness, Brian was coming up fast on the inside.

On the odd occasions when I was out of the house, or even out of town, the two of them would settle into a chatty, amiable relationship based, as far as I could tell, on the exchange of worldly information and the telling of jokes. Whereas I was more in the habit of carving out my own privacy while knocking around the house with Casey — I would read beside him, while he drew — he and Brian related head-on and embarked on ambitious schemes together. They enjoyed each other's company. "Oh right, dad, very funny," Casey would snort through his nose to some elaborate pun on Brian's part.

Our disciplinary styles have always differed. Brian is both more patient and more authoritarian. He considers me lax in the area of household discipline, which is true. Whatever amuses Casey and stops short of fatal injury is fine with me when I'm on the phone, for instance. I let him slide down the banister. I brought him a whip that he likes to crack in the dining room. Sometimes he dangles from the banister by this whip, like a rock climber. As long as it doesn't involve fire or live animals, he can do anything that keeps him happy and out of my hair in the course of a long day home with me. But sometimes Brian walks in at six, or seven, or nine, sees him Threatening the Furniture, and intervenes. This immediate clamp-down inevitably results in more trouble than whatever Casey was doing in the first place. It instigates a power struggle. Brian's response to this would be that I let Casey get away with murder. I do, but only after long, conscientious hours of saying no all day long.

Then something magical happened this summer. We rented a summer cottage, and they became obsessive about fishing. It's the biggest male cliché going, but I'm convinced that fishing made them fall in love. There's nothing phonily macho about this fishing business, either. A long and luminous tradition of fishing literature attests to the way in which fishing feeds the imagination.

They were out on the lake in the canoe every night, the two of them. They cast their hooks through the skin of the calm lake and imagined fish. For an hour of stillness, they imagined what the bottom of the lake was like; they imagined where the bass might be lurking, and then they cast hopefully in the direction of their desire.

The cottage was four hours from Toronto, and the family who owned it and spent their summers next door had outfitted the place with every kitchen utensil ever made, from melon baller to cherry pitter. There were bookshelves full of perfect summer reading, from Grey Owl to a biography of Priscilla Presley. There were three different editions of Monopoly (British, American, and Canadian) and framed native prints on the walls. A ginger-bread family cottage, a diorama of domesticity. The only organized activity, apart from my furtive trips into "town" — a marina and two stores four kilometers away — was fishing. This took place sometimes in the morning before breakfast, but always in the evening, after dinner.

The two of them would baste themselves in bug repellent, get the bait out of the fridge and take the tackle — a treasure trove of lures that reminded me of earrings — down to the dock. We had the use of an old wooden rowboat, still seaworthy, and an aluminum canoe. Casey had mastered the etiquette of not hooking your boat-mate. He had learned how to put the worms on the hook, and how to take the hook out of the transparent mouths of the small rock bass and throw them back. Most amazing, he learned to be quiet on the water, as they sat in the canoe, casting, handing the bait can back and forth, and concentrating on the task at hand.

If they caught a good one, they came back elated, ecstatic even. If they caught nothing, or the line got fouled, or the fish weren't nibbling, they came back flat and somber. Each night was different. There was a "hole," a small, elusive lucky trough, that they headed for each time. As soon as they left the cottage, I was happy to be alone, but before they came back in, I was ready to go find them. They would sit out by a point of land until it was so deep into twilight I would come down on the dock and let my voice echo over the water to them. I didn't want them to get caught out there by darkness. I had those dreary mother thoughts, while they were out there, imagining fish.

Soon they switched from worms to live leeches, available only in a town a half-hour's drive away, a trip Brian made every other day. There was much discussion of these leeches. Brian decided that because the leeches had a hole at one end and a sucker at the other, they were "cuter" and much more human, as it were, than worms. One night I went out with them in the boat as they pursued this leech talk.

"Leeches have real personality," Brian said.

"They kind of look nice on the hook, don't they, dad?" Casey ventured. They gazed at their undulating leeches, at home in the water despite the hook through one end. "They look almost happy."

"The trouble with worms is that basically they drown," Brian explained. "You're just dragging around a dead worm. Leeches live in the water."

"Until a fish eats them," I pointed out.

"Don't look at the leeches, mom, you won't like them."

I made a show of being absolutely unflustered by the animal life on the end of the hooks. I put a few writhing worms on the hooks for him, not with any great love of the act. Any fisherman who says worms feel no pain can't read body language.

"Leeches seem to move with intelligence," Brian enthused. "And they get big, and small, and stuff."

"I see," I said. "They get big, and then small." Sarcastic little grin on my face. The phallic subtext of fishing has not been lost on writers from Pliny on down.

"So," I went on, "you paddle out until you find the 'hole', you put a leech down into the big wet lake, and if you're lucky, the worm magically 'gets big', and ends up inside a long, firm fish that flops out of the water."

"Go ahead, reduce everything to sex," Brian said.

"Now I see why they call it fly fishing," I said.

*   *   *

While I felt it was my duty to make fun of this hierarchy of boneless, swelling things, there must be something to it. Sperm are little black wrigglers who hope to hook into something bigger, the wayward, shore-hugging ovum. There is so much dumb luck involved in fishing, in which the aggression of the hook is swamped in the passivity of the sport. Sperm swim upriver with the same hopeful, outnumbered blindness.

When the fish captures the leech, both are caught, in fact.

And to judge from the patient lingering of father and son on the water, chilled and slapping at mosquitoes, the fishermen are caught by the catching as well. There is more reciprocity here than meets the eye (unless you keep and kill the fish, which involves an unpleasant bonking with a lead weight). Bonking aside, there was something about their attentiveness in the boat that made me think I had underestimated fishing completely.

While dragging the drift-net of metaphor behind me in this fashion, I later came upon new research on sperm behavior and the mechanics of fertilization — which turns out to be a microscopic case of fishing. It seems that the sperm don't valiantly battle upstream until the best and strongest penetrates the passive egg. Both sperm and egg are "caught" in a chain of chemical reactions triggered when the two of them collide. In fact, sperm are indifferent swimmers, but great escape artists — those frantic whiplash movements may be attempts to escape the egg, not dive into it. The closer they come to the egg, the more evasive their movements become. Sound familiar? But given the right chemistry between egg and particular sperm, the ovum "hooks" one sperm and the process of fertilization begins. It may be more accurate to say that the egg catches the sperm: sperm as bait, as lively leech. They look at home on the hook.

This reciprocity makes sense to me — aggression and passivity may be blunt, inadequate terms for a much more intricate dance. If this new research is correct, we will have to shift metaphors and alter our descriptions. The sperm's behavior is not so much divide-and-conquer as search-and-evade. One could use the words fickle or coquettish to describe the way in which the sperm seem to be on the prowl for something — but the minute they run into a ripe egg, they thrash about like slam-dancers, desperately trying to escape. What is it that men want, anyway?

On this particular evening, in the boat, all they wanted to do was catch a fish. Rodless, I was bored, idling my oars as I tried to keep the boat over the "hole." This waiting, baiting, the triple-tiered box of iridescent, light-catching lures was all for that brief tug on the end of the line, when the fish takes the hook. This feeling is unambiguous, thrilling, and surprisingly strong. Every time I caught a fish, I wondered how something so small could have such clear, pure strength. It kept reminding me of another sensation, from another realm. The fish on the line, I eventually realized, felt like the baby, kicking inside you. Or the shocking, life-hungry pull of the baby on the breast. Perhaps fishing is like quickening for men, a long and patient wait for a few electric moments when they feel connected to another life.

I LOVED THE cottage kitchen, with its clean, cracked linoleum and the old Rubbermaid dish rack. There were brass hooks for the crocheted pot-holders, magnetized strips for the myriad knives, extra fuses on the sill, and a card of hand-lettered instructions for lighting the oil furnace on cold mornings. The same thinking had gone into the staging of the cottage as my parents had poured into the grouting and caulking, the bath mats and rubber doorstops of their home. I felt surrounded by somebody else's detailed imaginings, as if I had stepped inside a modest work of art. Here we would be able to play house, with all the necessary props.

I had brought up a reading lamp, just in case. A mistake; there were thirteen lamps in the cottage, divided among the five tiny rooms. Everything was padded. The dining table was protected by a quilted pad, which was then covered by a cloth, under an oilcloth, topped by vinyl place mats. Outside on the deck were boxed geraniums to ward off the raw nature a few steps away. There were lazy Susans in the cupboards and even in the microwave. It was the cloudless land of lazy Susans, delivered intact from my childhood.

On Monday, Brian would go back to the city to work while I stayed up north with Casey and his friend Nicholas. They would play, I would "work." (We maintain the illusion that my work is portable and can be done unobtrusively anywhere. This never happens.) The following week, Brian would play the cottage widow while I went down to the city to work. A friend's teen-age daughter, the accomplished and resourceful Maggie, would come up for a few days to help amuse the boys. On paper it all seemed unusually organized and idyllic.

After Brian left, the first two days were damp and thundery, which I secretly welcomed. This meant we could reconstruct life before TV. Out came the puzzles, the water colors, the drawing assignments. ("Draw five emotions. Begin with anger.") The rain made a pleasant din on the roof. We cut and assembled five complex paper planes from a kit designed by an aeronautical engineer. They flew.

When the rain let up, Casey caught a large toad and kept it in the salad spinner until pressure from Nick and me forced him to let it go. The boys were the best of friends and expressed their fondness for each other by staging daily versions of Wrestlemania that began in rapturous giggles and ended with me using all my strength to pull them apart before someone hit his front teeth on the iron bedstead.

Sometimes they obeyed me, and sometimes they didn't. The days of the omnipotent mother were coming to an end. I could feel their strength and will slowly creeping up on mine.

At eight, I noted, boys are obsessed with butts, farts, dicks, and bad words. Naughtiness of every sort, especially involving body fluids or gases, seems to nourish them in a special way. If Casey wanted to irritate Nick, he would call him "Dickolas" over and over, accompanied by salacious laughter. They were thrilled with the twenty-foot arc of a new water gun I bought them, an Uzi-like device that uses air pressure to send out a blast of water. They used this super-dick to write their names in the dirt, over and over.

At dinner one night, we started fooling around. I was indulgently going on about Kentucky Fried Leeches and so forth — their brand of conversation.

"What if we only knew two words and we had to talk with them?" Casey said. "What if we only knew the words . . . dicky fried?" He dissolved into laughter. Then he began to burble "Dicky fried, dicky fried, dicky fried," inflecting it like a regular conversation. This sort of thing can be irritating after a few days without adult conversation. But deep in my past, I remembered the intoxication of being this far gone on a summer's night, with your best friend laughing so hard her mouthful of milk goes up her nose. The dicky-fried monologue continued, and Nicholas looked to me, slit-eyed, for some gauge as to how this joke was going over.

"Okay, knock it off, guys, you'll choke," I said without much conviction as I forked up the boring brown rice and red cabbage I was determined to eat while a cottage widow.

"Dicky fried, dicky fried, dicky fried," Casey sang, barely able to get the words out for a champagne geyser of laughter. My mouth twitched, the boys slid down their chairs. With my head buried in my arms, I laughed weakly while the two of them fell about snorting and hiccupping.

*   *   *

The construction and deployment of missiles took up much of our days, between wrestling and bouts of butt-talk. Casey was big on his bow and arrow this summer. The wooden bow with the red leather hand guard was my own girlhood bow, inherited from my brother — the thing was fifty years old, and even with kitchen twine, it still worked perfectly. Casey used one tattered old blunt-nosed arrow over and over.

One day, on a rain-excursion to the nearest town, we were browsing through a sports store when Casey came upon a professional crossbow, and caressed it. A mustachioed salesman in an orange hunting vest came along and demonstrated the crossbow. Then he showed us his selection of real arrows. Casey tested the metal tips, and I had another flashforward: I'm reading on the dock, when I hear a muffled *thok* from behind the cottage, after which I drive to the phone booth.

"Hello, Pat? It's amazing, but the arrow passed right through Nick's rib cage and out again . . ."

After scouring the town for toy arrows to no avail, I gave in and bought the real ones. Much serious talk of weaponry and sudden death from me on the way home. We made a target out of a large pizza box and set it up behind the cottage. I drew lines in the dirt and made rules about the proper mounting of arrows and the importance of standing behind the person shooting, not in front. Then I did the dishes while staring out the window as they shot their arrows. They were good. Casey took fascistic delight in enforcing the rules. Embrace barbarism, I thought to myself, and there's always the chance you can squeeze a little civilization out of its rituals.

A day or two later, I gave out the art assignments. "Draw five emotions," I barked in the mode they preferred. "Begin with joy." Nicholas sweetly drew a figure with his arms around someone else. I looked at Casey's drawing. It was him, a target, a red arrow in the center, with rays of happiness haloing the archer.

"Joy is a bull's eye," he said.

*   *   *

On Friday night Brian arrived buoyant and energized by his time in the city. "You're going to have a great time on your own," he said. Since when is a week of solitary work supposed to be better than a vacation together, I semi-grumbled. "Time alone is great no matter how good your family life is," he said with unusual forthrightness (the result itself of time alone).

I was careful not to prune or tamper with this new outside energy of his. He had gone to the office, he said, "seen people" and "run into friends," dined out alone, left his dishes any old where in the house, sprawled across the king-sized bed. I doubted, but never eliminated the possibility, that much else happened. He would be much happier and more guiltily manic, I decided, if anything resembling infidelity had transpired.

But he had his own contours back, and that was fine with me. Beside him I felt shapeless and unsexed by my days and nights with the Dicky-fried Boys. It felt exotic to relate to another adult, who arrived with beer and gossip from town. "Who?" Casey kept interrupting. *"What* about Paul?" "Nobody," we'd answer, "nothing."

The week had passed, and I had scarcely done any work at all. Whenever I tried, blimp-thoughts kept crossing my mental screen: did they have their sunblock on, were we out of tuna? It is easy, so easy, to drown in family, inch by cozy inch.

Later on we managed to negotiate the mummified sex that the anti-libidinal Canadian cottage dictates, with its squeaky beds and half partitions. The rest of the weekend was peaceful, and when Monday came, Casey and his father dismissed me with barely a glance. I headed toward the city and my first week alone in the house.

At home a tricky euphoria set in. I felt myself expanding, made light and almost giddy by the freedom at my disposal. There was a deadline to meet but for once work didn't have to be arranged around school or other people's appetites.

But what *did* I want for lunch? I had forgotten. Since I could have anything or go anywhere, what would please me? Locating my true desires was not as easy as I had imagined. Sometimes, when I wasn't locked into work, I felt dangerously light, as if I might blow away like a piece of dandelion fluff.

The first two nights alone, going up to bed, reading, and falling asleep was delicious. The third night, I had a wrench of pity for my son up north, coughing in his sleep. The cottage was damp, and the dampness fed the asthma. I spent twenty minutes worrying about whether Brian would remember to creep in and put on an extra blanket. The cool air coming through my window became directly related in my mind to the clamminess of my son's skin, not to mine.

The fourth night, the bed began to feel too big, and I kept shifting. The skin of me felt thin and taut, like a balloon about to burst. I got up in the morning and fell into work. When I couldn't work any longer, I roamed aimlessly through the house, refusing to unpack. Instead of thinking I had a whole day left to myself, I was thinking, By tomorrow, I'll be there. I flowed out of myself too quickly, I almost seemed to hemorrhage. Even the writing turned manic and indiscriminate.

At 4 p.m. the next day, the phone rang. It was Casey, calling from the fly-buzzed booth down by the marina.

"How was the water slide in Haliburton?" I asked sweetly, maternally.

"It sucked," he said. Ah yes. That son. Then Brian got on the phone.

"Well, Hammy, uh, went up to the sky last night," he said without sarcasm, as Casey stood by. Hammy is one of several proudly non-creative pet names passed down through the Jackson family. He is — was — Casey's hamster.

Hammy was about a hundred and sixty-two in human years and had recently been observed making a real effort to curl up and die. Even his bones seemed lighter whenever I picked him up and felt the curve of his sharp little spine.

The week before, Brian had brought him up to the cottage in the car, with a towel over the cage. When I lifted him out, he looked like a shipwrecked rat. The water bottle had leaked, and the trip had left him wedged between his yellow plastic ranch-style house and the treadmill of his youth, the one he no longer used. I took him out, toweled him dry, and noted how stiff his hind legs were. Even such a tiny imminent death pinches the heart in a particular way.

"God, the grampster's almost dead," I said to Brian at the time. We had re-christened him this in light of his advanced years.

"But he always comes back," Casey said blithely, more interested in rummaging through the new groceries than resuscitating his pet. I put dry shavings in the hamster's cage, and with the sun on him he fluffed up again. The next day, we let him out on the ground under the big pines where he perked up, flipping pine needles around his head. Then he burrowed down into the dirt. The year before, he would have waddled off in pursuit of some dim memory of freedom. But this summer he delved into the ground, balled himself up, and heaved his breath in and out. Hammy's days were clearly numbered.

"We left him on the porch last night and it was a pretty cold night," Brian said on the phone. I could hear Casey in the background. "He was frozen stiff in the morning!"

"Yeah, we thought he was dead but Casey took him into bed and brought him around. He seemed okay. But this morning he was really dead."

"Gee," I said. I felt an absurd crest of sadness. What you care for and feed every day you love a little, against reason.

"Put Casey on."

"Hammy died today," Casey said in a funereal but palpably insincere voice.

"I know. That's too bad. But, you know, he was the oldest hamster in the world,"

"No, he wasn't, mom." Wrong again.

"At least he died in the woods," I said brightly.

"He died in his cage, mom."

"Well . . ."

"But we had a funeral," he said, with a little more animation. "We all went to our rooms and put on something black."

"Brian too?" I imagined the owners next door watching through the curtains, convinced they had leased their cottage to a satanic cult.

"Yeah. He played the drum, and Maggie said the twenty-third psalm. We made a tombstone and everything." I had a vision of Brian in a black "Terminator II" T-shirt, playing the death march, while Maggie and Casey inserted a Tetley's tea box into the ground.

"Well, that was nice."

"We buried him really deep, and made a cross. Here's dad."

"I hear you had quite the funeral." Assumed irony this time instead of assumed sincerity.

"This was definitely a first in hamster history. The only thing missing was a riderless horse."

"Was Casey sad?"

"Yes. There were lots of tears. Then he got into the whole funeral thing."

"I can imagine."

"I have to hang up," Brian said. "We have cones and they're melting all over."

I put the phone down. Now there was no further to go. My dear, kind, too-mute husband had mastered the pet funeral. His mind, too, had become colonized by thoughts of life preservers, Lyme tics, and melanoma. I felt grateful and relieved to know that death was going along so smoothly without me.

coming

through

33. Sickness

THE RULE with children is: never say you are out of the woods. Just as you are congratulating yourself on three straight months without antibiotics, you will be struck down again. Hubris loves families. Complacency will be punished. The Old Testament lives on in viruses that take root the day you book a non-refundable flight.

Last week I went to pick up Casey at his after-school day care. The director, a woman who is warm with kids in a way that doesn't make me grind my teeth, came over to chat. "Gee, Casey's asthma is a lot better this year," she said. I looked around in panic for something made of wood to knock on. Nothing is made of wood any more.

"I'm going to pretend you didn't say that." We observed him diving down the orange plastic tube at the top of the playground, hatless, coat flapping, in the raw November air. It was six weeks until Christmas. He had been motoring along with a tiny cough for about a week, but I was "on top of it." So I told myself.

The thing about managing a chronic illness like asthma — and manage is the verb they use — is that you must live with it without turning it into your personal adversary. Control comes down to tedious discipline (around preventive care or the administration of drugs) and acceptance of this flaw, this heart-bruising imperfection in your child. But even acceptance, once achieved, is fickle. As soon as your child gets better, you begin to think you just invented those nightmare dawns. Sooner or later the dark hours are erased, like the pain of childbirth. Then the illness comes back and brings you to your knees once again, and you remember what you tried to shut out for a while: he is like you, fallible and mortal.

But I do my best to disguise my fears; it's bad enough to have asthma without catching your mother's anxiety, too. When a friend in Freudian analysis suggested that Casey's asthma was probably just an expression of my own mothering neuroses — what, me neurotic? — I wanted to throw a bust of Melanie Klein at him. Emotions don't cause asthma. They can trigger attacks, but then so do the little turds of dust mites. Symbiotic as we are, Casey's asthma never seems wired to his own moods or fears, let alone mine. There is a genetic predisposition to asthma, and allergies are usually involved, too. He has both. Analysands, enough of mother-blame.

Shortly after our upbeat chat in the school yard, Casey's cough dug in and began to wake him up more often at night. He wasn't really sick, but I kept him home — a crafty preventive measure, I thought. I was on top of this! I increased his asthma drugs in the approved aggressive fashion, moving in with the new localized anti-inflammatory steroids, the ones that are not supposed to turn him into a dwarf, absolutely not.

At night he started to throw up the clear mucus that asthma generates. I took him off milk products. The word "mucus" began to figure in my thoughts and phone conversations. Friends were those willing to discuss the hues and consistencies of bodily fluids. This narrowed my social life considerably.

For the first week or two of illness, we were quite enterprising. We had our own twelve-step recovery program. Here is a list of what we did.

1. Ripped ads out of old Consumers Distributing catalogues to paste into his already voluminous album of Possible Christmas Gifts.
2. Sent a fax to a friend's beagle.

3. Got out the Christmas decorations and looked at them. Sewed Christmas stockings out of unsuitable blue corduroy.
4. Made very rudimentary cookies (pressed, not baked).
5. Looked at bread mold (easily harvested from bread box) under the microscope. Left agar gel in saucers to grow yet more mold.
6. Phoned grandmas one and two.
7. Erected Death Ramp for micro-machine cars on Ping-Pong table.
8. Planned to glue all loose photos into photo albums. Stopped after two pages.
9. Phoned Brian at work. (With some sarcasm, in my case.)
10. Went to the video store ("hello again!") and rented *Charlotte's Web* and *The Adventures of Baron von Munchausen.*
11. Rode exercise bike with headphone plugged into TV until succumbed to coughing fit.
12. Awoke in the middle of the night coughing, watched half-hour infomercial for Miracle Blades, guaranteed sharp for life, will let you create radish roses and palm trees out of zucchinis, comes with zester and tool for creating potato curls. I was so grateful to see Casey calmed and mesmerized by the Miracle Blade that I took my credit card out and ordered some. Nine weeks later, they arrived, thin and sharp and nasty as razors.

*   *   *

On his third week home, the first lash of winter arrived. The furnace, a dragon full of old spores and mouse dander, clicked on for the first time, and unseen allergens danced through the ducts. I don't especially trust the furnace. Its blue pilot flame is the heart of the mystery of the house, the id in the basement. Casey's cough got worse. I did the usual dreary anti-allergen things — wet-mopped the floors, swathed the mattresses in plastic. I paid The

Bay three hundred and fifty dollars to come and clean out the ducts, and two men arrived in a truck with air tubes that inflate into something that looks like Bart Simpson's brush cut. Afterward, one of them showed me a bag of dirt, ostensibly the fruit of our ducts, but perhaps just a single, sacred bag that he drives around from house to house to reassure mothers that nothing bad will ever happen to their children. So I had given our house a high colonic, swept the dirty world out of our sleeping chambers as best I could.

It's like a little animal, asthma. The beast has its active spells, and cat naps, and bouts of night-time scavenging. Just before bed, the cough steps up. It's like the ghouls leaving the graveyard at sundown, the way something tries to exit from his body every night at the same time. He tries to sleep, he coughs, the drugs he takes to dilate the airways make his heart race and keep him awake even when he's tired. Then he falls asleep, deeply. An hour later, an expulsive cough propels him upright in bed. I stand in the hall, waiting to see if more will follow, or if the paroxysm will pass and he can fall moaningly back to sleep.

Near dawn, it comes alive again. If it's bad, he'll wake up with a whitish mask around his mouth. We'll go to the doctor to make sure it's not pneumonia, which it isn't, this time. He won't complain, it's not like the near-suffocation of a severe asthma attack. I'll put my ear to his mouth to listen for the high whistling wheeze. I am like a bird watcher trained to distinguish between small nuances of bird song. There are harmless, on-the-mend rattles, and moist bubblings in the chest that signal something worse. I can tell the dry, innocuous-sounding pneumonia hack from the noisy, grandstanding but mechanical bronchitis. This time, there was something going on besides the asthma; I just didn't know what it was. But I always recognize the point when things are going to get worse before they get better.

I hate the intimacy of my knowledge and can never suppress the trapped, anxious feeling that comes with this intuition. My dread is double-sided: I know I'm going to have to give over to mothering again, and that I will succumb to the minor despair that goes along with "managing" the asthma. I am responsible for him.

One night I walk into his room, kneel beside his bed, and look at his face. He has been sweating, his dark brown hair lies in wet strands across his forehead. He sleeps propped up on three pillows, crookedly. He draws a breath, then he seems not to breathe at all. He clears his throat, draws another breath. I tell myself we're lucky that his asthma is not acute, not yet. But those fickle, ragged breaths unnerve me. Brian never imagines he might lose him. I do.

Just as I cover him and turn to go back to bed, he wakes up and coughs violently, as if a beast inside his chest is trying to get out. My hoping is over. I tilt over into nursing mode, a surrender to service.

34. Bodily Fluids

THE MYSTERY illness turned out to be a terrible case of whooping cough that dragged on for six months. After seven weeks of it, Casey began to call himself Mucusman. Mucusmom had lost ten pounds. We never went anywhere without our silver throw-up bowl and a box of Kleenex, because every time he went into a spasm of coughing, roughly every forty minutes during the night and twice as often during the day, it was a riveting event, it was near-asphyxiation, it was . . . the river of mucus. Stay with me here, I need to talk this out.

The bowl was about six inches wide, stainless steel, and curved on the bottom. Our more usual throw-up utensil was a big empty yogurt container. But this human Krazy Glue his body produced was thick, thicker than eggwhite, more tenacious than semen. It clung to plastic surfaces, hardened onto dishes, and turned tissues into papier-mâché. The paroxysms of coughing always ended in a terrible, brief strangulation as he tried to get the web of stuff up his windpipe and out.

Whooping cough is the Geraldo Rivera of coughs — tacky, moist, exhibitionist. The spasms of coughing are a scary sight, and surprisingly noisy, too, a tiny Dresden bombing in your own living room. At least, I thought, he's not an infant any more, with a windpipe the size of a pencil. Whooping cough can be fatal in infants. But the fact that my son had the build of a small halfback did not entirely comfort me.

The disease seemed to live in his windpipe like a rabid rodent, slumbering away, then roused to viciousness without warning. About an hour after he fell asleep, he would be launched awake by a violent chain of coughs, seven, eight, nine to a breath, ending with the eponymous whoop — the sound of air being sucked back into grateful lungs. Usually he would throw up, too. I would leap to his side to cheerlead and work the bowls. I began to live entirely in the present tense.

*　　*　　*

It's 1 a.m. three weeks into the siege. Calm, for the past two hours. I'm asleep. Then the cough strikes, the way a guard dog lunges barking against a fence. I whip into Casey's bedroom, where he is hunched over, flipping his hand, which is what he does when he can't speak, meaning "Bowl! Bowl!" I put the bowl under his chin. The cough is racketing through him like a seizure.

My hand is on his back, willing the stuff up like mercury in a thermometer.

"Get it out. Get it all out. Good, good for you."

He strains forward, his hand curling into a claw with the effort of the coughing. The veins in his temple stand out, the tiny capillaries in his eyes burst, his face turns a dusky red. Alarm, the old respiratory alarm, courses through my body. He is working it up now, he is the yoga of mucus. A string of the stuff, like clear gelatin, hangs out of his mouth. The cough stops, his breathing suspends, and he turns still, concentrating. His eyes roll back a little in his head. Then he delivers it, like an exorcism, into the silver bowl, and with a shuddery intake of air he falls back into the pillows.

"Oh mom," he says. "Mom." He sinks immediately into a peaceful sleep. Forty or fifty minutes later, the same scene will be repeated.

Like someone who has just had three cups of coffee injected into her veins, I teeter back to bed and wonder whether to wait for the next round or try to sleep, hitting REM just in time to be snatched awake again.

*   *   *

This is whooping cough, or pertussis (or the more euphemistic "parapertussis" if they're not sure) — the P in the childhood DPT inoculations. The fact is, the vaccine offers only partial protection. It's still possible to contract a mild case of it, and for some reason even inoculated children occasionally come down with full-blown whooping cough. Mini-epidemics swing round, every few years. Casey had had his DPT shots but we decided to skip the last booster; the shots always made him sick for a week and inevitably triggered a bout of asthma. The point is not that whooping cough is any better or worse than a dozen other ghastly illnesses that children get. It's gruesome, but rarely fatal. The point is that any incurable disease still comes as a surprise to parents.

It doesn't occur to us that only two generations ago, it was normal for babies to die of diphtheria, scarlet fever, and pneumonia. It was an ordinary case of the flu that sent my father's father to bed in 1919, where TB killed him two years later. It's only the last fifty years that have made us complacent about childhood disease, as if an anti-mortality vaccine is right around the corner. I associate this foolish optimism with the era of the birth-control pill; for a while there, it seemed nobody had to get old, or unnecessarily pregnant. Our one perfect child would never have green snot running down his face for an entire winter.

There was no need to make any deals with Nature at all. Instead, we sank our trust into Amoxil and Ceclor and vaccinations. Or else we refused the boosters and brewed up herbs, gargled Echinacea. Thoughts of mortality were now reserved for AIDS. When your own flesh and blood comes down with something *incurable*, it seems scandalous, like a tornado ripping through a summer picnic.

My generation did a good job of bricking our bodies in with a wall of contraceptives, anti-aging creams, parenting tomes, and amniocentesis, all of which give us the illusion that we're in control — of our fertility, our children's health, the aging process. But it takes only a nick in one chromosome or a night when the thermometer goes up over 104 degrees to bring the wall tumbling down.

First, you get mad at your fallible doctor, for not being able to cure everything. Then you get mad at the cool resignation with which the nurses in Emerg chalk your child's name up on the board, number 14, two hours down the line. You blame yourself, for making him go to school when he said his throat was sore. And naturally you are furious with your partner for not knowing exactly when to make the dash to the hospital, or where to park. The horrible truth is that everything doctors know is not enough, and sickness can take over, like a military coup, at any time. The democracy of health is an illusion.

It took weeks to even pin down the diagnosis. Everyone assumed it was bronchitis, or a virus, or stubborn asthma. Then my GP sent us to a specialist, the local King of Asthma. I took Casey, the bowl, and the box of Kleenex to his building, where we rode up in a crowded elevator. He coughed. The other people in the elevator moved against the wall and looked at me as if I were a madwoman. We walked down the hall, the sound ricocheting against the walls like a squash ball.

Ten per cent of the population have asthma; half of them appeared to be shoehorned into this specialist's waiting room. Finally, the doctor's door opened. "That's whooping cough, all right," he said smilingly before he even examined Casey. "I've seen lots of it this fall, it rolls around every three years like clockwork. All you can do is keep the asthma under control, and sit it out."

This was strangely cheering. A clear diagnosis always comes as a relief at first. We went home, assuming we were halfway through the typical six-week prognosis. But a few nights later, his asthma took a bad turn and we drove him to the hospital. "By the way," I said to one of the nurses, "he has whooping cough, too." She gave me a baleful look. "This could last for four months, you know," she said. "Oh, don't say that!" I chided her merrily. I assumed this was mere sadism on her part.

A friend later revised this estimate. "Six months," she hissed. "Robert coughed for six months straight." No, no, surely not in this case, I said, but it turned out to be true.

I began to see the wisdom and logic of personifying illness, the way native cultures do. The whooping cough had a distinct life span, like a creature that evolves from larva to worm to some winged thing. It also had a daily rhythm — quiet in mid-afternoon, hectic at 9 p.m. then again at 11, and 4 a.m., with many micro-bouts in between. I arranged our life around this rhythm. All this time, I repeated my mantra: not fatal, not fatal, rarely fatal. I thought of what it would be like to care for a child with cystic fibrosis, or any number of heartbreaking things. This was a manageable, passing crisis, but anything that attacks a child's breathing triggers instinctive alarm, and there's nothing you can do about it. I felt embarrassed by the depth of my anxiety. But it's there for a reason.

Around this time, Brian had to go to L.A. for eight or nine days on business. When he left, I clung to him and told him I was afraid that things were going to get worse before they got better. He tried to reassure me. I trembled. I was in the grip of premonition. When sickness takes root in a child's body, a little worm begins to grow in the mother's body, a larval fear. I felt infected myself by something that had no locus yet.

I kept reading the little paragraph in Spock over and over, like a catechism. "Six weeks," it said. "In most cases." Six weeks had seemed like a life sentence when I first read it. Now that sounded optimistic. "Sometimes the face will turn blue. If this happens, get them to a hospital immediately." I watched Casey's face as he coughed. Pink, red, deep bluish-red . . . but never blue, never completely blue. But they didn't mean sky blue, did they?

What did a blue face look like? I decided to wait until Casey felt scared himself, which would be my signal to do something. In the meantime, the noise, the sense of assault, the collection and transportation of bodily fluids kept us both busy.

Antibiotics eliminate the contagious factor, but don't necessarily alter the course of the disease. Before we knew what he had, a friend came over to visit, and in due time he got whooping cough, too. So did his mother and his sister. It destroyed their Christmas. I felt terrible, but everyone had reassured me at the time that he wasn't infectious. I had my doubts and should have listened to them. Never ignore your instincts, and never allow anyone else to ignore your instincts either.

But once he was no longer contagious, Casey's friends would come over to visit and watch. In the middle of a Nintendo game, he would go into his hurling-up routine, one hand on the bowl, one on the Nintendo controls. Some stopped coming. Who could blame them?

Meanwhile, Brian was interviewing movie stars and doing research on a piece about theme parks — i.e., he was going to Disneyland. I was as tolerant of this as I could be, under the circumstances. How was Casey doing, he asked, how were things at home. I replied in a voice of styrofoam, my empty mother's voice. Things were not great at all, I said, things were bad. He offered to fly back. No, I said, I will let you know when that becomes necessary. Not much more was said.

Casey and I now spent the nights down in the living room, because that way he could sleep sitting up on the couch, which helped clear his chest. I bedded down in a sleeping bag, more or less under the coffee table. We were also closer to the Home Shopping Channel and the hair-product infomercials that only run at 3 a.m.

I was now starting to resemble one of those see-through Invisible Women, with the red nervous system that lights up like a tree. I felt flayed. Casey was mostly unscarred by it all, although it's hard work, to cough around the clock. It left his ribs sore, and his eyes so bloodshot he looked like somebody in a bad photograph. He ate this and that, but solids wouldn't stay down. And each night was just a tiny bit worse than the last.

I never knew whether the asthma was getting worse underneath the whooping cough, so I kept dragging him into Emerg. One night I drove him to the door of the hospital. I had to park the car, so I asked him to walk through the automatic doors and stand inside, where he could wait for me. He took his silver bowl. He walked gently, so as not to stir the beast inside. But the cold air got him going, and I watched him stand still, his shoulders curved like an old man's. He leaned one hand on a pillar and steeled himself against the force of the cough. Over in her cockpit, the triage nurse eyed him with a small glint of compassion. He furtively threw up and looked around, embarrassed to be in public. Then he carried his silver bowl over to the admissions desk and sat down, tucking his chin into the high collar of his winter coat, ready to wait.

As we went through admissions, I kept saying "pertussis." They looked at us dubiously and put us in our own quarantined stall.

"Isn't this nice?" I chirped. "We have our own room and our own gurney this time."

The only way you can truly diagnose whooping cough is with a sputum culture — charming phrase — and anyway, what's the point, since there's no cure. So they wrote "pertussis?" on our charts and went away. One doctor, then another came in, talking to me in that weary, opaque manner that interning residents have as they work their way down a list of worst-case scenarios. At the very least, they decided, his asthma was out of control. They gave him not one but three successive Ventolin masks. This let him breathe more easily, although the cough attacks persisted. I was proud of how he handled himself, of how brave he was. Then the pediatrician on call, an elegant East Indian woman, came in and said he ought to go on prednisone, an oral steroid, for four or five days.

This was bad news. Oral steroids are anti-inflammatory drugs, very effective for asthma, but with extended use they have nasty side effects. They can stunt bone development and all sorts of unpleasant things. Four days was nothing to worry about. I wouldn't notice anything, the doctor said. But still, it signaled an escalation.

Then the thing happened that always happens. I began to hope that the prednisone might cure everything, and that he wasn't very sick at all. I put my faith in the drug.

We went home. The hated steroid did control the asthma, which only served to clarify and isolate the whooping cough. I was now administering ten different drugs in the course of a day: bronchodilators, inhaled steroids, oral steroids, decongestants, antibiotics, as well as assorted supplements, Vitamin C, zinc, and any herbal potion I thought might pamper his immune system. I kept track of it all on a little pad of paper. I became whooping cough's secretary.

There was one terrible night when Casey lost his personality. It was the only time I have seen him overtaken, unable to muster his usual humor. He was so exhausted that whenever he was awakened by the cough, he would glower at me or mutely kick me in the leg. In response to this I made a face, a kind of groveling, pouting face. We didn't speak, we just made these mask-faces at each other. It was the end of five weeks of being up night after night, as if someone had roughly shaken us awake over and over: a fine strategy for torture. I spent the day getting soup and liquids into him, and then getting most of it back in bowls and yogurt jars. It's amazing how much effluvia the human body can produce. A cycle had taken root and we simply had to follow the curve of it.

It scared me. Early on, when I wasn't sure what was going on, and I thought he might just seize up and stop breathing, I phoned people. One night I phoned four friends. Three had their answering machines on, a fourth didn't answer — phone unplugged to sleep. I was furious at the way people could disappear like this. What kind of fucking community do I live in, anyway, I thought, where you can't get a voice on the line at night? I felt absurdly betrayed. I had my doctor's home phone and her pager number, too, but there was, after all, nothing she could do. Brian called every night, subdued and worried. I alternately reassured and punished him. Sometimes I phoned the all-night information number at the hospital just to hear the night nurse's voice. I didn't think I could stand to hear Casey turn himself inside out for one more night.

Down in the very valley of the illness, once again I faced the thing I had avoided from the beginning: my fear of losing him. I felt there would be some terrible justice, some lesson about the random mutability of life involved, if this gift of a son were to be taken away.

There was another Casey, the brother of a close friend, who had died in his teens. Terrible things did happen to people. I was afraid that the more deeply you loved, the more likely it was that you would have the love snatched away. I wasn't interested in what this revealed about my vexed relationship to happiness. I just kept thinking about how natural death can be, in the scheme of things.

One night it was particularly cold. I was in my usual living-room station, half in, half out of the sleeping bag more or less under the coffee table. Casey slept sitting up, his head tipped over to one side awkwardly. Around his mouth was the familiar white raccoon's mask, the pallor of asthma. Apart from that, he scarcely looked sick at all. I was so tuned in to his body now that I nearly always woke a split second before he began to cough. The attack came, hurtling him forward. I leaped up to reach the bowl and stepped on my glasses, which were on the rug beside me. They shattered. The cough seemed almost to pull him apart from the inside. Afterwards, Casey was upset about my glasses, but I wasn't. I was transparent, only there for him.

"Now you won't be able to drive to the hospital, mom," he said somberly.

Oh, it was pathetic.

The next morning, he was looking worse and acting lethargic. I decided it was time for a daylight excursion to the hospital. If we were in a hospital, I reasoned, close to much sicker people, maybe I could get some perspective on this thing. I was tired of waiting until I came to the absolute end of my resources before asking for help.

So I propped the Gagging One up on the couch, supplied him with all his mucoid accessories, and said I was going out to get the ice off the windshield and warm up the car. I stepped out into the sudden clasp of deep winter air. It was bracing, almost tonic. There was sunlight, for a change, and the fall of snow reflected more light. I had a little surge of well-being, noting all the while how odd it was to feel my mood lift. Then I reached my car and discovered that someone had broken into it. They had smashed the no-draft, reached in and stolen the tape deck and radio. Broken wires dangled out of the cavity in the dashboard. How dully I took all this in. More mundane catastrophe. This was small potatoes, I wanted the thief to know, compared to biological vandalism. Go ahead, smash the other window, take the pant-saver mats while you're at it. What a rush of bitter, anonymous anger I felt at this accretion of bad luck. Had I thrown out a chain letter, not been good enough?

We took a cab to the hospital, and in the course of the day, Casey improved. When we got home, several women friends had come to my rescue. They arrived with beer, dinner, and things for Casey to do, bringing a gust of health and humor through the door. I no longer noticed the mounds of crumpled Kleenex, the home nebulizer with its hospital overtones, the old Raggedy Ann crib quilt I wrapped Casey in on the couch, the camped-in look of the living room. Their presence waved a wand of normalcy over the house for a few hours.

One weekend morning when they came by, the phone rang. It was Brian, logging in for the daily report. Briefly invigorated by the influx of new people, Casey rose up from the couch and went to find something from the basement. Tippily, he made his way down the stairs. Brian was telling me, with all due irony, about Disneyland, about having to take the Dumbo Ride that very morning. Then we heard a terrible sequence of thumps, followed by silence. I dropped the phone, leaving Brian dangling as he listened to three women screaming, and raced down the stairs where I saw Casey still heaped on the concrete floor, unable to breathe.

"Breathe!" I shouted.

My horrified friends watched from the top of the stairs. He gasped, and the breath came back. Everything kept shattering, shattering like this, I thought, rocking and murmuring to him in this amazingly normal voice.

"What are you trying to do, scare me to death?"

"I'm okay, I'm okay," he said, seeing the alarm in my face anyway. He shivered and we clung.

"Somebody get the phone." Brian was still hanging there, wondering if a gas line had erupted and his entire family had been wiped out. Judith answered the phone and gave him the latest health bulletin. He told me later that he aged about seven years between the time I dropped the phone and she picked it up. There was an eruption of faintly hysterical laughter in the kitchen, and more than a few Disneyland jokes.

"We're on a sort of Dumbo Ride of our own," I said to Brian. He sounded as if he were in mild shock. That got him, I thought meanly. Now he knows.

I led Casey to the couch. The fall had scared him, but his eyes looked all right. The color, what little he had in the first place, was coming back to his face.

I poured myself a stiff scotch, one of the things I now did in mid-afternoon to stop the march of my thoughts.

"God, this is a horror show," someone said.

"Isn't it?" We laughed. I cursed my husband, who would be home the next day. He was standing at an outdoor phone booth in California, heartsick, helpless and punished by distance.

AS CHRISTMAS loomed, Casey slowly improved but was still housebound. Brian came home from L.A. and did massive penance. Holiday plans proceeded as usual; the juggernaut of Christmas will not be stopped.

One night I left Brian home dealing with the ebb and flow of fluids while I went out tree-hunting. One of these years, I thought, we must switch to an artificial tree. Somewhere in the back of my mind was a scrap of knowledge about pine trees and allergies, but Casey had never had any problems with trees.

I pulled into one of those fly-by-night corner lots and a very nice man discussed stand strategies with me, the merits of scotch pine vs. spruce, and tricks with sugar to prolong freshness. Which one is best for allergies, I inquired, just to be sure.

"Oh, you better ask the old man about that," he said. I looked around. No old man in sight.

"He's in the trailer." I opened the door to a large sort of van and inside I found the very soul of a tree farmer — a fat ruddy man in a tuque and a maroon sweater, dipping a tea bag up and down in a mug of hot water. He was wearing galoshes and his stomach showed.

"Is it asthma?" he asked professionally. I nodded yes.

"You'll be better off with spruce, then. My daughter's asthmatic. It goes much easier with spruce. Is your house cold?"

"Oh, we keep it cool!"

"Give it plenty of water and aspirin — Bufferin, if you have it."

Feeling as if I had just visited an eye, ear, and nose specialist, I closed the door and picked out a nice seven-foot spruce, symmetrical and bushy. The good-hearted helper humped the tree to my car and packed it into the hatch-back like somebody stuffing a turkey.

By the time I got home, I was feeling pretty Christmasy. The tree went into the wretched tree stand like magic, for the first time in memory. It was straight, it didn't wobble, each side looked great. I looked at my husband. We couldn't believe our luck. Later that night, I even got to race off to a magazine office party, while father and son decorated the tree.

When I came home, the tree was up and tenderly trimmed. I had no urge to move the angels or anything. My son was ecstatic, leaping about, coughing only a little, scarcely more than usual. I dosed him with his asthma drugs and put him to bed.

An hour later, he sat up like a vampire going on duty, whooped, coughed, spun, and expectorated in a classic asthma attack. Mucus began to pour out of his nose and rise up his throat like the Bay of Fundy tides. After another binge of this at l a.m., I gave him the vile, wicked cough suppressant, which only made him more talkative and speedy.

"Let's go ice-fishing this winter!" he said when he woke up at two. Then he burbled on about the exact dimensions of a tree house he planned to construct. He drew a diagram, with arrows. He swooned back into the pillows. At 4 a.m., another assault.

Normally the cough went into hibernation by midday. But not this time. Hack, hack, hack. My eyes swiveled toward the spruce, our best tree yet. I opened the newspaper, where, spookily, I read an item about the problem with asthmatics and Christmas, about how mold in the tree bark was thought to be the culprit. Over in the corner, needles fell to the floor with a soft ping. I looked at Casey, box to the right, bowl to the left, and I knew. I knew as dolphins feel the tsunami coming, as small rodents scurry for cover before the first tremors of an earthquake. Our Christmas tree was poisoning him.

I didn't despair, I took action. I phoned The Bay and reserved the last of the non-pink artificial trees. Then I snatched the ornaments off our tree like a hairdresser pulling clips off a client and dragged the son-of-a-bitch out the sundeck door, shedding needles all the way. I refused to recycle it. I was going to let it die a slow death.

Off we went with the bowl, to the doctor, and then to pick up our new plastic tree. I was full of crazy good cheer as we drove through the frantic pre-Christmas traffic to The Bay. Life was wild! What more could happen?

*　　*　　*

Close to Christmas, I went to a friend's house party. Brian offered to stay home. "Now don't talk about the whooping cough," he said, in the hope that I might forget about it for an hour or two. "I won't," I promised.

I walked into the party and two wild-eyed mothers accosted me. "We heard about your son," one of them said, "and we have to talk to you about whooping cough."

I am sorry to say that this news gladdened my heart. One woman had just been through a siege of pertussis with her five-month-old baby. She fixed her dark eyes on mine. "I went mental," she said. "My husband had to physically shut me away in a room one night, I couldn't bear to watch her cough any more." The other woman dandled her baby on her knee and gave me a somewhat demented smile. "All three of my children had it, one after the other," she said, "and so did I. It was the single hardest thing I've ever done in my life."

We spent the next hour discussing cough patterns, marital collapse, and the universal reluctance of doctors to diagnosis incurable conditions. But hospitals and doctors were not the main problem. I had a family doctor who would see me at the drop of a hat and the best pediatric hospital in the country ten minutes away. What I needed most of all was an hour of conversation with two women who had been through the same thing.

*   *   *

Christmas Day was almost over. We drove home from our second family gathering, at Brian's house. Despite bloodshot eyes that looked exactly like two cranberries, The Invalid had done well. Bowl at the ready, he had no problem forcing down his grandmother's excellent English dinner, including the bread sauce, gravy, stuffing balls, and sherry-drenched trifle with the spears of real angelica. There were Christmas crackers at the table — cherry bombs crossed with loot bags, his favorite. This year his grandmother had given him Gameboy. All of which left him deeply, deeply gratified on the ride back home. I even allowed myself a leakage of Christmas spirit now that everything was almost over.

There was no snow, but it was a cold night. I hustled Casey from the car to the house and up to bed, relieved that we had made it through two dinners and the required commuting without too much damage. The beast of burden, the weary man of the house, carried parcels and gifts up the stairs — the usual military bivouac necessary to unpack the car and get everything into the house.

As he put things away, Brian took one of my gifts, a bottle of Giorgio's Red, into the bathroom and put it with the other bottles on the windowsill. It tipped, fell, and broke. Sturdy little molecules of perfume began to waft down the hall and through the house.

"What's that smell?" I shouted.

I went into the bathroom and found Brian on his knees, frantically swabbing up the perfume as I went absolutely, end-of-my-Christmas-tether crazy. If there is a more potent asthma trigger than spruce mold, it is perfume.

"We have to evacuate!" I shrieked. "We'll have to book into a hotel! Open all the windows, scour everything — I'll phone you!"

I woke up Casey, wrapped him in a quilt, and strapped him into the front seat of the car. His head lolled to one side. Right, he probably thought, another festive spin to the hospital. I left Brian like Bob Cratchit in the bathroom with mop and pail, swabbing away.

I drove off in the direction of downtown, swerving over the streetcar rails on Gerrard Street. Banished from our own home on Christmas night. Only the most pathetic people were still on the streets. Everyone else was home pawing through the medicine cabinet, looking for the Rolaids. Casey slept and coughed. I drove by a hotel lobby, where the bored staff were all sitting in huge armchairs watching TV. If we did book in, I thought, Casey would only wake up and want to order room service. The hotel room would probably have potpourri, off-gassing night tables or something just as bad as Red.

In the end, I drove around the city for a few hours, with the car radio playing late-night reggae carols. It was peaceful, in a grim sort of way. It gave me the illusion that I was leaving things behind. After a while, I began to feel badly for Brian, home alone on perfume duty. I hoped he liked Red, at least.

When I got back to the house, Brian carried Casey up to bed. He had opened all the doors and windows, so it was cold as a manger inside the house.

"The smell kept spreading, it was like a horror movie," he moaned. "I scrubbed the entire bathroom, but I couldn't get it out of the shower curtain, so I put it in a garbage bag. Then I had to take off all my clothes and seal them in a bag, too. But the bag smelled, so I had to put everything outside . . ."

We embraced. He was completely odorless. Casey stirred, mumbled, and stayed asleep. We jacked up the heat, poured two bowls of cereal, read the paper in the kitchen for a long time, and went to bed.

36.　　　More Weaning

IT'S THE DAY before my forty-fifth birthday. Just yesterday the trees released their green, and our long-suffering tulips at the back of the yard are hard-budded and ready to bloom. I have much to do and no desire to work. Instead I read *The Myth of the Bad Mother* by Jane Swigart this morning at the kitchen table and got all teary around the chapter "Love and Relinquishment." Casey is now back at school after our winter of illness. I notice that his departure, combined with my age, has brewed up a predictable bout of sadness in me.

Last night while Brian prepared for his impending interview with Sharon Stone (a strange and subtle task), I sat downstairs watching "Switched at Birth," a TV movie about two babies who ended up going home with the wrong families. By the end of it, the mother is trying to reclaim her biological child, and the father of the switched baby may have to give up "his" child. The script was maudlin (graveside monologues, always a bad sign) but the combination of the search for the lost natal child with the loss of another loved child was quite unbearable. My fast-flowing tears were easily explained. I was in the middle of losing not just the baby but the child in Casey, who is now a boy, a guy, a pre-teen.

This morning I came down and he was playing delinquent Nintendo, pale-faced and focused. I mildly chastised him and he came into the kitchen where he stood on a chair and hugged me. I went on a bit about how rough it must be on his poor brain to put it through all those mazes before it's even awake. I took out a grapefruit for him and had the knife poised.

"No," he said with absolute authority, "no grapefruit. It will hurt my canker sore." He stretched open his mouth and gave me an excellent view of this particular feature. Then he got up on his stool, pulled out the big frying pan, cracked a couple of eggs and made scrambled eggs. "Put the toast down . . . now!" he commanded. The timing of the eggs and toast was vital. Once in a blue moon, he will even make and bring this breakfast up to us in bed, with tea. So much for childhood.

At the table I grumbled aloud about the paper not being delivered again. "Well, don't blame me for waking up to a bad day," he said, somewhat churlishly. I looked at him and saw his strong, roundish blue eyes, a flash of someone else, so firmly defined. It is almost as if I have emptied out my clarity into him, and now he stands firm and I am hopelessly soft and blurred. The person he is I have no claim on. His big wide rib cage, his square hands, bear no resemblance to either Brian or me. He goes back to the Big Men in my mother's family. Last night, watching "Switched at Birth," I thought, It's completely understandable how the nurses could pick up one swaddled infant, change him, and lay him down in the wrong basket. You fall in love anyway. It could happen. One's children could be strangers.

I've always seen this son of mine as distinct and clear, and he always has been. But now that he's eight, he makes a point of distinctions. A while ago, after some altercation concerning the purchase of an advanced chemistry set with skull and crossbone warnings all over the experiments, he pushed a printed note under my office door: "Sometimes you jest dont understan mom."

Recently, we have fights over rules and chores. The winter of at-home illness destroyed any semblance of structure. He goes to bed fairly docilely, but the piano practice, the clothes on the floor, chores . . . he thinks he deserves money, cold cash, every time he lifts a finger. If I leave his clothes precisely where he lets them fall and never wash them, he goes on wearing them until they're stiff with dirt. If I point out that everybody has to pitch in around the house, he says, "Sorry, mom, but it cuts into my time."

*   *   *

Tomorrow I will be forty-five and, as far as I'm concerned, officially over the hill for reproduction. Up until now, if I got pregnant, I would have enjoyed the long-shot aspect of it, the miracle edge. As I give up the possibility of another child, other aspects of my age sink in. To me, forty-five is the age of people in *New Yorker* cartoons. It is when people have begun to turn into caricatures of themselves. It suggests arrival, status, circular drive-ways, stepped-up grooming and highlighting jobs, the mainte-nance and dilution of middle age.

When I was younger, I had terrible assumptions about people who were forty-five, and some of them, I must admit, have come true. I am less adventurous. I have more fear. I have more opinions and less access to fresh experience.

This morning, I felt I had to hold a new baby, or somehow get out of my musty life. I missed romance and new love. Brian was gearing up to write, which always feels like a genuine deser-tion; he might as well be in Tunisia. My son was off and running, which fed my mood of irrelevance. When I picked him up yesterday, he immediately hit me with requests and began to grouse until I snapped and said, "Stop asking for things, and *be nice to me*" in a vile snarl. He gave me that "what's *your* problem" look and sat beside me in the car in stoical silence.

It struck me that we now have entrenched differences of opinion. His consumerism drives me wild. I know it's almost unavoidable, given these canyons and quarries of commodity that surround us. Stuff — it's our form of wilderness. But his inability to anchor his pleasure anywhere else alarms me. He likes books, but reading is not yet an oasis. His perfectionism — which springs from the only-child syndrome of getting lots of attention and imagining that he is a short adult — abides no failure or frustration.

No sooner did he begin piano lessons than he wanted to quit because he couldn't master it right away. "Wait three weeks and then we'll decide," I said. The crisis passed. He doesn't like to be caught in the act of learning, of being imperfect. Instead he thinks in terms of immediate solutions, and the dialectical Nintendo buttons — A for forward, B for jump. Getting him to practice the piano is like some scene out of a Norman Rockwell illustration. I stand over him with my arms folded while he sits on the edge of the piano bench, morosely fingering away. I could cast about for somebody to teach him on a synthesizer, I suppose, but music theory is drudgery no matter how you do it, and the drudgery is necessary. I want him not to be a spoiled little wussy about this, I admit. There is no Nintendo Power magazine with cheater codes for cracking the piano, and he might as well figure that out now. (How bitterly parental that sounds, how we resent having to unbliss their lives, bit by bit.)

Then again, he's only eight. Modesty has set in, but at bedtime, dawdling between clothes and pajamas, he lies there like an elongated cupid, spider-round in the belly, long-legged, almost as long as the bed now. His hair is shaggy and long and needs to be cut. His fingernails are dirty, and a big front tooth is jagged on the bottom. They sometimes comes in jagged, and then get smooth, the dentist reassures me.

He still tutors me in simple physical epiphanies. He sighs with rapture if I pull off his socks at night. "Ahh, that feels so good to have my feet free." I throw his pajamas at him. I'm hoping to get out of the bedroom because I want to go down and watch part two of "Switched at Birth," but he persuades me to read another page of *The History of the Sumerians*, some musty garage-sale book. As I read, I realize that he is hearing about Egyptian civilization for the first time in his life. It seems a little less boring, thinking that. For a second, he curls his hand under my chin, as he has since he was a baby. "Nnnnnn, your neck feels so good," he says. This last vestige of the physical intimacy, the way he puts his hand on the side of my neck. Now that he's not sick, his skin has a warm, healthy feel, there's sun inside him, despite the ongoing asthma. Poor drug-stuffed little guy. As I watched him tear around the gym in school the other day, he was as energetic as anybody else, but he ended with a cough, a hand to the chest, and the forward curving of his shoulders that only began with the whooping cough. That inner listening that sickness breeds. But he has no self-protecting stiffness, no holding back physically. Being sick hasn't put a dent in him.

The consequences of being an only child, however, are both obvious and subtle. Obviously, he gets bored with no one to play with, and we must organize and chauffeur and schedule in friends. No big deal. It also means we actually try to *play* with him, although his tolerance for our soggy reflexes is already on the wane. He is acutely conscious of his lack of power, just because he's the child in this household. "You get to stay up as late as you want," he says, unaware that I long to go to sleep when he does. "It's not fair being a kid!" This last statement, again and again. Occasionally, I glimpse the truth of that statement. He *feels* so much in control that the disparity between his imperial sense of self-propulsion and the strange ways in which the world condescends to children makes no sense to him.

Veterans of permissiveness, both of us jump through hoops not to lay down arbitrary rules. ("Of course I trust you, but the oil in the pan might catch on fire, and you would get first-degree burns, and be in a burn bed, and have to have skin grafts, and would miss floor hockey, and so making french fries is not a good idea for you.") But we now point out to him, with some feeling, that we have to do things we don't want to, all the time.

"You know, Casey, we spend lots of our time doing things we don't want to. Lots and lots of time."

"Like what?"

"Well, like work. We have to work. You don't have to."

"I have to go to school."

"Well, I don't get recess." (Lowering ourselves, already.)

"You get to go out to parties and stay up late, and I have to go to bed."

"You go to parties. Your whole life is a party." (An overstatement, amounting to parent-child competition to see who is most oppressed.)

"Why can't I just . . ."

"Live on your own?"

"Yes. Then I wouldn't bug you."

Uh-oh. Reee!Reee!Reee! Guilt alarm goes off.

"Oh, darling, you don't bug me. Don't say that."

(Sensing he has hit pay dirt.) "Yes, I do. I'm just a nuisance. You'd be better off without me."

(Detecting manipulation but still alarmed.) "I would miss you horribly if you moved into your own apartment. You're not a nuisance."

He looks out the car window. Far too early, the stores have Easter paraphernalia displayed.

"It's not fair that you rule me."

37.　　　　Joy

A FRIEND is having a family birthday party for her teen-age daughter, and Casey and I are invited to drop by. The get-together involves a complicated genealogy of one father, two mothers, two half-siblings, two cats, and a biased godmother. But it works, because there is an architecture of friendship holding it up, and because they make it work. There are chill currents, bonfires of resentment now and then among the adults, but all this has been made secondary to the protection and loving of the children. They go on thriving, the two suns of this complicated solar system, as the family falls apart, re-shapes itself, forges on.

Broken hearts are not forgiven, no phony deals are struck. But the birthdays and rituals continue and seem to have more meaning for the arranging, the ferrying to and fro that must be done to make these evenings happen.

This agreement to remain a family actually manufactures love like oxygen, you can feel it in the room when they're all together. They remind me that family is not a given but something that is perpetually negotiated and renewed.

Casey brings over his Casio to play "Happy Birthday" to the birthday girl, who sings "The Lion Sleeps Tonight" for us in French, to warm applause. Her godmother has given her many copious and wonderful cosmetics. Then the daughter agrees to baby-sit/torture the two boys. They head out the door with the ghetto blaster to dance on the lawn as darkness falls. I know Casey is coatless and it's past his bedtime, but I stay in the kitchen anyway, drinking beer with the three mothers, god- and maternal. There are many jokes. Their behavior through all these Christmases and graduations, bad nights and good, remains tactful and raucous, queenly and subversive. Every household harbors sadness, hidden or manifest, but in their kitchens, there are no shibboleths, no conventions to protect.

Finally I drag Casey home long after his bedtime. "That was fun," he declares with satisfaction. He loves a party. As he moonwalks toward bed, it occurs to me that we are getting along again.

*   *   *

Bad patches come and go and are completely convincing for as long as they last. This is especially true when you live with a first or only child, and none of the landmarks are familiar. As children grow up, they pass through stages that seem like permanent disfigurements of character. The worries peak, the parents make a list of remedial actions — stiff rules, new book shelves, a chat with the teacher — and then something happens. For no discernible reason, the unhappy one breaks through to a new plateau, and the mood in the house lightens.

This pattern is dramatically clear in infancy, when a baby will turn cantankerous just before some surge in development — before she walks or talks. She longs to grasp the world in a new way and gets furious when it remains out of her reach. Then it happens. She takes three steps or utters the words and her happiness and ageless pride are palpable.

In a more cluttered way, adults go through the same thing. They stall in cloudy, congested passages, then break through to an inexplicable clarity. Sometimes they "take steps," too — change careers, stop drinking, start therapy. Sometimes they do absolutely nothing at all, and it still happens, like perennials that push up each spring through the litter in a neglected yard. The cyclical is much underrated in our lives.

After the party, Casey warbles away in the bathroom, brushing his teeth — a prolonged activity that leaves the mirror looking like a Jackson Pollock painting. The three of us are meshing more easily now, although I'm not sure why. There are a few obvious factors. Casey's health has improved. He and Brian have a solid bond that doesn't depend on my intermediary presence. I can see light at the end of my work tunnel. New worries always percolate away — an air pollution problem in Casey's school, debts, unpainted walls. But recently there has been less clamoring from Casey for the next new toy, fewer monologues from me about the domestic habits of my housemates, an ebbing of work angst on Brian's part. Touch wood, knock on particleboard. Going through family is like traveling on pack ice; you leap from ice floe to ice floe and once in a while everyone converges on a chunk so big it feels like the mainland. You pitch camp, admire the sunset. Then a new chasm appears and you move on.

Last week, for instance, Casey was home with a run-of-the-mill virus for four days, just when I had to meet a deadline, and . . . it was fine. He even got tired of television. I gathered up all his far-flung Lego and he settled in to build aircraft carriers and intergalactic freighters, for hours. Quietly, calmly, with workmanlike delight. Then one night, out of the blue, he began to read real books, on his own. He had been doing expedient reading for a couple of years — instructions, Trivial Pursuit cards, school reading. But this time he sat up in bed with a Hardy Boys book, *The Secret of Sigma Seven*. One day he was stumbling over sentences and diphthongs, the next he was able to deftly make his way through a paragraph containing the word "memorabilia." The reading gene kicked in.

All of a sudden, his previous behavior made more sense. For two months, he had flounced around, restless and unresponsive to our attempts to get him into something — art lessons, birdhouse-building, keeping a diary. Now, mysteriously, he is capable of being satisfied. And he seems so pleased and happy, to be happy. Perhaps he knows it's rare. These moments feel like skating on a frozen river — the momentum is actually an accumulation of strokes, but there is the brief illusion of gliding, of flight.

Last night I went out with friends while Brian and Casey had dinner at home. I had left the two of them some revolting health-food purchase, an organic turkey thigh or something. Instead Brian went out and bought fish to barbecue and six oysters for the two of them. It was later reported to me that Casey gamely sucked in his first oyster and said, "I can't eat this, dad, it's like chewing one of my balls." Their world spins off and out of my view.

Brian spent the rest of the evening writing a TV script, four minutes long, with lines two inches wide. He rephrased some of it to me later in bed, with a near-hysterical fit of self-parody. He misses real writing. He is gearing up to "walk," too, and the creative frustration shows. I've been the fat one on the seesaw lately, sitting at the computer not moving. He's tired of dangling up there in the air.

This point where the balance pivots and the weight in the family shifts arrives stealthily. The prodome is always an overwhelming sense of exasperation, an end to patience. Two people lying in bed, eyes to the ceiling, talking: *We've got to do something about the bank/the yard/our future/his nightmares/school/dust mites/your attitude/our bodies.* They give in, they say it.

In the morning, the same problems remain, but they no longer seem insurmountable. For an hour, or a day, your son is all uncorrupted sweetness, your mate a peerless wit, and the weight of them in your life feels satisfying, like the handle of a good knife.

38.   All Happy Families

I'T'S NOT quite spring. My son is now almost nine. The book is almost done. I am handing out bits of it, hoping that the people in it can live with my fun-house-mirror version of our past.

We go to visit my parents. I'm not sure they see the point of telling these stories, which is understandable, since on many days the point eludes me, too. In any case, being written about, boiled down to a page here or there, is a strange sensation, and I want to tell them they don't have to pretend otherwise.

I leave a few sections for them to read. I warn them that the book is more revealing than they may like, although not about them. This only makes my mother look more worried. Still, I say, it's pretty personal.

"But everything's like that these days, isn't it," says my mother. "So personal. I keep reading these stories about stars who describe all the terrible things their mothers did to them."

"Well, this is not that sort of book."

Then, instead of asking me what compelled me to turn the whole family into grist for the mill, my mother starts to talk about how she didn't know a thing about babies when she had her first child, my older brother.

"I was the youngest in my family, I'd never taken care of a baby before," she said incredulously, fifty-seven years later. "And a colicky baby at that." Then she rolled her eyes and mentioned a time when she got angry at me for accidentally dumping my lunch on the rug while I was glued to a radio show. "I *still* feel bad about that," she said. It is such a tiny, such a minor transgression, as motherhood crimes go, that I can't believe my ears. Here I am, feeling apologetic for writing a book about motherhood — an experience that runs so much deeper and wider in her life than mine — while she sits there questioning the things she did raising us. Two mothers a generation apart, still united and divided by guilt.

The moment passed. My father strolled in and said it must be swell to be getting near the end, and my mother went off to get some clippings she'd kept for me.

*　　*　　*

We're driving back to Toronto at night. Brian has spent the weekend reading this book in draft form. He had been through other sections before but this is the first time he's read my version of our courtship. It's just a story, but I'm worried about the power of the unconscious to slay. Writing is soul-snatching at the best of times. Having put all my rages and grudges into words, now I see him as so tolerant and blameless driving beside me in the dark. The old furies are gone. I await new ones. Writing is a strange process, as strange as the history of love.

Casey has fallen asleep in the back seat. Brian says reassuring things to me about the book, about its power to console. I think he means them.

But?

"Well, I think you leave yourself open to being misunderstood in places."

Such as?

"It leaves the impression that I was away most of the time, which isn't true. It's not that I think there has to be more of me in the story, but right now it sounds like I was never around."

"Well, you *were* away a lot, in the beginning."

We skate the thin ice around that one again.

"But things have changed," he says.

Yes. That's true.

"You don't want to make me sound like some AWOL male, off on the road all the time. The point is that this stuff happens even in so-called happy families."

"It's just that all the good stories come out of the worst times, and they happened when you were away."

"But I'm around a lot these days. It's pretty even now. Things have changed."

That's true.

"Anybody reading this would think I never made a meal, for instance."

"Well — "

"I *always* end up cooking when people come over. You know, I don't mind if you take some cheap shots at my cooking —"

"Like your thing about garnishes, or the way you fillet fish, or not trusting ripe tomatoes — "

"Whatever. I don't mind if you exaggerate, or make things up, as long it sounds like me."

"Okay, that's no problem. I'll put more of you in toward the end. You can start off absent and end up present. That's sort of what happened . . ."

We passed little blue lights winking like a constellation on the Ford plant. Empty Sunday parking lots. In the rearview mirror, Casey slept.

"The angry parts don't bother me — the more hateful the better, really. But it's so easy for people to latch on to one thing and forget the rest. You know, if you complain about sex on one page, they'll assume we never have it. We'll end up on Joan Rivers."

"Right. But if you only say good things, people will think you're lying. And if you don't talk about it at all, they'll assume there's a problem. It's impossible either way."

I wait until I see the big curve of the lake, west of the city, until I say what's been on my mind all weekend.

"The problem is, I'm superstitious now. I'm afraid that if I say we're happy, an eighteen-wheeler will loom out of the dusk and crush us. I can't bear to have the last word. Why can't you write the ending?"

"Pay me and I will."

The traffic is steady and heavy on either side of us.

"But you know," I say, smoothing out the little rip on one finger of my leather gloves, "it's a book about mothers, not fathers. And there's a lot of you in it, considering."

"Fishing, driving, and phoning home?"

"It's the problems that are interesting, not the easy parts. You know — all happy families resemble one another."

"I'm not saying it should be happier. I don't think you should go with a happy ending."

No, I say looking out the window at the tidy elegance of the city at night. That would be asking for trouble.

*　　*　　*

Later in the bedroom. He puts down his magazine.

"You know the part near the beginning where you said I wasn't curious about you, when we had that first conversation in the diner, in the falafel place on Yonge?"

"Yes."

"I don't remember talking all the time. I remember you interviewing me. You didn't want to talk about yourself."

"Really?"

"You just kept asking me questions."

"Really?"

"We have completely different memories of that time."

Someone's car alarm goes off up the street, and I get up to close the window.

"You make it sound like all you wanted to do when you met me was get pregnant, but it wasn't that clear-cut. You were fairly ambivalent yourself, as I recall. You were just as obsessive about your work as I was. And now you're using hindsight to describe things."

I sigh.

"Well, I can still change the names and turn it into fiction."

"You don't have to change the names. To anyone who doesn't know us, we're just characters in a story."

Some staring at the bedroom walls, which still need to be painted. I put my feet against his calves. He turns toward me.

"Maybe the ending should come back to us," he says.

I look at him, impressed by the fact that he is still here, in bed with me. I can't believe we've come this far.

"I'm afraid that when the book ends, we'll end."

"Well, don't worry about that," he said. "Just make something up."

"There is no ending, that's the problem."

"Use that," he says. "That's good."

Afterword

THAT last conversation on the Queen Elizabeth Expressway took place ten years ago. The boy who was asleep in the back seat is now eighteen years old, in first year university, and living in Montreal. In eleven days, he's coming home for Christmas. This has allowed me to go out and buy him some new clothes, as a gift. (Two sweaters — Montreal can get cold, especially down by the water.) In the meantime, I have been busy getting my bearings in a whole new suburb of the mother zone — the leaving-home latitudes.

Once again, the "overwhelmingness of the dominant" obscures any clear view of the landscape. I am so in the middle of un-mothering that I have no idea how to describe it. Too bad there aren't any books or manuals for this bit. Of course, I miss him terribly. (There is much less music in the house.) But it's a totally distinct category of pulling apart. The small acts of daring that he is involved in every day, as he moves out into the world, feel like reciprocal acts of daring on our part too, as we feel our way into changed roles. It's sad, and exciting. It also reminds me that the process of leaving begins long before the event of departure. Like continental drift, it is incremental: things happen before they happen. The goodbyes begin face to face and don't even register as attempts to separate. All last year, there was a strong desire among the three of us for nothing ever to change. But change we must, and so we did.

Leonard Cohen has a new song that offers explicit instructions on how to handle the departure of a loved one:

As someone long prepared for this to happen
Go firmly to the window. Drink it in.
Exquisite music. Alexandra laughing.
Your firm commitments tangible again.

Going off to college made our first commitments tangible again. The newness of settling our son into his room at residence — lugging up the computer and the two guitars, along with some of my old books — had a Christmas-Eve feel, as if his father and I were assembling an especially complicated tree house or train set. Slide Tab A into Slot B for your new life apart. All around us were other middle-aged couples, unmistakably parents, like us. No sooner did we completely look the part than we began to embark on the business of unlearning it.

Oh, and by the way, his father and I are still together, pleasantly surprised to have survived not only the family years but also the first few months of setting the table for two. Jokes come in handy during this stage; they help offset a certain self-consciousness. (*The empty-nesters find themselves gamely cooking an over-elaborate dinner, asking, "But what do YOU want to listen to?"*)

When my son was still small, I began writing this book because I felt excluded from the books that offered parenting tips, when my first burning question, upon being handed a newborn, was not how to, but who. Who mothers? The alchemy of motherhood is one of life's most profound transformations, and it is an open-ended one. Ten years later, I find my original conclusion still applies: "There is no ending, that's the problem." Departures are not to be confused with endings.

I was amazed and touched by the range of women who wrote to me about their own lives after reading *The Mother*

Zone. They told me all about themselves. I was afraid my single-child, urban life might not connect with women living different lives, but I heard from mothers isolated on prairie farms or up in the Yukon, and from madly competent women who had five children and were also trying to write books. A number of fathers wrote to thank me for not leaving them out.

I am gratified to find that a new generation of mothers can recognize themselves in this story, too. It demonstrates what I suspected when I was in the thick of it myself, namely that the laws of evolution don't seem to apply to motherhood. Every new mother is new in the same old way; the core experience does not get passed down, because we like to forget, or we revise the truth of what it felt like. Each generation marches into the zone with lofty new ideals and expectations, to find that motherhood is the great leveler — and the thing that lifts us up.

Now and then I run into a curious reader who will ask, "And how is Casey?" As in, how did he turn out? What sweet revenge he could wreak on a mother who dished. My son is not quite out of the muffin tin yet, but I can offer one or two answers. The childhood asthma that provided such lurid interludes in this book has quieted down; this year he was able to play on an intramural hockey team for the first time. As for his nature, when he was three months old, I thought he had the kindest smile in the world, and this remains true. The older your child becomes, the more you get objective glimpses of him and I am struck by what a good soul he is: open, reflective, and generous. I just hope the world he inherits is not too stunned and harsh to make proper use of him. He loves learning but is wary of anything too removed from ordinary life. The other day on the phone, after he had spent a restorative weekend in the country hauling logs around, he announced that "chores are really the answer." This is something my mother has said to me more than once. Perhaps in reaction to our own postmodern rootlessness, he is drawn to the hidden center of things — the roots of music, the roots of history, and to trees, including the family tree. I note the deep bond between him and his father, a bond that pivots on a different sort of humor as well as on their shared passions.

And of course, the mothering continues. I wish there was a book for this stage too — the other zone. I am still learning when to zip my lip, when to speak from the heart, when to cut through the existential dilemmas with something brisk and, well, parental.

New ground.